WHAT THE
BIBLE
IS ALL ABOUT

for young explorers

HE CARETH for you.

I PETER 5:7

WHAT THE BIBLE IS ALL ABOUT

for young explorers

Based on the best-selling classic by
Dr. Henrietta Mears

Author and General Editor,
Frances Blankenbaker

Foreword
Billy and Ruth Graham

Gospel Light

Cover Design, Barbara Fisher
Interior Design, Christina Wilson
Illustrator, Chizuko Yasuda
Author and General Editor, Frances Blankenbaker
Biblical Researcher and Contributing Writer, Dr. Robert J. Choun, Jr.
Editorial Contributors, Sheryl Haystead, Wes Haystead, Alice Huffaker, Karen Stimer

Contact GLINT for other editions in foreign languages at Glintint@aol.com or at www.Glint.org for more information.

For more information on the life of Henrietta Mears, see *Dream Big: The Henrietta Mears Story* (Ventura, CA: Regal Books, 1990). ISBN 0-8307-1254-2

Library of Congress Cataloging-in-Publication Data
Blankenbaker, Frances.
    What the Bible is all about for young explorers: based on the best-selling classic by Henrietta Mears/author and general editor.
Frances Blankenbaker: foreword, Billy and Ruth Graham. —Rev. ed.
        p. cm.
    "This special version—for young explorers—is written to help children and young people discover for themselves what the Bible is all about."
    Summary: A discussion of the origin, significance and contents of the Bible, with a book-by-book analysis of events, as well as time lines, photographs and maps to pinpoint when and where they happened.

    ISBN 0-8307-2363-3 (pbk.)

    1. Bible—Juvenile literature. [1. Bible.] I. Mears, Henrietta C. (Henrietta Cornelia), 1890-1963   What the Bible is all about.
II. Title.
BS539.B57   1998
220.6′ 1—dc21   98-12360
                                                                CIP
                                                                AC

6 7 8 9 10 11 12 13 14 15 / 09 08 07 06 05 04 03 02 01

Rights for publishing this book in other languages are contracted by Gospel Literature International (GLINT). GLINT also provides technical help for the adaptation, translation and publishing of Bible study resources and books in scores of languages worldwide. For further information, contact GLINT, P.O. Box 4060, Ontario, CA 91761-1003, U.S.A., or the publisher.

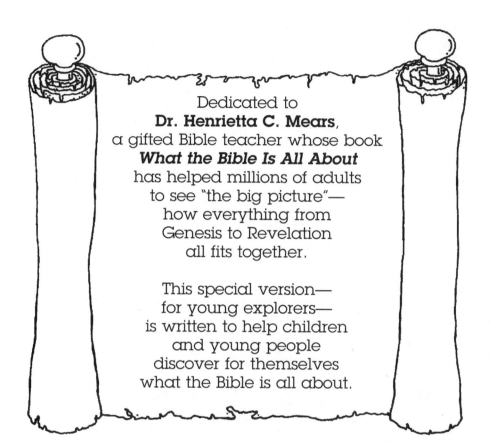

Dedicated to
Dr. Henrietta C. Mears,
a gifted Bible teacher whose book
What the Bible Is All About
has helped millions of adults
to see "the big picture"—
how everything from
Genesis to Revelation
all fits together.

This special version—
for young explorers—
is written to help children
and young people
discover for themselves
what the Bible is all about.

Foreword

You may be buying this book for a young explorer, or you may be one yourself. In any case, you know that the Bible is an exciting book. As we study the Bible it is easy to become so involved in the details of each event or chapter that we lose sight of the "big picture." This book will help you see the "big picture"—how everything in the Bible all fits together.

You will see that throughout the entire Bible God has a plan
   —a plan for the nation of Israel,
   —a plan for providing mankind with forgiveness
      and eternal life,
   —a plan for YOU!

This book will also help you understand the events that happened in the Bible. The time lines tell WHEN events happened, and the photographs and maps show WHERE it all happened.

It will all come to life for you as you discover the meanings of Bible words and customs—and as you read what archaeologists have discovered by digging in Bible lands. The charts and diagrams help to tie together how things relate to each other.

This is a book you'll use over and over again as you study God's Word. It will help you understand not only what happened in Bible times but also how to apply it to your own life.

We cannot recommend it too highly, whether for personal Bible study, family devotions or group study.

Billy and Ruth Graham

Contents

Adventure Ahead!

When starting an adventure, it's a good idea to look ahead before you start exploring. So, get ready to

✳ investigate the creation of the universe!

✳ check out narrow escapes and courageous showdowns!

✳ and hunt down heroes, villains and ordinary folk!

All that (and more!) happens in the **Old Testament** part of the Bible.

Then, with the flip of a few pages, you will

✳ meet evil kings and powerful leaders!

✳ discover an angel who opens prison doors!

✳ and find the Person who will make your whole life different!

Now we're talking about the **New Testament** part of the Bible.

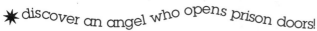

All the stories in the Bible—from Adam and Eve to the very end—fit together to show us God's great plan for our world and for our own lives. That's an **adventure** you won't want to miss!

BUT WAIT! THERE'S MORE! →

IT'S A MESSAGE!
IT'S A STORY!
IT'S A LIBRARY!
IT'S—THE BIBLE!

IT'S A MESSAGE!

Over many hundreds of years God used many different writers to produce this book. The writers were different ages and had different backgrounds, but what they all wrote carried the same wonderful **message**—

The Savior will come!

Old Testament

The Savior has come!

New Testament

What are some names you have heard people call the Bible? Do you know what those names mean?

✚ Bible (book)　　　　　　✚ Scripture (writings)

✚ God's Word (God's truth)　✚ Holy Bible (special book)

✚ The Gospel (good news)　　✚ The Law (God's rules)

The word "Bible" is from the Greek word that simply means "book," but the Bible is no ordinary book. That's why most Bibles have the word "Holy" ("special or chosen by God") in the title.

IT'S A STORY!

The Bible tells us what God wants us to know about Himself and His plan for us. This exciting, true story is God's **story.**

THE BIG PICTURE OF THE BIBLE

Old Testament   **New Testament**

Creation   Jesus promised   JESUS! Great things that happened   Us
                  to come   because of Jesus

IT'S A LIBRARY!

When you hold a Bible in your hands and thumb through its pages (or check out the contents page in the front), you see that the Bible is a collection of 66 books—a **library**!

A Library with Two Sections

There are 39 books in the first section. This section makes up about three-fourths of the whole library. It's called the **Old Testament**.

$$\begin{array}{r} 39 \\ +27 \\ \hline 66 \end{array}$$

There are 27 books in the second section. This part makes up the last fourth of the library. It's called the **New Testament.**

A Library That's Easy to Use

Besides having only two parts, this library of books in the Bible is easy to use.

So that you can quickly find your way around, nearly all of the books are divided into chapters; and all of the chapters are divided into verses.

To find something in the Bible, all you have to do is look up its **reference**— just like you look up an address! For example, the reference Genesis 1:1 means look in the book of Genesis, chapter 1, verse 1. It's that easy!

Part One: Old Testament

Think **promise**—the word "testament" means a promise. The entire **Old Testament** is the story of the parts of a wonderful **promise** God made! There are five sections in the Old Testament and that **promise** is found in every section!

SECTION 1:

The first **five** books are called the books of the **Law**. These books tell about the creation of the world and how God chose a family that grew into a nation—Israel—to help fulfill His **promise**. It tells how God freed Israel from slavery, cared for them through 40 years in a desert and gave them His laws. (That didn't mean they always obeyed!)

Right from the start, people disobeyed Him, causing one problem after another. But also right from the start, God **promised** a way **to make things right** again.

SECTION 2:

The next **12** books are called the books of **History.** They tell the story of God's nation, Israel, and start at the time the Israelites entered the land God had promised.

When the Israelites obeyed Him, God defeated their enemies. But **more** often, God's people **disobeyed** and got in serious trouble! There were a few kings and queens who did right—and many who didn't! The disobedience led to fighting; the fighting led to Israel splitting in two, and both halves

ended up **captured** by enemies who sent many away to foreign lands. The books of History **end** at the time some of those people **returned** to the land of Israel.

SECTION 3:

In the very middle of the Bible are **five** books called **Poetry.** These poems and songs were written by many different people—including David king of Israel and his son Solomon. This **poetry**

describes the greatness of God and the beauty of His creation, gives wise **advice** and **answers** many hard questions. The books of Poetry also give **more promises of the great leader** God would send His people!

SECTIONS 4 & 5:

During the years we read about in the books of History, God sent many messengers, called **prophets,** to His people. These prophets spoke or wrote what God wanted His people to know. They gave many

warnings to obey God and many **more promises** about the **great King and Savior who was coming!**

The first five books of prophecy are called the "Major Prophets" because these books are longer than the "Minor Prophets," 12 smaller books that complete the Old Testament.

Part Two: New Testament

The New Testament tells about **how** God's promise came **true** and how God's keeping of His promise **changes everything!**

The word "gospel" means "good news." The **four Gospels** tell the **good news**—the King and Savior God had **promised** really did come!

They tell about **Jesus'** birth, life and teachings—and how **many** of God's promises came **true** when Jesus died on the cross to take the punishment for our sins. **More** of God's **promises** came true when Jesus came back to life!

The **Acts of the Apostles** tells what God's **Holy Spirit** did through people who took the **good news** about Jesus to the rest of the world! It tells how Peter, Philip and then Paul spread the **good news**, sharing God's **promise** with everyone—and causing such a stir that people said they were **turning the world upside down!**

The Bible ends with **Letters. Thirteen** are from **Paul**—most written to **churches** and a few written to **people**

Paul knew. These letters **encouraged** and **taught** those people more about Jesus. Those letters still **teach us** how God's **promise** changes our lives!

Eight letters were written by other **leaders** in the **early church** and were sent from **church to church.**

The **last book** of the Bible is a **letter**, too. It's addressed to **seven churches.** It tells of a **prophecy** (or revelation) given to John about the **future.** A lot of this book may be hard to understand, but the great, big **promise** here is clear: **Jesus** will come back to earth, and **everyone** will know He really is the **King of kings** and **Lord of lords!**

Becoming God's Child

Exploring the Bible is more than just discovering exciting stories or meeting interesting people. It's also more than uncovering interesting information about God and Jesus. Exploring the Bible leads to the amazing discovery that God has gone to a great deal of trouble so that you can become His child.

Some people claim that everyone is already God's child. They say that because God created people, He's obviously everyone's Heavenly Father. People who say that are only partly right. They miss some very important information that everyone needs to know. By exploring the Bible, we discover the rest of the story. Here are the highlights.

God knew you before you were born.

God spoke to the prophet Jeremiah saying, "Before I formed you in the womb I knew you, before you were born I set you apart" (Jeremiah 1:5). God knew all about you even before you were born, just as He knew about Jeremiah.

God made you.

God didn't just create the first two people and then let nature take over. God's Word tells us, "For you created my inmost being; you knit me together in my mother's womb. I praise you because I am fearfully and wonderfully made; your works are wonderful, I know that full well" (Psalm 139:13,14). God made you to be a special, unique person.

God knows you today.

God knows who you are. His Word says, "O Lord, you have searched me and you know me. You know when I sit and when I rise; you perceive my thoughts from afar. You discern my going out and my lying down; you are familiar with all my ways" (Psalm 139:1-3). God knows you, what you are doing and even what you are thinking. Thus He knows when you want to do things your own way instead of His way. You can't fool Him, nor do you have to try to impress Him. He knows you at your best and at your worst.

God wants you to become His child.

Since He made you and knows you, God wants you to know Him. He doesn't only want you to know things about Him, He wants you to get to know Him as a loving and good Father. He wants you to live as His child.

You know what it's like to be part of your own family. You know about ways that family members love and care for each other. You also know that family members sometimes don't get along with each other. God's family, the family He wants you to join, does not depend on imperfect people. It is held together by God's perfect love, the love that has been shown to us by Jesus.

How do you become God's child?

There are a few important things you need to know and then some steps you need to take. Then God will do what He promised, making you His much-loved child!

1. Do you know that the God who made the universe loves you?

He does!

He loves you so much, He wants you to be His child!

God's Word, the Bible, says, "God is love." 1 John 4:8

2. But, do you know that you and I, and all the other people in the world, have done wrong things

- like forgetting God
- and disobeying Him
- and being selfish
- and hurting others?

We have.

3. In the Bible, the word for doing wrong is "sin." God says that you have sinned, and I have sinned. Our sin keeps us away from God's great love for us.

God's Word says, "All have sinned and fall short of the glory of God." Romans 3:23

4. So God sent His Son, Jesus, to show how much He loves you. Did you know that Jesus took the punishment for your sin?

He did!

Jesus died on the cross so that all the wrong things you've done could be forgiven. Because Jesus never sinned, He is the only One who could take the punishment for your sin.

God's Word says, "Christ died for our sins." 1 Corinthians 15:3

5. Do you know that God is ready to forgive you right now?

He is!

If you admit that you've done wrong things and if you believe that Jesus died for you, God will forgive all your sin.

God's Word says, "If we confess our sins, he is faithful and just and will forgive us our sins." 1 John 1:9

"Everyone who believes in him receives forgiveness of sins." Acts 10:43

6. Do you know that when God forgives you, you become His child?

That's right!

God wants you to be in His family!

God's Word says, "To all who received him, to those who believed in his name, he gave the right to become children of God." John 1:12

"How great is the love the Father has lavished on us, that we should be called children of God! And that is what we are!" 1 John 3:1

7. Do you know that when you become a part of God's family, God gives you an awesome gift — eternal life?

He does!

This means Jesus will be with you now and forever! God's Word says, "For God so loved the world that he gave his one and only Son, that whoever believes in him shall not perish but have eternal life." John 3:16

8. How do you ask to be God's child?

You can talk to God in your own words.

1. Tell God that you need to be forgiven.

2. Thank God that Jesus died for you.

3. Ask God to forgive you and to help you turn away from doing wrong.

4. Thank God that Jesus will be with you forever.

If you believe God's promise to you, you are now a child of God.

- God has forgiven you!

- He has made everything right between YOU and HIM!

- He looks at you as if you had never sinned!

- He gives you the gift of everlasting life.

This means God is with you now and forever!

Welcome to God's Family

To remind yourself, and everyone else
who looks at this book, that you have
become a child of God, fill in this certificate.

I want everyone to know that

on _____
Month/Day

of _____
Year

I, _____ ,
Name

became a child of God by
asking Jesus to forgive my sin
and to be with me forever.

You can talk to God any time!

Talking to God is called praying. You can pray out loud or just with your thoughts.

It's great to talk to God when
- you're angry, sad or worried;
- you're happy and glad;
- you've done something wrong and are sorry;
- you're thankful that He loves and forgives you!

It's even greater to know that God always listens!

You can get to know God better!

God gave us a wonderful book, the Bible, that tells about God and what He wants us to do. A good place to start reading is the Gospel of Mark, one of four books about Jesus.

You can show His love to others!

Other people can learn that God loves them when you are kind and tell what you know about Jesus.

Your Bible may use some different words for these Bible verses. Look them up in your own Bible.

The Bible—A Library of Smaller Books

OLD TESTAMENT

THE LAW

- Genesis
- Exodus
- Leviticus
- Numbers
- Deuteronomy

HISTORY
- Joshua
- Judges
- Ruth
- First Samuel
- Second Samuel
- First Kings
- Second Kings
- First Chronicles
- Second Chronicles
- Ezra
- Nehemiah
- Esther

POETRY
- Job
- Psalms
- Proverbs
- Ecclesiastes
- Song of Songs

MAJOR PROPHETS
- Isaiah
- Jeremiah
- Lamentations
- Ezekiel
- Daniel

MINOR PROPHETS
- Hosea
- Joel
- Amos
- Obadiah
- Jonah
- Micah
- Nahum
- Habakkuk
- Zephaniah
- Haggai
- Zechariah
- Malachi

NEW TESTAMENT

GOSPELS

- Matthew
- Mark
- Luke
- John

HISTORY
- Acts

LETTERS BY PAUL to Churches

- Romans
- First Corinthians
- Second Corinthians
- Galatians
- Ephesians
- Philippians
- Colossians
- First Thessalonians
- Second Thessalonians

LETTERS BY PAUL to Others
- First Timothy
- Second Timothy
- Titus
- Philemon

GENERAL LETTERS
- Hebrews
- James
- First Peter
- Second Peter
- First John
- Second John
- Third John
- Jude

PROPHECY

- Revelation

Let's Look at the Books of the Law

The first five books of the Old Testament are called the books of the Law. They tell about creation, the entrance of sin into the world and the early years of the nation through whom God would send the Savior.

The Books of the Law

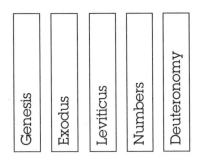

Genesis Exodus Leviticus Numbers Deuteronomy

What is "the Law?" Most of us think of "the Law" as the Ten Commandments God gave Moses on Mt. Sinai. But Leviticus and Deuteronomy record many other instructions God gave to Moses at the same time. These first five books are often called "the Pentateuch," which means "five volumes." They all make up what Israel recognized as the Law.

Why did God give Israel the Law? The Law was given to show God's holiness and people's sinfulness. The Law made Israel different from all the other nations and marked them as God's chosen people. The Law also prepared Israel for the coming of the Savior by showing that a sacrifice was necessary for forgiveness.

What does the New Testament say about the Law?
1. Jesus said He came to fulfill the Law, not to do away with it (Matthew 5:17). He is the only person who has ever kept the Law perfectly.
2. The Law shows us our sin and points us to Christ (Romans 7:7; Galatians 3:24). God gave the Law so that we could see our own sinfulness. Then He sent His Son, Jesus, to perfectly fulfill the Law and die as the payment for our sin.

Genesis

WRITER: Luke 24:27 and John 5:46 tell us that Moses wrote part of the Old Testament. Guided by the Holy Spirit of God, Moses wrote the first five books of the Bible.

TITLE: "Genesis" means "beginnings." Genesis tells us about the beginning of everything except God. God was always there. Genesis tells us about the beginning of:

- ☐ the world (Genesis 1:1-25)
- ☐ people (Genesis 1:26—2:25)
- ☐ sin in the world (Genesis 3:1-7)
- ☐ God's promise of salvation (Genesis 3:8-24)
- ☐ living as a family (Genesis 4:1-15)
- ☐ civilization (Genesis 4:16—9:29)
- ☐ the nations and languages of the world (Genesis 10,11)
- ☐ the Hebrew people—the nation of Israel (Genesis 12—50)

LOCATION: Genesis is the first book of the Bible. It is the first of five Bible books called the Books of the Law.

The Books of the Law

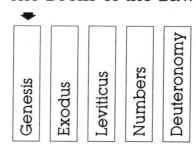

MAIN PEOPLE: Adam, Eve, Noah, Abraham, Isaac, Jacob and Joseph

OUTLINE:
- ☐ The creation of the world (Genesis 1,2)
- ☐ Sin in the world (Genesis 3,4)
- ☐ Noah and the flood (Genesis 5—9)
- ☐ The beginning of nations and languages (Genesis 10,11)
- ☐ Abraham's family: God's people in the land God gave them (Genesis 12—38)
- ☐ Joseph: God's people going to Egypt (Genesis 39—50)

When Events Happened

IN THE BEGINNING GOD CREATED THE HEAVEN AND EARTH

2100 BC

2000

FLOOD   BABEL   ABRAHAM   ISAAC

Main Events

■ The Creation, the Flood, the Beginning of Nations and Languages

Chapters 1—11 The first eleven chapters of Genesis tell about the beginning of the world, people, nations and languages. These chapters set the stage for what God plans to do through one nation—the nation of Israel. You will read about that part of God's plan in Chapter 12.

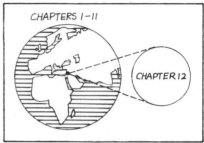

CHAPTERS 1–11

CHAPTER 12

Chapters 1,2: God created the heaven and the earth and all that is in them.

Chapter 3: The first man and woman, Adam and Eve, sinned. They did not obey God's command.

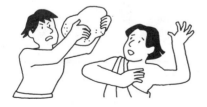

Chapter 4: Adam's son Cain killed his brother Abel.

Chapter 5: Adam's family grew. Here is Noah who was 500 years old before he became the father of Shem, Ham and Japheth.

1900

JACOB   JOSEPH

1800

Chapters 6—8: The people did not obey God. God was going to destroy the earth with a great flood. He told Noah to build an ark.

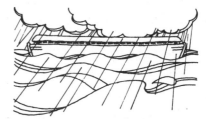

When Noah, his family and the animals were inside, the great flood came. Only those inside the ark were kept safe.

Chapter 9: God told Noah that never again would a flood destroy all life. God set His rainbow in the sky to show that promise to all people.

Chapter 10: This chapter tells about the families of Noah's sons: Japheth, Ham and Shem.

Chapter 11: The people were proud. They began to build a tower to reach into the heavens. God gave them different languages so they could not under-

stand one another. The people could not finish their tower. They went to different parts of the earth.

■ God's People in the Land God Gave Them

Chapters 12—38 God began a great nation—the nation of Israel. God's plan was that through this nation ALL people on earth would be blessed. God gave His people a land. It was in this land and through this people that God would keep His promise—hundreds of years later—to send a Savior.

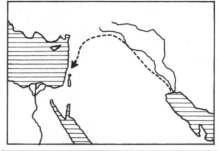

Chapter 12: God called Abraham to be the leader of the great nation. Abraham and his family went to the new land that God promised to them.

Chapters 13,14: Abraham divided his new homeland with his nephew Lot. Then Abraham rescued Lot who had been captured by enemy soldiers.

Chapter 15: Abraham and Sarah were old and had no children. God said that someday the people in their family would be as hard to count as the stars.

Chapters 16—18: Abraham's first son was born. He was called Ishmael, but was not the son God had promised. God then promised Abraham another son.

Chapters 18,19: The people in Sodom and Gomorrah did not obey God. These cities were destroyed.

Chapter 20: Abraham lied about his wife Sarah. Then he admitted he had done wrong.

Chapter 21: Abraham's second son was born. He was called Isaac, and was the son God promised to Abraham.

Chapter 22: God told Abraham to take Isaac and use him as an offering. Abraham obeyed God. God provided a ram to kill instead.

Chapters 23,24: Abraham's wife Sarah died and was buried. Their son, Isaac, married Rebekah.

Chapter 25: Abraham died at age 175. Isaac and Rebekah had twin sons—Jacob and Esau. Esau sold his birthright to Jacob for a bowl of stew.

Chapter 26: Isaac patiently refused to fight with his neighbors. God repeated His promise to Isaac.

Chapter 27: Jacob tricked his father Isaac into giving him the blessing that should have gone to Esau. Esau was furious.

Chapter 28: Jacob ran away to Haran. Along the way, God told Jacob in a dream that He would protect Jacob and bring him back again to this land.

Chapters 29,30: Jacob married Leah and Rachel. He had many children. One of them was Joseph.

Chapters 31—33: Jacob returned to Canaan, the land God promised to His people. Jacob made friends again with Esau, his brother.

Chapter 35: Jacob built an altar at Bethel to remember God's promise. God changed Jacob's name to Israel. God said, "I will give your family this land."

■ God's People Going to Egypt

Chapters 37—50 God continued to build the great nation He promised. Joseph, the favorite son of Jacob, is the main person in this section. First Joseph—then ALL of Jacob's family—went to Egypt. In Egypt God built the FAMILY of Israel (Jacob's new name) into the great NATION of Israel.

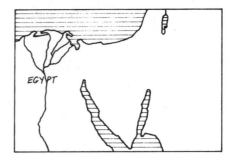

Chapter 37: Joseph was his father's favorite son. His brothers sold him as a slave. He was taken to Egypt and resold to Potiphar, the Egyptian captain.

Chapter 39: Joseph was accused of something he did not do. He was thrown into jail. But God was with Joseph.

Chapter 40: When Joseph was in jail, God helped him explain dreams.

Chapter 41: Joseph was called to explain Pharaoh's dream. Pharaoh put Joseph in charge of collecting food for the famine Joseph told him was coming.

Chapter 42: Joseph's brothers came to Egypt to buy food. Joseph knew who they were, but they did not know who he was.

Chapter 43: Joseph's brothers took food home to Canaan. When it was gone, they returned to Egypt. They brought Benjamin as Joseph demanded.

Chapter 44: Joseph falsely accused Benjamin and threatened to keep him a prisoner in Egypt. He did this to see if his brothers had changed.

Chapter 45: Joseph told his brothers who he was and invited his family to live in Egypt.

Chapters 46,47: Joseph's family moved to Goshen, the place in Egypt where Pharaoh said they could live.

Chapter 47: Joseph served Pharaoh well during the time of the great famine in Egypt.

Chapters 48,49: Jacob blessed Joseph's sons and his own sons. Jacob then died.

Chapter 50: Joseph's brothers were afraid he might still be angry with them. But he was not angry; he was kind. When he died, he was buried in Egypt.

Discoveries from the Past

People have made discoveries which show us that what is written in Genesis is true. Here are just a few of those discoveries.

Creation

About a hundred years ago, tablets were discovered in the ruins of Babylonia. They show the story of creation from the Babylonian point of view. (Look for Babylonia on the map on page 33.) These tablets tell us that other people besides the Israelites believed in a special CREATION of the world.

The Flood

The Babylonian story of the flood was found on the tablets that were discovered over a hundred years ago. The tablets describe the ark and the flood. The Babylonians did not worship the God of the Israelites. But they believed that the flood was planned by a power greater than human beings. These records from long ago tell about the same events we read about in our Bible. These records help to show that the Bible writings are true.

Cities in Genesis

Tablets that are thousands of years old have been found in the Syrian city of Ebla. They contain the names of some of the Canaanite cities we read about in Genesis.

The Destruction of Sodom and Gomorrah

The Bible tells us that the cities of Sodom and Gomorrah were destroyed by burning sulphur. The burning sulphur made smoke like the smoke that comes out of a furnace. Scientists have studied the area where these cities were. They report that chemicals in the ground mixed together and exploded. This sent red-hot salt and sulphur into the air. In this case, it is not written records but physical science that proves the Bible record is true.

Where It All Happened

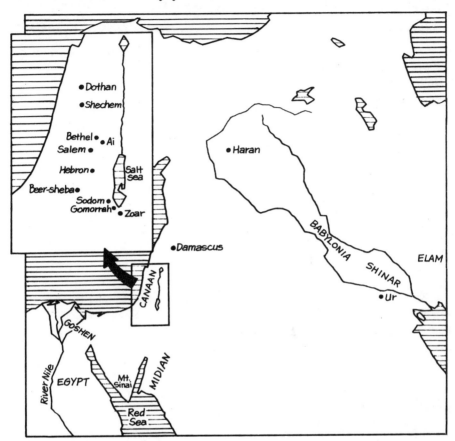

Genesis

and God's Plan to Send a Savior

God's First Promise to Send a Savior

Near the very beginning of this book, chapter 3, we see the sin of the first people. The woman was tempted by the serpent to eat of the fruit of the tree. "She took some and ate it. She also gave some to her husband, who was with her, and he ate it" (Genesis 3:6). When the first man and woman were tempted by the serpent—Satan—they sinned. They did not do as God had told them.

God said that Satan would be crushed by a child born to the woman. This promise came true many years later when Jesus died on the cross. Genesis 3:15 is the first promise of the coming Savior.

God Chose a People Through Whom the Savior Would Come

God promised that the Savior would come through Abraham (Genesis 12:1-3), Isaac (Genesis 17:19-20), Jacob (Genesis 28:10-14), Judah (Genesis 49:10) and (hundreds of years later) David (2 Samuel 7:5-17). Matthew 1:1 says that Jesus Christ is from the family of Abraham and David—just as God promised.

Abraham

Isaac

Jacob (Israel)

Judah

(hundreds of years later)

David

(hundreds of years later)

Jesus

As you read through the book of Genesis, look for these names: Abraham, Isaac, Jacob, Judah. These are people in the family from which Jesus came. Imagine, God had already planned to send a Savior to die for us. He loved His people very much even at the beginning of the world!

Pictures of the Coming Savior

Genesis has some exciting stories which are like pictures of what Jesus came to be. Adam and Eve's son Abel was killed, even though he had done nothing against his brother. Jesus also was killed, and He did nothing wrong at all. Noah's ark saved his family; Jesus is like the ark, saving from sin all who are in God's family. Joseph gives another picture of Jesus. Joseph was mistreated, and unfairly put into prison, yet he did not try to "get even." He forgave his brothers and saved them from famine. Jesus also forgave those who mistreated him. He offers salvation from the punishment for sin.

Exodus

WRITER: Luke 24:27 and John 5:46 tell us that Moses wrote part of the Old Testament. Guided by the Holy Spirit of God, Moses wrote the first five books of the Bible, which include Exodus.

TITLE: "Exodus" comes from a Greek word that means "the way out." This book tells how God delivered His people out of slavery and led them out of Egypt.

LOCATION: Exodus is the second book of the Bible. It is the second of the Bible books called the Books of the Law.

The Books of the Law

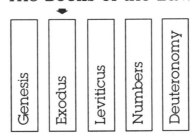

Genesis | Exodus | Leviticus | Numbers | Deuteronomy

MAIN PEOPLE: Moses and Aaron. The families of Israel were becoming a nation.

OUTLINE:
- [ ] The slavery of God's people (Exodus 1)
- [ ] The call of Moses to be the leader of God's people (Exodus 2—4)
- [ ] The challenge for Pharaoh to release God's people (Exodus 5—11)
- [ ] The passover for God's people—a picture of Jesus as our Savior (Exodus 12,13)
- [ ] The exodus of God's people from Egypt (Exodus 14—19)
- [ ] The giving of the Law to God's people (Exodus 20—24)
- [ ] The building of the Tabernacle by God's people (Exodus 25—40)

When Events Happened

1600BC   *1400BC*

MOSES

35

Main Events

■ God's People Are Freed from Slavery

Chapters 1—13 Many years passed. Jacob (Israel) and his children were dead. But their descendants (children's children's children) still lived in Egypt. A new Pharaoh made the people of Israel slaves. They prayed to God and He answered them. God chose Moses to lead His people out of Egypt.

Family of Jacob (Israel)

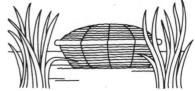

Descendants of Jacob (Israel)

Chapter 1: The people of Israel (also called the Hebrew people) were made slaves in Egypt. The Egyptians were very cruel to them.

Chapter 2: Moses was born and hidden from Pharaoh's soldiers. The princess adopted him. When Moses grew up, he killed an Egyptian and ran away to Midian.

Chapters 3,4: God spoke to Moses from a burning bush. He told Moses to go back to Egypt and lead the people of Israel out of slavery.

Chapters 5,6: Moses asked Pharaoh to let the people of Israel go. Pharaoh said no.

Chapters 7—10: God sent disasters upon the people of Egypt to make Pharaoh set the Israelites free. Still Pharaoh said no.

Chapters 11—13: God took the lives of all the first-born in Egypt. He spared the first-born of Israel (Passover). Pharaoh finally said yes.

■ God's People Leave Egypt

Chapters 13—18 God led His people through the Sinai wilderness. The photos on page 351 show what the Sinai wilderness looks like. Can you imagine what it would be like to travel in this wilderness?

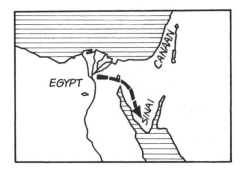

Chapter 13: Moses led the people out of Egypt. God guided them in a cloud by day and fire by night.

Chapters 14,15: Pharaoh changed his mind and chased after the Israelites. God protected the people by opening a path for them in the Red Sea.

Chapters 16,17: God provided food and water for His people.

Chapter 18: Moses met his family in Midian. Moses picked other men to help him lead the people.

■ God's People Camp at Mount Sinai

Chapters 19—40 Look at the photos on page 351. This is the mountain many people think is Mount Sinai. Find the large flat area where the people of Israel could have set up their camp.

Chapters 19—24: God gave His people the Ten Commandments and many other laws that they must live by. The people promised to obey God.

Chapters 25—31: God gave His people directions for building a Tabernacle. The Tabernacle was a tent that would be a holy place for worshiping God.

Chapter 32: The people sinned by worshiping a calf made of gold. In anger, Moses broke the tablets of Law. Moses asked God to forgive the people for their sin.

Chapters 33,34: God promised to go with Moses and the people as they traveled. Moses wrote the Ten Commandments on two stone tablets as God told him to.

Chapters 35—39: The Tabernacle was built. The people made special clothing for the priests who would serve God in the Tabernacle.

Chapter 40: The Tabernacle was set up. A cloud by day and fire by night proved to the people that God was pleased with the Tabernacle.

The Tabernacle Furniture

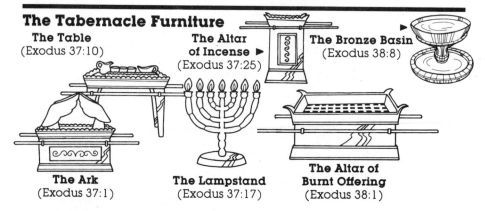

The Table
(Exodus 37:10)

The Altar of Incense ▶
(Exodus 37:25)

The Bronze Basin
(Exodus 38:8)

The Ark
(Exodus 37:1)

The Lampstand
(Exodus 37:17)

The Altar of Burnt Offering
(Exodus 38:1)

Discoveries from the Past

People have made discoveries which show that what is written in the book of Exodus is true. Here are just a few of these discoveries.

The Hebrew People (the People of Israel) in Egypt

Paintings found in the Egyptian tombs show Hebrew slaves making and laying bricks.

Discoveries have proven that many of the cities and places mentioned in Exodus did exist at the time of the Hebrews. The cities of Pithom and Rameses, built by Hebrew slaves, have bricks made without straw. Exodus 5:6-8 says that Pharaoh did not give the slaves the straw they needed to make their bricks.

The Hebrew People in Canaan

Written records tell us that invaders called "Habiru" (Hebrews) entered the land called Canaan. About one hundred years ago some letters from a military leader were found in Canaan. These letters ask the Egyptian Pharaoh for help against the Habiru.

Date of the Exodus

The exodus from Egypt probably took place around the year 1441 B.C. The Pharaoh at that time was Amenhotep II.

Where It All Happened

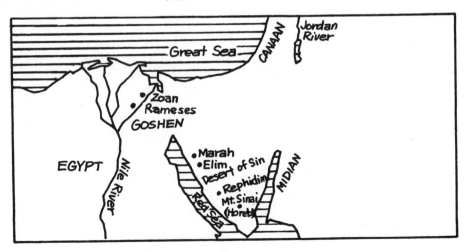

Exodus

and God's Plan for a Savior

The book of Exodus gives us four different pictures of the coming of Jesus Christ.

Moses

The life and ministry of Moses shows us how salvation for many is found through one man. Like Jesus, Moses was chosen and cared for by God. Like Jesus, Moses had a special ministry to do to save God's people. Moses saved his people from death. Jesus Christ saves us from death and gives us eternal life—if we are a part of God's family.

The Passover Lamb

The lamb used in the Passover was to be perfect. The lamb was killed and the blood was placed at the door of the Hebrew home as a sign that protected the people inside. The Passover Feast helps us understand God's plan to send Jesus Christ, the Lamb of God (John 1:29).

The Tabernacle

The Tabernacle was the gathering place of the people of God. The parts of the Tabernacle show us Jesus Christ. The golden lampstands (Exodus 25:31-40) remind us that Jesus is our Light. The laver (a large bowl used for washing—Exodus 30:18-21) reminds us that Jesus washed His people free of their sins. The bronze altar (Exodus 27:1-8) reminds us that Jesus took our sins as He died on the cross.

The Priesthood

Aaron, the high priest, reminds us of Jesus Christ. Aaron's breastplate, robe and golden headplate were made of beautiful colors and precious stones which show the glory and beauty of Jesus Christ. Hebrews 2:17 tells us that Jesus is our high priest.

Exodus

and You

As you read the book of Exodus, look for ways God led His people out of Egypt. Look for ways God cared for His people. As you read, ask yourself how God has taken care of you. God is ready to save you—through Jesus Christ.

Leviticus

WRITER: Luke 24:27 and John 5:46 tell us that Moses wrote part of the Old Testament. Guided by the Holy Spirit of God, Moses wrote the first five books of the Bible, which include Leviticus.

TITLE: Leviticus received its name from the word "Levites." The Levites were the people God chose to be priests and workers at the Tabernacle. Leviticus is called the "Book of the Atonement." (Atonement means that God makes people to be His friends.) Leviticus is God's picture book for the people of Israel to help them learn of God's forgiveness for sin. Every picture points to Jesus Christ.

LOCATION: Leviticus is the third book of the Bible. It is the third book in the Bible books called the Law.

The Books of the Law

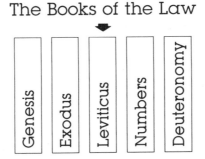

Genesis Exodus Leviticus Numbers Deuteronomy

MAIN PEOPLE: The people who bring the offerings (people of God) and the people who sacrifice the offerings (priests)

OUTLINE: ☐ **Sacrifice and Separation**—How can an unholy person come to a holy God? (Leviticus 1:1—6:7)

☐ **The Priest**—The priest went to God with the prayers and praises of the people. (Leviticus 8—10)

☐ **Rules About Daily Living** (Leviticus 11—22)

☐ **The Day of Atonement** (Leviticus 16)

☐ **The Feasts** (Leviticus 23—25)

When Events Happened

See time line at bottom of page 35.

Main Events

■ Leviticus—God's Laws for His People

Chapters 1—27 The book of Leviticus has laws about:
- offerings
- priests, food, health and daily life
- feasts (holidays)
- rewards and punishments

Chapters 1—7: Laws about Offerings. The laws required that the people make offerings to God at the Tabernacle.

These offerings included animals, grain and other items that would be placed on the altar. Different sacrifices were required for different purposes.

Chapters 8—10: Laws about the Priests. There were strict laws about the duties and behavior of the priests.

Chapters 11—22: Laws about Food, Health and Daily Life. Many of the laws concerned standards of health and the cleanliness of the camp.

Chapters 23—25: Laws about Feasts (Holidays). God also gave careful directions about how the people should celebrate holy days.

Chapters 26,27: Rewards, Punishments, Rules. Directions were given for how to make a promise, how to give to God, what to expect when God was not obeyed.

The Feasts and the Farming Year

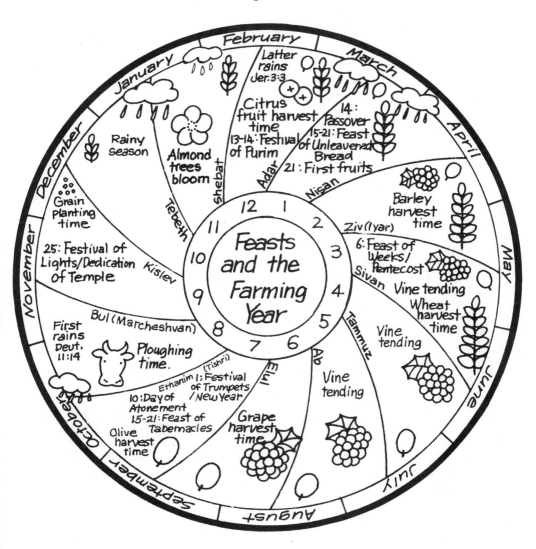

Discoveries from the Past

Records have been discovered in the ruins of civilizations from the time of Moses. They show that other nations had laws that were much like those found in Leviticus. The purpose of the Laws of Moses, however, was to dedicate the people to God.

Where It All Happened

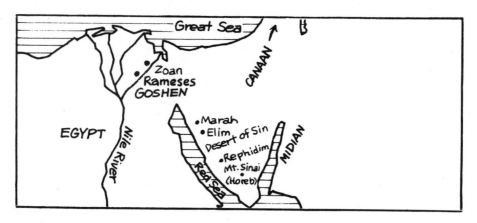

Leviticus

and God's Plan to Send a Savior

When we looked at the Tabernacle in the book of Exodus, we saw that the different parts make us think of Jesus and His ministry.

Here, in the laws of Leviticus, we again see pictures of Jesus Christ. Let's look at some of the laws to see what they tell us about the Savior.

☐ Offerings and Sacrifices	Reminders of Jesus' sacrifice
☐ Burnt Offering (1:3)	Jesus offered Himself as a perfect person to God.
☐ Meal (Grain) Offering (2:1)	Jesus was a perfect offering to God—a sweet-smelling aroma
☐ Peace Offering (3:1)	Jesus' death brought peace between God and man.
☐ Sin Offering (4:2)	Jesus died for the sins of all people. Jesus died in our place.
☐ Trespass Offering (5:1-4)	Jesus died for our trespasses (sins) that we might live.

As you read the book of Leviticus, look for the ways in which perfect sacrifices were needed in order to get forgiveness from God. Remember, Jesus offered Himself to be our sacrifice. He was a perfect offering to God the Father. Do you believe that He gave up His life for you? If you do, will you tell that to God? Will you respond to Him by thanking Him?

Numbers

WRITER: Luke 24:27 and John 5:46 tell us that Moses wrote part of the Old Testament. Guided by the Holy Spirit of God, Moses wrote the first five books of the Bible, which include Numbers.

TITLE: Numbers got its name from the census lists in chapters 1 and 26. Numbers is called the "Book of the March" or "Roll Call." It is about the wilderness wanderings of the people of Israel from Mount Sinai to the border of Canaan. (Canaan was the land God promised to His people.)

LOCATION: Numbers is the fourth book of the Bible. It is the fourth book in the Bible books called the Law.

The Books of the Law

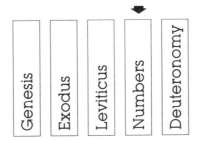

Genesis | Exodus | Leviticus | Numbers | Deuteronomy

MAIN PEOPLE: Moses, Aaron, Joshua, Caleb, Miriam and the Priests

OUTLINE: The events in the book of Numbers took about 40 years.

- ☐ The preparation for the journey (Numbers 1—10)
- ☐ The wilderness wanderings (Numbers 10—20)
- ☐ The journey to Canaan (Numbers 21—36)

When Events Happened

◄ *1450 BC*   *1400 BC* ►

JOSHUA, CALEB   *MOSES, JOSHUA*

Main Events

■ The Preparation for the Journey

Chapters 1—10 The people of Israel were in the Sinai wilderness. The Law was given and the Tabernacle was built. God was preparing the nation of Israel for its work. God led the people to move their camp to Kadesh.

Naphtali Asher Dan

Ephraim Merarites Judah

Manasseh Gershonites Tabernacle Moses Aaron Issachar

Benjamin Kohathites Zebulun

Gad Simeon Reuben

N W E S

Chapters 1—4: The people prepared to leave Mount Sinai by counting everyone.

They also planned how the 12 tribes would line up for the long march. Careful directions were given as to how the contents of the Tabernacle should be moved.

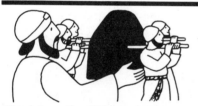

Chapters 5—10: The people were careful to obey every law so that they would be ready to march.

Just before leaving, the people celebrated the Feast of the Passover. This helped them remember how God freed them from slavery in Egypt.

■ The Wilderness Wanderings

Chapters 10—20 The people of Israel did not believe God would give them the Promised Land (Canaan). And so they had to wander in the wilderness for 40 years.

Chapters 10—12: The people set out with God leading just as He did before they camped at Mount Sinai.

The people complained that they had not eaten meat for a long time. God gave them meat, but also punished them for complaining.

Chapters 13—15: Twelve spies were sent to scout out the Promised Land (Canaan). Joshua and Caleb returned saying the people should go into the land.

But the other ten said no. And the people said no. They did not trust God. God said they would wander in the wilderness 40 years instead of going into the land.

Chapters 16—20: A group of people who disobeyed God were swallowed up by the earth. A sign from God proved that God had chosen Aaron to be High Priest.

Moses sinned because he did not obey God's exact command. Aaron died at Mount Hor. Eleazar, Aaron's son, became High Priest.

■ The Journey to Canaan

Chapters 21—36 The people of Israel traveled from Kadesh to the Plains of Moab. They were right across the river from the Promised Land (Canaan).

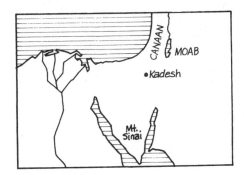

Chapter 21: The people grumbled and complained against God. God sent snakes whose bites killed people.

The people were sorry for their sin. Moses prayed. God had Moses make a bronze snake on a pole. Looking at it would cure a snake bite.

Chapters 22—24: When the Israelites camped in Moab, the Moabites were afraid. The king sent for Balaam to come and put a curse on the Israelites.

When Balaam was on his way to do this, an angel warned him to say only what God told him to say.

Balaam blessed the people of Israel and said good things about them. He did not put a curse on them. The king of Moab was angry.

Chapter 25: God provided protection against Israel's enemies, but the people sinned by worshiping idols.

Chapter 26: A new counting of the people took place. It showed that those who doubted God's promise had died in the 40 years of wandering.

Chapters 27—36: God chose Joshua to be the new leader after Moses. God gave the boundaries of the new land. He chose men to divide the land among the people.

Where It All Happened

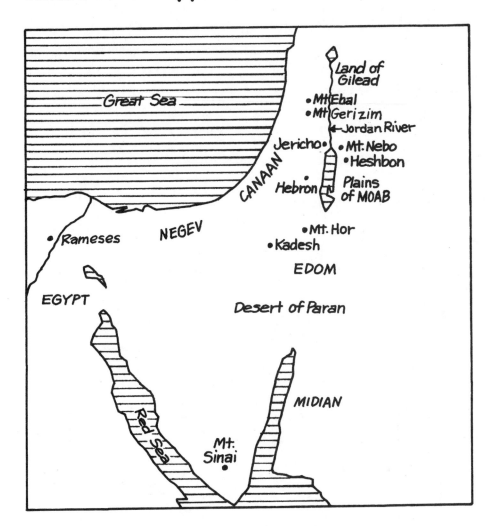

Numbers

and the Coming of the Savior

The bronze serpent (Numbers 21:1-9) gives us a picture of Jesus. The serpent high on the pole before the people makes us think of how Jesus on the cross was made to bear our sins. Those who believed God's promise to heal them looked at the bronze serpent and were saved. Those who believe in God and the sending of His only Son to die on the cross will be saved.

Sinai Wilderness and the Promised Land

Bible Lands Information

Camping at Mount Sinai

As the people of Israel traveled back to the land God promised them, they spent a long time camped near Mount Sinai. It was here that they built the Tabernacle, following the instructions God gave Moses. God even told Moses how the people were to camp around the Tabernacle (see Numbers 2:1-31; 3:21-38).

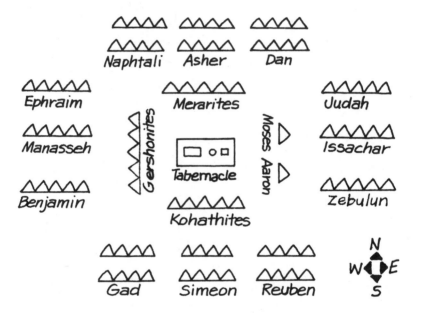

Note: Moses, Aaron and the Merarites, Gershonites and Kohathites were Levites. God chose the tribe of Levi to serve as priests and to care for the Tabernacle. They also carried the Tabernacle and its furnishings when the Israelites moved from place to place. God chose Moses to lead the Israelites, and Aaron to serve as high priest.

Look at the photos on page 351. Many people think this is the location of Mount Sinai and the place where the people of Israel camped. Can you picture in your mind how the Israelite camp must have looked?

Deuteronomy

WRITER: Luke 24:27 and John 5:46 tell us that Moses wrote part of the Old Testament. Guided by the Holy Spirit of God, Moses wrote the first five books of the Bible, which include Deuteronomy.

TITLE: Deuteronomy means "second law." Here the law is given again. Moses did this to remind the people of what God did for them. They were to serve Him when they reached the Promised Land (Canaan).

LOCATION: Deuteronomy is the fifth book of the Bible. It is fifth of the five Bible books called the Books of Law.

The Books of the Law

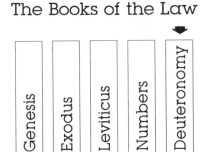

Genesis   Exodus   Leviticus   Numbers   Deuteronomy

MAIN PEOPLE: Moses, Joshua

OUTLINE: ☐ Moses' First Speech to the People
"Looking Back" (Deuteronomy 1—4)
☐ Moses' Second Speech to the People
"Looking Up" (Deuteronomy 5—26)
☐ Moses' Third Speech to the People
"Looking Out" (Deuteronomy 27—33)
☐ Moses' Death (Deuteronomy 34)

When Events Happened

1475 BC   *1400 BC*

MOSES

Main Events

■ The Law Is Given Again

Chapters 1—34 Deuteronomy is divided into three speeches by Moses and a description of Moses' death.

Chapters 1—4: Moses' First Speech—Looking Back. Moses reminded the people of God's faithfulness throughout the journey from Egypt.

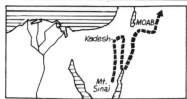

Moses reviewed the trip from Sinai to Kadesh and on to Moab. He promised the people portions of the land on which they stood. He told them to obey God.

Chapters 5—26: Moses' Second Speech—Looking Up. Moses reviewed God's laws and warned the people not to anger God by disobeying Him.

Chapters 27—33: Moses' Third Speech—Looking Out. Moses reviewed the agreement between God and the people. He assured the people of God's protection.

Chapter 34: Moses' Death. God let Moses see Canaan from the top of Mount Nebo. God said, "This is the land I promised to Abraham, Isaac and Jacob."

Moses died and was buried in Moab at the age of 120. The people of Israel were very sad because Moses was gone. Joshua became their new leader.

Discoveries from the Past

Copper in the Land

When Moses was giving directions from the Lord, he told the people that Canaan was "a land where the rocks are iron and you can dig copper out of the hills" (Deuteronomy 8:9). Recent discoveries have proven that there is copper in the hills of which Moses spoke. In fact, these copper mines were probably worked in the days of Solomon. God's Word is correct in everything.

Death of Moses

The first five books of the Old Testament, the Law, were written by Moses. How could chapter 34, telling about his death, have been written by the man himself? It is most likely that Joshua, who would take over for Moses, wrote the story of Moses' death. It was put at the end of Deuteronomy as a record of this important event.

Where It All Happened

The people remained where they were at the end of Leviticus.

Deuteronomy

and God's Plan to Send a Savior

Moses told the people of a coming prophet who would speak God's words just as Moses did. Deuteronomy 18:18 says, "I will raise up for them a prophet like you from among their brothers; I will put my words in his mouth, and he will tell them everything I command him."

Joshua was the first of many people God chose to speak His words as Moses had. But Jesus was to be even greater than Moses or the prophets.

Let's Look at the Books of History

The next 12 books of the Old Testament are the books of History. They record what happened to the people of Israel from the time they reached the Promised Land until the Old Testament closes—almost 900 years of history!

The Books of History

Joshua | Judges | Ruth | First Samuel | Second Samuel | First Kings | Second Kings | First Chronicles | Second Chronicles | Ezra | Nehemiah | Esther

Events	Book
Israel crosses the Jordan River to claim the Promised Land.	Joshua
Israel forgets God's instructions; God allows enemies to invade Israel.	Judges Ruth
Israel asks for a king; Samuel anoints Saul and then David. David reigns in Jerusalem.	1 Samuel 2 Samuel 1 Chronicles
King Solomon builds the Temple; Israel divides into two kingdoms after his death; both kingdoms are carried away as prisoners by enemies.	1 Kings 2 Kings 2 Chronicles
After 70 years, Cyrus, king of Persia, allows the Israelites in his land to return to Jerusalem and rebuild the Temple.	Ezra Nehemiah Esther

How do the books of History fit in with the rest of the Old Testament?

The next five books of the Old Testament are the books of Poetry. They are songs and stories written mostly during the kingdom years of Israel. See the overview on page 120 for more information.

The last 17 books of the Old Testament are the books of Prophecy. They contain the messages God sent Israel through the prophets during the years covered by the books of History. Pages 136-140 explain how the two sections fit together.

What does the New Testament say about the history of Israel?

Paul wrote the Corinthians: "These things happened to them as examples and were written down as warnings for us" (1 Corinthians 10:11). God wants us to learn from Israel's example to trust Him and follow Him faithfully.

Joshua

WRITER: We do not know who the writer was. It may have been Joshua, the man who led the people of Israel into the Promised Land.

TITLE: The book bears the name "Joshua," meaning "the Lord's Salvation." Joshua was the leader God chose to take over when Moses died.

LOCATION: When we open the book of Joshua, we are beginning the second division of the Old Testament, the books of History. Joshua is the sixth book of the Old Testament and the first book of the History division.

The Books of History

Joshua | Judges | Ruth | First Samuel | Second Samuel | First Kings | Second Kings | First Chronicles | Second Chronicles | Ezra | Nehemiah | Esther

MAIN PEOPLE: Joshua, Rahab

OUTLINE:
- ☐ The mobilization of the army (Joshua 1,2)
- ☐ The forward march (Joshua 3—5)
- ☐ The fall of Jericho (Joshua 6)
- ☐ The campaign at Ai (Joshua 7,8)
- ☐ The southern campaign (Joshua 9)
- ☐ The central campaign (Joshua 10)
- ☐ The northern campaign (Joshua 11)
- ☐ The defeated kings (Joshua 12)
- ☐ The division of the land (Joshua 13—22)
- ☐ Joshua's farewell and death (Joshua 23,24)

When Events Happened

1400 BC

RAHAB   ACHAN

Main Events
■ Conquering the Land

Chapters 1—12 Joshua took command of the people and prepared them for the battles ahead. They crossed the Jordan and conquered the cities of Canaan. Canaan was the land God promised to Abraham, Isaac and Jacob.

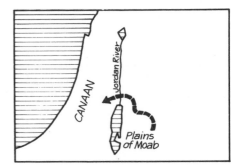

Chapter 1: Joshua took over and prepared his army for battle against the armies of Canaan—nations that God was judging for their great wickedness.

Chapter 2: Spies were sent to scout out the city of Jericho and were helped by the woman Rahab.

Chapters 3—5: Joshua's army crossed the Jordan, bringing with them the Ark of the Covenant.

Chapter 6: God destroyed the walls of Jericho to help Joshua capture the city.

JOSHUA

Chapters 7,8: The army of Joshua was defeated at the city of Ai. It was discovered that the soldier Achan had sinned.

Achan kept for himself treasure from Jericho that should have been given to the Tabernacle. After Achan was punished, Joshua conquered the city of Ai.

Chapters 9—12: Joshua was tricked into defending the Canaanite city of Gibeon against its enemies, the Amorites.

Joshua defeated the Amorites and many Canaanite kings. At last there was peace!

■ Dividing the Land

Chapters 13—22 Joshua divided the conquered land of Canaan among the tribes of Israel. A tribe is a group of families that descended from one of Jacob's sons. The tribe of one of Jacob's sons, Levi, was chosen to serve as priests and helpers in the Tabernacle. And so you will not find their name on the map that shows the sections given to each tribe. You will not find the name of Joseph, another of Jacob's sons, either. This is because Joseph is represented by his sons Ephraim and Manasseh. Look at the map on page 59 to see if you can find the twelve tribes of Israel.

■ Joshua's Farewell and Death

Chapters 23,24 Joshua called the people together to remind them of what had happened since they left Egypt. He told them of the goodness of God and their duty to obey His laws. Joshua died at the age of 110 in the land given to his family.

Joshua

and God's Plan to Send a Savior

The first five books of the Bible told us about God's plan for people. In Genesis, we learn that people sinned and were separated from God. In Exodus, Leviticus, Numbers and Deuteronomy we see God working with His people to bring them back to Himself. We saw Moses as a picture of Jesus Christ. As Moses led the people out of their slavery in Egypt, so Jesus Christ has led His people out of their sin. Jesus died for our sins so that we can be members of God's family.

In the book of Joshua we see the leader Joshua bringing God's people into the Promised Land. To keep the land, the people had to obey God. In the New Testament we see another leader who came to take God's people into the promised land—eternal life in heaven. This leader is Jesus Christ.

Knowing that Jesus Christ died for your sins, you can thank God for Jesus and His death. Also, thank God that you will go to the new promised land (heaven) if you become a member of God's family.

Where It All Happened

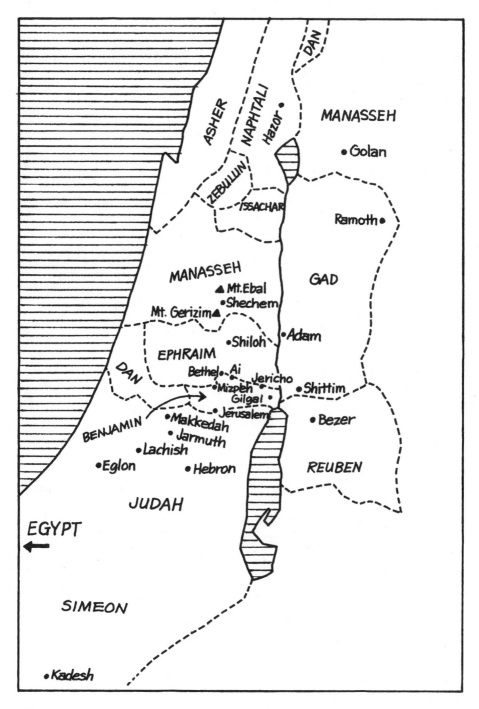

Discoveries from the Past

The Name of Joshua

The name "Joshua" was found in Egyptian tablets (writings) that were from the time of the conquest of Canaan. Since the writings were done at the time of the battles recorded in the Bible, this "Joshua" of the Egyptian reports could very well be the captain of the Israelites.

The Cities of the Conquest

The men and women who search for cities of the past are called archaeologists. When it is first located, an ancient city may look like no more than a mound of earth. Homes, streets and walls used for defense are uncovered by digging down into the mound. The remains of older cities are sometimes found beneath newer cities built on the same spot. Archaeologists can learn a great deal about the history of a city by studying the layers of the mound.

Layers of ashes and ruins were found in some Canaanite cities. But none can be clearly identified with the conquest by Joshua's armies. One reason for this may be that the Israelites often occupied Canaanite towns alongside the people who already lived there. We could not expect to find signs of violent attacks in these places.

Walls and houses made from mud-bricks are often worn down by winter winds and heavy rains. This may have happened to the deserted city of Jericho over a period of hundreds of years.

Archaeologists continue to look for clues that will tell us more about the people who lived in Canaan before and after it was conquered by the Israelites.

Judges

WRITER: The writer of the book of Judges is unknown.

TITLE: In the book of Joshua we saw a people obeying God by taking the Promised Land. They trusted God and His power. Here, in the book of Judges, we see a people not obeying God. They worshiped idols. They were defeated every time they sinned. They did not trust in God. The title means "judges, rulers and saviors." The judges were leaders chosen by God to deliver the Israelites and then rule with justice.

LOCATION: When we open the book of Judges, we are in the second division of the Old Testament, the books of History. Judges is the seventh book of the Old Testament and the second book of the History division.

The Books of History

Joshua | Judges | Ruth | First Samuel | Second Samuel | First Kings | Second Kings | First Chronicles | Second Chronicles | Ezra | Nehemiah | Esther

MAIN PEOPLE: The judges. The chief judges were Deborah, Gideon, Samson and (in the book of 1 Samuel) Samuel.

OUTLINE: ☐ The Israelites did not possess all the land (Judges 1,2)
☐ God sent judges (Judges 3—16)
- Othniel and Ehud (Judges 3)
- Deborah (Judges 4,5)
- Gideon (Judges 6—8)
- The wickedness of Abimelech (Judges 9)
- Jephthah (Judges 10—12)
- Samson (Judges 13—16)

☐ The Israelites did not keep God's laws (Judges 17—21)

When Events Happened

1375 BC

OTHNIEL   DEBORAH

Main Events
■ The Israelites Did Not Possess the Land

Chapters 1,2 After Joshua's death, the people of Israel (Israelites) needed to finish the job God gave them to do. God had commanded them to drive out of Canaan the wicked people who lived there. The Israelites were to possess the land and destroy the altars where the people of Canaan worshiped idols. (God was judging the people of Canaan for their great wickedness.)

The Israelites did not drive out the wicked people of Canaan (Canaanites) as God commanded. The Israelites decided to live with their Canaanite neighbors.

Then the Israelites started worshiping the Canaanite idols. God was angry. He said, "I will not help my people drive the Canaanites out of the land."

■ God Sent Judges

Chapters 3—16 The Israelites' enemies made life very hard for them. When the Israelites prayed for help, God showed them mercy. He sent strong leaders (judges) to help and guide them. But as soon as a judge died, the people disobeyed God again. This happened again and again.

The Israelites disobeyed God.

God allowed their enemies to make life hard for them.

God sent a judge to help them.

The Israelites prayed to God for help.

1050 BC

GIDEON   JEPHTHAH   SAMSON

Chapter 3: When the Israelites worshiped idols, God allowed their enemies to conquer them. When they prayed for help, God sent Othniel to free them.

The Israelites disobeyed God again. And again they were made slaves. When they prayed for help, God sent Ehud to free them.

Chapters 4,5: The people sinned again and were punished by Sisera's army. Sisera and his army were destroyed through the leadership of Deborah and Barak.

Chapters 6—8: The people were next overcome by the Midianites.

God chose Gideon to take charge of the army even though Gideon wanted many proofs of God's faithfulness.

God led Gideon to defeat the Midianites.

63

Chapter 9: Abimelech ruled Israel after murdering the sons of Gideon. Abimelech was punished by being killed trying to conquer the city of Thebez.

Chapters 10—12: God sent more leaders to help the people in their battles against the Canaanites. Jephthah led the Israelites against the Ammonites.

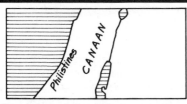

Chapters 13—16: Israel's enemies, the Philistines, lived along the coast. God sent Samson to deliver the Israelites from the Philistines.

Samson used his great strength to win victories over the Philistines, but he foolishly wasted his ability.

He let a Philistine woman put him in the power of his enemies. They blinded him and made him a slave.

God returned Samson's strength. Samson died as he destroyed the building in which he was a prisoner—killing the enemies who were in that building.

■ The Israelites Did Not Keep God's Laws

Chapters 17—21 The Israelites continued to disobey God. Judges 21:25 tells us: "In those days Israel had no king; everyone did as he saw fit."

Chapter 17,18: Micah worshiped an idol that was stolen from him by the men of the tribe of Dan.

Chapters 19—21: The evil deeds done by the tribe of Benjamin caused war with other Israelites. The Benjaminites stole wives at a festival in Shiloh.

Where It All Happened

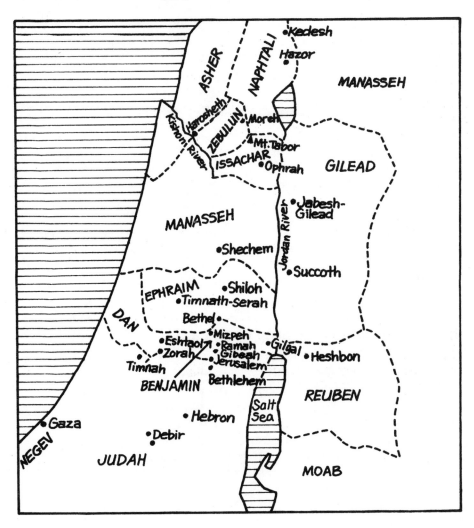

Discoveries from the Past

Evidence from the Egyptians

The name "Israel" has been found in the writings of the Egyptians during the time of peace after Ehud defeated the Moabites. Egyptian writings also tell of the power of the Philistines against whom Israel fought. Records from other nations mention the same persons and places that we find in our Bible. These records help us know the Bible is true.

Evidence from Old Writings

Judges 8 says that Gideon had a young man write down the names of the men in his city. Some people used to believe that the Israelites could not read and write well enough for this to have happened. Archaeologists have found enough Hebrew writings from that time to state that the Bible story is true, after all.

Judges

and God's Plan to Send a Savior

Each judge was a ruler, a person who protected the people, and a savior. The judges gave us a picture of what the promised Savior will be like. That person is Jesus Christ. The book of Judges shows the need for a person who is righteous (pure in mind and life).

When we look at the list of Israel's judges, we see some who were rulers (Othniel and Gideon). In the book of First Samuel, we also see Eli who was a priest and Samuel who was a prophet. This shows us the many jobs of leaders at that time. Jesus, the one who came in New Testament times, was a Prophet, Priest and King.

In the book of Judges we remember that everyone did what was right in his own eyes. We also remember the trouble that kind of living brings on a person. Are you living a life that pleases God? Or are you doing what is right in your own eyes? God wants us to live a pure life. Ask Him right now to help you live a life that pleases Him.

Ruth

WRITER: The writer of the book of Ruth is unknown.

TITLE: The book of Ruth is a story that took place in the time of the judges. It is about Ruth, a woman from the country of Moab. Ruth worshiped the God of Israel instead of the idols of Moab.

LOCATION: When we open the book of Ruth, we are in the second division of the Old Testament, the books of History. Ruth is the eighth book of the Old Testament and the third book of the History division.

The Books of History

Joshua | Judges | Ruth | First Samuel | Second Samuel | First Kings | Second Kings | First Chronicles | Second Chronicles | Ezra | Nehemiah | Esther

MAIN PEOPLE: Ruth, Naomi, Boaz

OUTLINE:
- ☐ Ruth's husband, Mahlon, an Israelite, died in Moab (Ruth 1).
- ☐ Ruth decided to go to Israel with Mahlon's mother, Naomi (Ruth 1:1-18).
- ☐ Ruth cared for Naomi (Ruth 1:19—2:23).
- ☐ Ruth wanted to be with Boaz (Ruth 3:1-18).
- ☐ Ruth married Boaz and had a son (Ruth 4:1-22).

When Events Happened

1375 BC   1050 BC

RUTH, NAOMI   BOAZ

Main Events

■ The Story of Ruth

Chapters 1—4 Ruth was faithful to God in a time when most people had no faith in God. God rewarded her by giving her a husband (Boaz) and a son (Obed). She became David's great-grandmother and an ancestor of our Lord Jesus Christ.

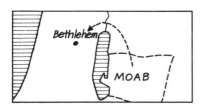

Chapter 1: Naomi and her daughter-in-law, Ruth, went from Moab to Judah after Ruth's husband died. Ruth made Naomi's homeland and God her own.

Chapter 2: Boaz, a rich relative of Naomi, was friendly to Ruth. He allowed her to gather grain from his fields.

Chapter 3: Boaz decided to marry Ruth. That right belonged to another man who was a closer relative. Boaz was not sure what to do.

Chapter 4: Boaz received the right to marry Ruth. He also purchased the land once owned by Naomi's dead husband. Ruth and Boaz married and had a child.

Where It All Happened

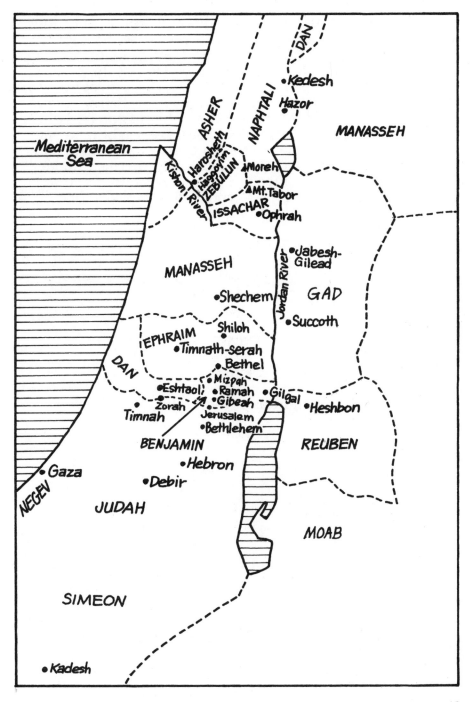

Ruth

and God's Plan to Send a Savior

The story of Ruth is about a stranger in a strange land. Ruth was taken care of by someone willing to pay the price for her safety and well-being. Boaz, a close relative, paid for the right to marry and protect Ruth. He volunteered to pay this price even though he did not have to. Jesus, like Boaz, gives freely to buy eternal life for us. The price Jesus paid was His own life.

It is exciting to know that this picture of Jesus can be seen in a man who was an ancestor of our Lord. The son born to Ruth and Boaz was named Obed. The son of Obed was Jesse, and the son of Jesse was David. The son of David was the famous King Solomon. From Solomon's son the line of fathers and sons can be followed to Jesus. The Gospel writers Matthew and Luke trace the line of Jesus' ancestors.

Boaz and Ruth
|
Obed
|
Jesse
|
David
|
Solomon
|
(hundreds of years later)
|
Jesus

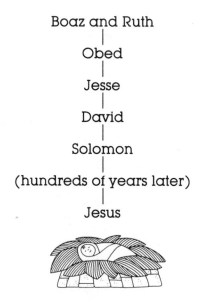

First Samuel

WRITER: The author of the first book of Samuel is unknown.

TITLE: The book of First Samuel describes the transition of great leadership in Israel from the judges to the kings. When this book was first written, it was together with Second Samuel. (The book was probably divided to make it easier to fit on the scrolls. Scrolls were the form in which books were written then.) The name "Samuel" means "asked of God." Samuel was born in answer to his mother's prayer for a son.

LOCATION: When we open the book of First Samuel, we are in the second division of the Old Testament, the books of History. First Samuel is the ninth book of the Old Testament and the fourth book of the History division.

The Books of History

Joshua | Judges | Ruth | First Samuel | Second Samuel | First Kings | Second Kings | First Chronicles | Second Chronicles | Ezra | Nehemiah | Esther

MAIN PEOPLE: Eli, Samuel, Saul, David

OUTLINE: ☐ Samuel—The last of the judges (1 Samuel 1—8)
☐ Saul—Israel's first king (1 Samuel 9—15)
☐ David—A new king chosen (1 Samuel 16—31)

When Events Happened

1100 BC   1050 BC

ELI, SAMUEL   SAMUEL   SAUL   DAVID

Main Events
■ Samuel—the Last of the Judges

Chapters 1—8 Samuel was the last judge. The people asked for a king like all the nations around them. Samuel was sad. He prayed to God. God said, "It is not you they have rejected. They have rejected me. Let them have a king, but warn them of the bad things that will happen." Samuel did as God said.

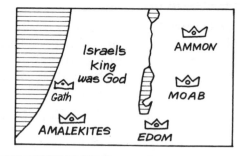

Israel's king was God

Gath

AMMON

MOAB

AMALEKITES

EDOM

Chapters 1—3: Hannah prayed for a child. God answered her prayer. Hannah gave her son Samuel to God so he would have a ministry with God's people.

God called Samuel to serve Him as a prophet and later as a judge. Samuel told the people what God told him to say.

Chapters 4—6: The ark of the covenant was captured by the Philistines. They returned the ark to Israel after suffering many disasters.

Chapters 7,8: Samuel served the people as a judge, but they asked him for a king.

1010 BC

SAUL'S DEATH

■ Saul—Israel's First King

Chapters 9—15 God chose Samuel, Israel's last judge, to anoint Israel's first two kings. The first king was Saul. Samuel anointed Saul by pouring some oil on Saul's head. This showed that Saul had been chosen by God to be the next leader of Israel.

Chapters 9,10: Samuel anointed Saul to be king. Samuel presented Saul to the people as their first king.

Chapters 11,12: The Israelites rejoiced when their new king defeated the Ammonites. Samuel warned the people to serve God and not to worship idols.

Chapters 13—15: Saul did not follow Samuel's orders. Samuel told Saul his kingdom would not last a long time because he disobeyed God.

Saul's son Jonathan made a daring raid on the Philistine camp. Saul's foolish vow almost cost Jonathan his life.

Saul disobeyed God again by not destroying all that he took from his enemies, the Amalekites.

God was sorry that He had made Saul king. Samuel told Saul that because of his disobedience God would choose a new king.

■ David—a New King Is Chosen

Chapters 16—31 God told Samuel to anoint a young shepherd, David, to be the next king. Samuel obeyed God. David did not become king until King Saul died.

Chapter 16: Samuel found and anointed David, the son of Jesse, to be the new king.

Chapter 17: Young David killed Goliath, the giant champion of the Philistines.

Chapters 18—20: David became best friends with Jonathan, Saul's son. Saul was jealous because the people loved David. Saul tried to kill David.

Jonathan and Samuel protected David. David promised to take care of Jonathan's family.

Chapters 21—23: David and his men escaped from Saul, who was chasing them through the wilderness. Saul killed those whom he suspected of helping David.

Chapter 24: David had a chance to kill Saul in a cave at En Gedi. But he spared Saul's life.

Chapters 25,26: David married Abigail. David spared Saul's life a second time when he found Saul asleep in Saul's camp.

Chapters 27,28: David lived with the Philistines and became the Philistine king's bodyguard.

Samuel died in Israel. Saul learned from a fortune-teller about his coming downfall.

Chapter 29: The Philistines did not trust David and his men to fight in their army. David and his men returned to their home.

Chapter 30: The Amalekites kidnapped the wives of David and his men. David chased the Amalekites and got back everything that had been taken.

Chapter 31: Saul and his three sons died in battle with the Philistines.

Where It All Happened

Tyre · ASSYRIA↑ · Damascus

NORTHERN
KINGDOM
ISRAEL

Mt. Carmel

· Megiddo
· Jezreel
▲ Mt. Gilboa · Ramoth Gilead
· Bezek · Jabesh

· Samaria
· Shechem

Mediterranean Sea

· Shiloh · Mahanaim
Bethel

PERSIA
BABYLON
Euphrates →

Mizpah · Micmash · Rabbah
Ramah · Gibeah · Jericho
Gibeon · Nob · Gilgal
· Bahurim
· Beth
Shemesh · Jerusalem
Gath · Bethlehem
· Adullam
· Tekoa
· Hebron MOAB
· Ziph

PHILISTINES

· Carmel En
Ziklag · Maon Gedi
· Beersheba

SOUTHERN KINGDOM
JUDAH EDOM

← EGYPT

Note: Israel was all one kingdom at
the time of Saul, David and Solomon.
After Solomon's death, the kingdom
was divided as shown here.

Elath · · Ezion Geber

Discoveries from the Past

The Ark of the Covenant

The Philistines took the ark of the covenant from the Israelites. They put it in the temple of the god Dagon, an idol (1 Samuel 5:1,2). The next day they found the idol on its face on the ground—before the ark of the covenant. When other disasters happened to the Philistines, they took the ark back to the Israelites.

Men who have been exploring old cities have found a temple of Dagon in the city of Ugarit (Ras Shamra). The name "Dagon" can still be found written on artifacts from the days of Saul and David. (Artifacts are objects made by the people of a particular period of time.)

David's Music

David's love of music is told in 1 Samuel 16:17,18,23. Discoveries by archaeologists show us that music was used in David's time and even earlier. The tombs of some Egyptians had musical instruments in them. One tomb even contained a lyre which was one thousand years old before the days of David.

First Samuel

and God's Plan to Send a Savior

Samuel

The leader Samuel gives us a picture of Jesus Christ. Samuel was a prophet, priest and judge. Jesus was the greatest of the prophets, priests and judges.

David

The leader David is one of the most important pictures of Jesus Christ that we have in the Old Testament. David was born in Bethlehem, served as a shepherd and became the king of Israel. In 1 Samuel 13:14 God calls David "a man after his own heart."

Second Samuel

WRITER: The author of the second book of Samuel is unknown.

TITLE: The book of Second Samuel describes the events of David's reign over Judah and then over the whole nation of Israel. When this book was first written, it was together with First Samuel. (The book was probably divided to make it easier to fit on the scroll.) The name "Samuel" means "asked of God." Samuel was born in answer to his mother's prayer for a son.

LOCATION: When we open the book of Second Samuel, we are in the second division of the Old Testament, the books of History. Second Samuel is the tenth book of the Old Testament and the fifth book of the History division.

The Books of History

Joshua	Judges	Ruth	First Samuel	Second Samuel	First Kings	Second Kings	First Chronicles	Second Chronicles	Ezra	Nehemiah	Esther

MAIN PEOPLE: David, Ish-bosheth, Abner, Mephibosheth, Uriah, Bathsheba, Nathan, Joab, Amnon, Absalom

OUTLINE:
- ☐ David's rise—king and ruler (2 Samuel 1—10)
- ☐ David's fall—sin and problems (2 Samuel 11—20)
- ☐ David's last days—troubles in David's family and kingdom (2 Samuel 21—24)

Main Events

■ David's Rise—King and Ruler

Chapters 1—10 David was made king, first of Judah (the two southern tribes) and then of all Israel (all twelve tribes). He reigned over Judah for seven years. He reigned over all Israel for another 33 years. With God's help, David defeated Israel's enemies.

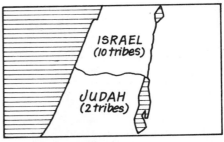

Chapters 1,2: David was sorry to hear of King Saul's death. The people of Judah (the southern tribes) made David their king.

But Ish-bosheth, Saul's son, ruled over Israel (the northern tribes). David's men battled the men of Abner, the servant of Ish-bosheth.

Chapters 3,4: Abner, who had commanded Saul's army, left Ish-bosheth and joined David.

Abner was killed by Joab, one of David's men, in revenge for those killed in the battles. Two of Ish-bosheth's men murdered Ish-bosheth.

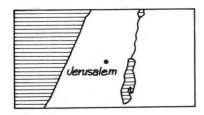

Chapters 5,6: David ruled over all the tribes and made his capital in the city of Jerusalem.

He made war against the Philistines and brought the ark of the covenant to Jerusalem.

When Events Happened

1010 BC

DAVID

NATHAN

MEPHIBOSHETH

Chapter 7: David offered to build a beautiful Temple. But God said it is He who will build a house (family) for David.

Speaking through the prophet Nathan, God promised that a son of David will have a kingdom without end.

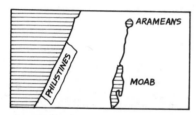

Chapters 8—10: David finally defeated the Philistines, Moab, Zobah and the Arameans. He made his nation strong and ruled with justice.

Remembering his promise to Jonathan, David took care of Jonathan's son, Mephibosheth. The armies of Ammon, joined by Aramean rebels, were defeated.

■ David's Fall—Sin and Problems

Chapters 11—20 David sinned and God had to punish him. God forgave David when David confessed his sin and turned from it (2 Samuel 12:13,14). David did not train his sons well and they became selfish and disobedient. They plotted against David and caused him much sadness and trouble.

970 BC

BATHSHEBA

Chapters 11,12: David sinned by taking the wife of another man. He then planned for her husband to be killed in battle.

David admitted he had done wrong. He confessed this to God and God forgave him. But God punished David by allowing his child to die.

Chapters 13—18: David's son Absalom ran away after killing his brother. David had Absalom brought back to Jerusalem and, after a while, forgave him.

Absalom plotted to take away David's power, forcing David and his household to escape from Jerusalem. David's men found and killed Absalom.

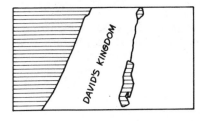

DAVID'S KINGDOM

Chapters 19,20: The people of Judah called David back as king. Joab, David's servant, put down an uprising among the men of Israel.

Judah and Israel were together again.

81

■ David's Last Days

Chapters 21—24 The last four chapters of Second Samuel tell some things David did and said toward the end of his life. However, David's death is not recorded until the beginning of the next book—First Kings.

Chapter 21: David was almost killed in a battle with the Philistines.

Chapters 22—24: David sang a song in which he thanked God for His protection.

Soon, however, David began to doubt God's protection. He counted his people to make sure that his nation was strong.

Angered by David's doubt, God sent a plague and many people died. David built an altar and made peace offerings. God forgave him and stopped the plague.

Discoveries from the Past

Archaeologists have found much evidence about David and his life. They have found references to the music and worship used during David's time. They have also found the City of David, which was called the fortress or stronghold of Zion (2 Samuel 5:7). The City of David was only part of the city we know today as Jerusalem (see pages 341, 353 and 354).

Second Samuel

and God's Plan to Send a Savior

Samuel

In chapter 7 of Second Samuel, the prophet Nathan told David God's words. God promised that a descendant of David would have a Kingdom that would last forever. Nathan was talking about Solomon, David's son. But he was also pointing us toward David's greatest son—Jesus Christ. Matthew 1:1 calls Jesus Christ the son of David because Jesus was from David's family. But Jesus was born hundreds of years later.

Where It All Happened

See the map on page 76.

First Kings

WRITER: No author is named for the books of Kings. Some people think these books may have been written by the prophet Jeremiah or by someone else of his time. The writer was familiar with the history of the people of Israel.

TITLE: The books of Kings were originally one book. First Kings covers over 100 years—from the end of King David's reign to the end of King Ahaziah's reign. In the first half of the book, Israel was one kingdom. In the last half of the book, Israel was divided into two separately-ruled kingdoms.

LOCATION: The book of First Kings is in the History division of the Old Testament. It is the sixth book of History and the eleventh book of the Old Testament.

The Books of History

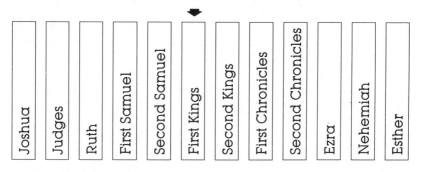

Joshua | Judges | Ruth | First Samuel | Second Samuel | First Kings | Second Kings | First Chronicles | Second Chronicles | Ezra | Nehemiah | Esther

MAIN PEOPLE: David, Solomon, Rehoboam, Nathan, Jeroboam, Ahab, Jezebel, Elijah, Elisha

OUTLINE:
- ☐ The reign of Solomon (1 Kings 1—10)
- ☐ The death of Solomon and division of the kingdom (1 Kings 11—16)
- ☐ King Ahab and his wife Jezebel introduce Baal worship (1 Kings 16)
- ☐ The Prophet Elijah defeats the prophets of Baal (1 Kings 17,18)
- ☐ Ahab does evil (1 Kings 19—22)

Main Events

◼ The Reign of Solomon

Chapters 1—8 Before King David died, he chose his son Solomon to be king. Solomon asked God for wisdom and understanding so that he could rule God's people well. God gave Solomon wisdom, riches and fame. The first 10 chapters of this book tell of God's great blessing on Solomon.

Chapters 1,2: David died, leaving the kingdom to Solomon, his son. To keep his throne, Solomon executed his brother and others who plotted against him.

Chapters 3,4: Solomon asked God for wisdom and understanding. His request pleased God, who gave him wisdom, riches and fame.

People from all over came to hear the wisdom of Solomon and get his help.

Chapters 5—8: God had told David that Solomon would build a great Temple for the Lord God. And Solomon did. Only the finest materials were used.

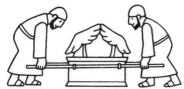

Thousands of people worked to complete the Temple. When the Temple was finished, the ark of the covenant was brought into it.

Chapters 8,9: The king and the people had a celebration that lasted for 14 days. God promised to protect Solomon as long as he and the people obeyed God.

When Events Happened

970 BC   930 BC

SOLOMON   JEROBOAM (I) / REHOBOAM (J)

Chapter 9: Solomon built a strong army and navy, and built many cities throughout his kingdom.

Chapter 10: The Queen of Sheba visited Solomon to hear his wisdom and bring him gifts. Solomon became known as the wisest and richest king on earth.

■ The Division of the Kingdom

Chapters 11—16 Solomon turned from God and worshiped idols. God told Solomon He would take most of the kingdom away from Solomon's son and give it to someone else. After Solomon's death, his son Rehoboam became king of Judah. But Jeroboam, one of Solomon's leaders, became king of Israel.

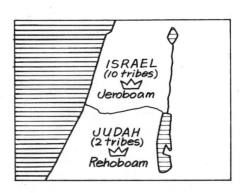

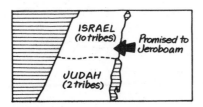

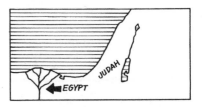

Chapters 11: God promised the rule of the ten northern tribes (Israel) to Jeroboam as soon as Solomon died. Jeroboam was one of Solomon's leaders.

Solomon tried to kill Jeroboam, but Jeroboam escaped to Egypt. Jeroboam stayed in Egypt until Solomon died.

870BC   853BC

AHAB(I)/JEZEBEL   ELIJAH   ELIJAH/ELISHA   AHAB(I)

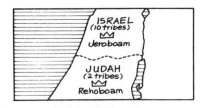

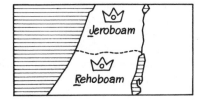

Chapters 12,13: After Solomon's death, his son **Rehoboam** was made king in Judah (two tribes). But the ten tribes of Israel made **Jeroboam** their king.

These two kings' names are a lot alike. Here's a way to remember which man ruled which kingdom. When written on a map, the names are in alphabetical order.

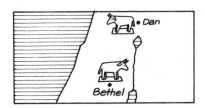

ISRAEL—Jeroboam had golden calves set up at Bethel and Dan. He told the people of Israel to offer sacrifices to these golden calves.

God was angry because Jeroboam was leading the people to worship idols. He sent a prophet with a message for Jeroboam. But Jeroboam kept on doing wrong.

Chapter 14: ISRAEL and JUDAH— God was angered by the sins of both Jeroboam and Rehoboam. The people of both Israel and Judah worshiped idols.

The king of Egypt attacked Jerusalem and carried away the treasures of the palace and the Temple.

JUDAH:	**ISRAEL:**
Rehoboam (Solomon's son)	Jeroboam
|	|
Abijah	(many kings)
|	|
Asa (a good king)	Ahab (a very wicked king)

Chapters 15,16: JUDAH—When Rehoboam died, his son and his grandson Asa followed as kings in Judah. Asa did what was right in God's eyes.

ISRAEL—As the years passed, other men became kings of Israel. Most of them did not obey God's commands. The worst was Ahab who built temples for idol worship.

■ The Reign of Wicked King Ahab

Chapters 17—22 The rest of First Kings focuses on the reign of wicked King Ahab of Israel. He and his wife Jezebel led the people to worship the false god, Baal. The Lord God used His prophet Elijah to show that He alone is the one true God. But Ahab and Jezebel continued in their wicked ways.

Chapters 17—19: ISRAEL—The prophet Elijah challenged and defeated the prophets of the false god Baal.

Elijah fled from Ahab and his evil queen, Jezebel. Elijah ran to the wilderness where God took care of him.

Elisha was chosen to follow Elijah. (Elijah trained Elisha to be ready to take his place as God's prophet when Elijah died.)

ELIJAH
ELISHA

The names of these two men are a lot alike. You can remember which came first if you notice that their names are in alphabetical order.

Chapters 20—22: Ahab battled and defeated the Arameans. Ahab took possession of a vineyard that belonged to a man that Jezebel arranged to have killed.

God said He would punish Ahab and Jezebel. Ahab died in a battle that a prophet of God warned him not to fight. Ahab's son continued to disobey God's laws.

Kings and Prophets

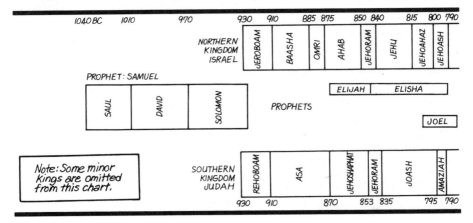

| 1040 BC | 1010 | 970 | 930 | 910 | 885 | 875 | 850 | 840 | 815 | 800 | 790 |

NORTHERN KINGDOM ISRAEL: JEROBOAM, BAASHA, OMRI, AHAB, JEHORAM, JEHU, JEHOAHAZ, JEHOASH

PROPHET: SAMUEL

SAUL, DAVID, SOLOMON

PROPHETS

ELIJAH, ELISHA

JOEL

Note: Some minor kings are omitted from this chart.

SOUTHERN KINGDOM JUDAH: REHOBOAM, ASA, JEHOSHAPHAT, JEHORAM, JOASH, AMAZIAH

| 930 | 910 | 870 | 853 | 835 | 795 | 790 |

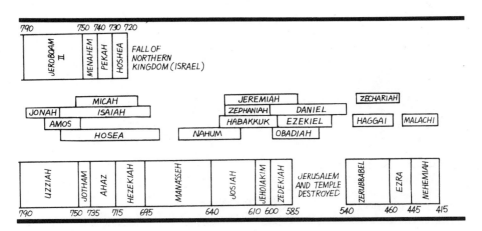

| 790 | 750 | 740 | 730 | 720 |

JEROBOAM II, MENAHEM, PEKAH, HOSHEA, FALL OF NORTHERN KINGDOM (ISRAEL)

JONAH, MICAH, ISAIAH, AMOS, HOSEA, JEREMIAH, ZEPHANIAH, DANIEL, HABAKKUK, EZEKIEL, NAHUM, OBADIAH, ZECHARIAH, HAGGAI, MALACHI

UZZIAH, JOTHAM, AHAZ, HEZEKIAH, MANASSEH, JOSIAH, JEHOIAKIM, ZEDEKIAH, JERUSALEM AND TEMPLE DESTROYED, ZERUBBABEL, EZRA, NEHEMIAH

| 790 | 750 | 735 | 715 | 695 | 640 | 610 | 600 | 585 | 540 | 460 | 445 | 415 |

Where It All Happened

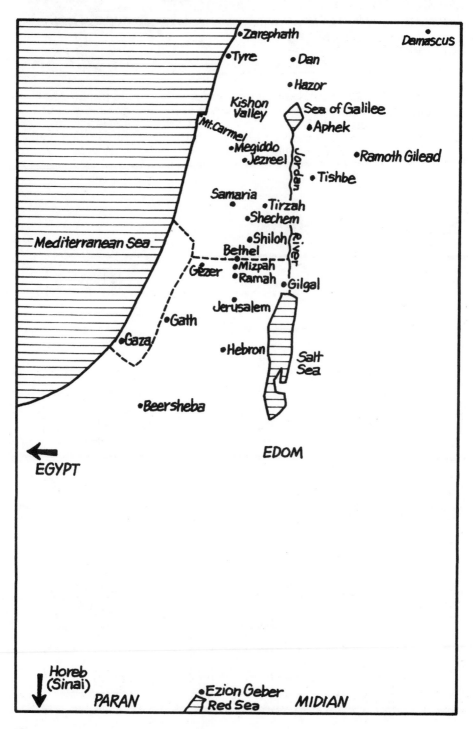

Discoveries from the Past

Solomon's Temple

The Temple built by Solomon must have been a very beautiful building. It was about twice the size of the Tabernacle (see Exodus 26:16,18 and First Kings 6:2). The Temple was divided into two parts. The outer room was the holy place. The inner room was the most holy place. The floors and walls were made from stone and cedar wood. They were covered with gold. At the front of the Temple there was a large porch with two tall pillars.

Although archaeologists are not able to date any remains of the Temple of Solomon's time, many other buildings of his day have been uncovered. They match the style and building materials described in the Bible.

Canaanite Religion

Writings and other remains found in Canaanite cities tell about their religion. The people worshiped idols (false gods) of wood and stone. They sacrificed even their little children to these idols. The worship of false gods was a bad example to the people of Israel.

The Moabite Stone

The Moabite Stone, set up by King Mesha of Moab, shows the importance of Chemosh, the god of Moab. It also names Omri (Ahab's father) as king of Israel.

Second Kings

WRITER: No author is named for the books of Kings. Some people think these books may have been written by the prophet Jeremiah or by someone else of his time. The writer was familiar with the history of the people of Israel.

TITLE: The books of Kings were originally one book. Second Kings covers over 200 years—from the ministry of Elisha under Ahaziah, king of Israel, and Jehoram, king of Judah, to the fall of the kingdom of Judah.

LOCATION: The book of Second Kings is in the History division of the Old Testament. It is the seventh book of History and the twelfth book of the Old Testament.

The Books of History

Joshua | Judges | Ruth | First Samuel | Second Samuel | First Kings | Second Kings | First Chronicles | Second Chronicles | Ezra | Nehemiah | Esther

MAIN PEOPLE: In ISRAEL—Elisha, Jehu, Jeroboam II
In JUDAH—Joash, Ahaz, Hezekiah, Isaiah, Manasseh, Josiah

OUTLINE: ☐ The ministry of Elijah (1 Kings 17—22; 2 Kings 1,2)
☐ The ministry of Elisha (2 Kings 1—9:13)
☐ The last days of Israel (2 Kings 10—17)
☐ The last days of Judah (2 Kings 18—25)

Main Events

■ The Ministries of Elijah and Elisha

Chapters 1—9 These chapters tell ways God used two prophets, Elijah and Elisha, to help people and to give people His messages.

ELIJAH   ELISHA

Chapter 1: ISRAEL—Ahaziah died. His younger brother Jehoram (also spelled Joram) became king of Israel.

Chapter 2: Elijah was taken up to heaven in a whirlwind, leaving Elisha to take over his work as a prophet of the Lord.

Chapter 3: The kings of Israel, Judah and Edom joined in fighting against Moab. Elisha gave them God's instructions.

Chapter 4: Elisha helped a widow pay money she owed. He helped another woman by asking God to bring her son back from death. And God did.

Chapter 5: Naaman, an Aramean commander, had leprosy. He came to Elisha to be healed. When he followed Elisha's instructions, God healed him.

Chapter 6: Elisha helped a man who had lost an axhead. Elisha made it float to the surface of the river.

When Events Happened (I)=KING OF ISRAEL   (J)=KING OF JUDAH

| 850 BC | 840 BC | 830 BC | 722 BC |

KINGS OF   ELIJAH/ELISHA   JEHU(I)   JOASH(J)   END OF
ISRAEL/JUDAH   NORTHERN KINGDOM

Elisha warned the king of Israel about an attack by the Arameans.

The Arameans tried to capture Elisha but were struck blind. Elisha led the blind men to Israel, where they were fed and set free.

Chapters 6,7: God protected the city of Samaria from attack. He made the attackers believe they heard the sounds of a great army coming against them.

Chapters 8,9: Elisha anointed Jehu king of Israel. Jehu killed the wicked kings of Israel and Judah. He ordered that Jezebel, Ahab's wicked queen, be killed.

■ The Last Days of Israel

Chapters 10—17 God told His people that if they obeyed Him, He would bless them in the land He gave them. But if they disobeyed Him, He would send them out of this land (1 Kings 9:6-9). God kept warning them, but they wouldn't listen. The 10 northern tribes (Israel) were the first to be sent out of the land.

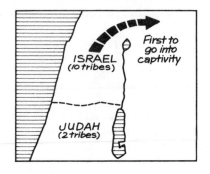

Chapter 10: ISRAEL—Jehu killed all who remained loyal to the family of dead King Ahab. He also slew the worshipers of Baal.

God promised the kingdom of Israel to Jehu's family for four generations. But Jehu didn't fully obey God, and Aram (Syria) overpowered areas of Israel.

Chapter 11: JUDAH—Joash, the son of Ahaziah, was hidden from his evil grandmother Athaliah. Athaliah wanted the throne of Judah for herself.

When Joash was seven years old, he was crowned king. His wicked grandmother was killed.

Chapter 12: Joash, who became known as Jehoash, made sure that the Temple was repaired.

However, when the king of Aram threatened to attack, Jehoash gave him all the treasures of the Temple and the palace to make him go away.

When Jehoash was killed, his son became king.

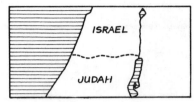

Chapters 13—16: ISRAEL and JUDAH—The kings of Israel and Judah continued to disobey God, but God protected these two kingdoms for the time being.

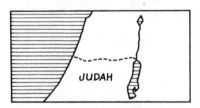

The places where the false gods were worshiped were still not destroyed.

Chapter 17: ISRAEL—The king of Assyria captured Israel and took the people of Israel to Assyria as prisoners.

God was punishing the people because they did not obey Him. The kingdom of Israel had now ended!

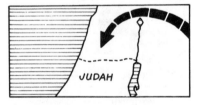

The king of Assyria sent people from other lands to live in the land of Israel.

■ The Last Days of Judah

Chapters 18—25 God continued to show mercy to the people of Judah. There were some good kings and some wicked kings. God warned the people what would happen if they continued to disobey Him. But they would not listen. And so the people of Judah were also sent out of the land God gave them.

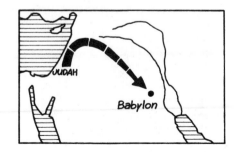

Chapters 18,19: Hezekiah, the new king of Judah, obeyed God by destroying places of idol worship. He would not serve the king of Assyria.

The Assyrian army came to attack Jerusalem, but God promised Hezekiah that the city would be saved. God sent an angel to kill the Assyrian army at night.

Chapter 20: God answered the prayer of a dying Hezekiah by making him well.

The prophet Isaiah warned Hezekiah that the Babylonians only pretended to be friendly. They would someday carry away the treasures and people of Judah.

After a long reign, Hezekiah died.

Chapter 21: Hezekiah's son Manasseh angered God by bringing back idols and many evil practices. His son Amon also worshiped idols.

When Amon was killed, the people crowned his eight-year-old son Josiah.

Chapter 22: King Josiah repaired the Temple. While repairs were being made, the workers found the Book of the Law. It contained the commands of God.

Josiah was sad because he knew he and the people had not followed God's laws.

Chapter 23: Josiah promised to keep God's laws. He also destroyed the idols.

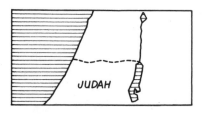

Josiah loved God, but God was still angry with the people. God said He would destroy Judah as He had destroyed Israel.

After Josiah died, his son was captured by the army of Egypt. The Egyptians made another of Josiah's sons the king of Judah.

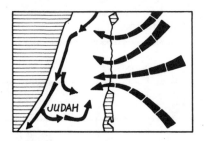

Chapters 24,25: God allowed other nations to attack Judah.

The king of Babylon captured Judah. He carried away the king, all the treasures and all but the poorest people. The kingdom of Judah had also ended!

Where It All Happened

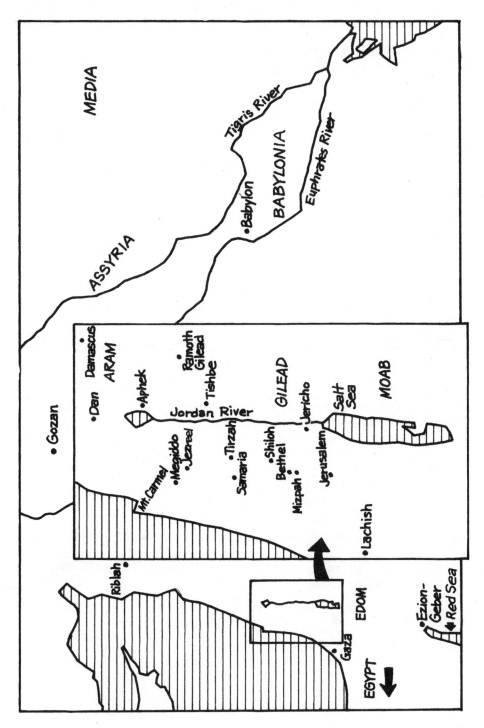

Discoveries from the Past

Jehu and the Assyrian Emperor

A stone that was found in the palace of Nimrud actually shows the Israelite king Jehu kneeling before an Assyrian emperor. The writing on the stone tells how the Israelites came bringing gifts of tribute. While this incident is not described in 2 Kings, Jehu was probably seeking Assyrian help against their common enemy Hazael, king of Syria (2 Kings 10:32).

Writings found from the Assyrians show that what is written in the books of Kings is true. These writings list people and events that are also described in the Bible.

The City of Babylon

At the end of the book of Second Kings the people of Judah were carried off to Babylon because of their sin. The great city of Babylon has been discovered and many of the ruins uncovered. See information and photos on pages 342, 356.

God's People

and the Land God Gave Them

In the books of First and Second Kings we have seen the people of Israel leaving the land God gave them. God had to punish the people for their great sin. In the book of Second Chronicles you will read another account of these events. Then, in the books of Ezra and Nehemiah, you will see God doing a very wonderful thing. After allowing His people to be held captive in foreign lands, He brings some of them back again to the land He promised them. For it was God's plan that in this land and through this people He would send the promised Savior—His Son, Jesus Christ.

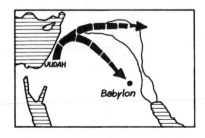

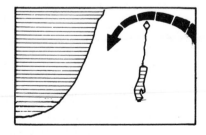

1 KINGS, 2 KINGS, 2 CHRONICLES   EZRA, NEHEMIAH

First Chronicles

WRITER: First and Second Chronicles were once together as one book. Ezra has often been named as the writer of this book. Ezra was a teacher God chose to teach His people about His faithfulness to them. Here we have lessons on God's activities in history. The writer gives us another look at many of the events described in earlier books.

TITLE: The name "Chronicles" means "the words of the days." First Chronicles lists families and leaders from Adam through the captivity. It gives details of the life of David.

LOCATION: First Chronicles is in the History division of the Old Testament. It is the eighth book of History and the thirteenth book of the Old Testament.

The Books of History

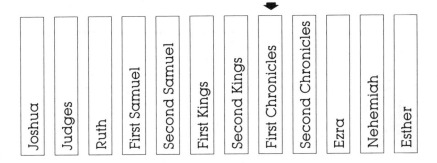

Joshua | Judges | Ruth | First Samuel | Second Samuel | First Kings | Second Kings | First Chronicles | Second Chronicles | Ezra | Nehemiah | Esther

MAIN PEOPLE: Adam, Abraham, Jacob, Saul, David

OUTLINE: ☐ Lists of families and leaders (1 Chronicles 1—9)
☐ The reign of David (1 Chronicles 10—29)
  • The death of Saul (1 Chronicles 10)
  • David's rise to power (1 Chronicles 11,12)
  • The ark of the covenant (1 Chronicles 13—16)
  • God's promise and David's prayer (1 Chronicles 17)
  • The victories of David (1 Chronicles 18—20)
  • David's Census (1 Chronicles 21)
  • Preparations for the Temple (1 Chronicles 22—27)
  • David's last days and death (1 Chronicles 28,29)

When Events Happened

FIRST CHRONICLES

1010 BC

970 BC

Long live King Solomon!

SAUL   DAVID   NATHAN   SOLOMON

Main Events
■ Another Look at Jewish History

Chapters 1—29 The books of Chronicles give another view of Jewish history that was recorded in Second Samuel through Second Kings. The writer reminded the Jewish people of their special relationship to God. Usually, brief accounts in First Chronicles can be found in more detail in Second Samuel.

Second Samuel | First Kings | Second Kings

another view ▶

First Chronicles | Second Chronicles

Chapters 1—9: The writer listed the people of God from Adam through the captivity.

Chapters 10—12: Saul was killed as his army fought the Philistines. David replaced Saul as king of Israel.

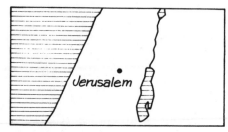

Jerusalem

Chapters 13—16: King David defeated the enemies of Israel and brought the ark of God back to Jerusalem.

Chapter 17: Speaking through the prophet Nathan, God promised that a son of David will have a kingdom without end.

SECOND CHRONICLES

605 BC   586 BC   538 BC

DIVIDED KINGDOM   CAPTIVES TAKEN   FALL OF JERUSALEM   CYRUS
TO BABYLON

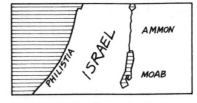

David thanked God for His goodness and His wonderful promise.

Chapters 18—20: David and his
army won victories against the
Philistines, the Moabites, the king
of Zobah, the Ammonites and
other surrounding nations.

Chapter 21: David sinned by
counting his army, rather than
trusting God.

Chapters 22—27: David began
preparation for building the Temple. He organized workmen,
priests, singers and other officials.

Chapters 28—29: David gave
final instructions for building the
Temple. He gave gifts and asked
the people to give gifts so Solomon could complete the work.

Solomon was made king. Then
David died.

Where It All Happened

See the map on page 76.

First Chronicles

and God's Plan to Send a Savior

In First Chronicles, chapters 1—3, we are given the royal line of King David. The writer goes back to Adam and traces the family line through Abraham and Jacob and on through the many kings from David's family.

In Matthew, chapter 1, we are given the family line of Jesus Christ. Matthew 1:17 says, "Thus there were fourteen generations in all from Abraham to David, fourteen from David to the exile to Babylon, and fourteen from the exile to the Christ."

It's exciting to see how long God planned to send a Savior. God cares very much for you. He proved this by sending His Son Jesus Christ to be your Savior.

Second Chronicles

WRITER: First and Second Chronicles were once together as one book. Ezra has often been named as the writer of this book. Ezra was a teacher God chose to teach His people about His faithfulness to them. Here we have lessons on God's activities in history. The writer gives us another look at many of the events described in earlier books.

TITLE: "Chronicles" means "the words of the days." Second Chronicles tells the history of Solomon and the kings of Judah.

LOCATION: Second Chronicles is in the History division of the Old Testament. It is the ninth book of History and the fourteenth book of the Old Testament.

The Books of History

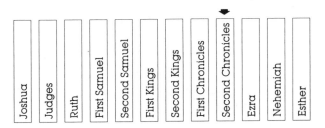

MAIN PEOPLE: Solomon and the rulers of Judah

OUTLINE: The numbers in parentheses are chapter numbers.

☐ The reign of Solomon (1—9)
- Solomon's request (1)
- Solomon's Temple (2—7)
- Solomon's success (8,9)

☐ The rulers of Judah (10—36)
- Rehoboam (10—12)
- Abijah (13)
- Asa (14—16)
- Jehoshaphat (17—20)
- Jehoram (21)
- Ahaziah, Athaliah,
- Joash (22—24)
- Amaziah (25)
- Uzziah (26)
- Jotham (27)
- Ahaz (28)
- Hezekiah (29—32)
- Manasseh, Amon (33)
- The fall of Jerusalem (36)

Main Events

■ Another Look at Solomon and the Kings of Judah

Chapters 1—36 Second Chronicles repeats many stories from the books of Kings. It focuses on kings in David's family—Solomon and the kings of Judah. You will need to read the books of Kings for stories of the kings of Israel.

Chapters 1—9: Solomon, David's son, became the richest and wisest king on earth.

He made the nation strong and built a beautiful Temple in Jerusalem.

Chapters 10—35: The people of Israel were divided into two nations—Israel and Judah. These chapters tell about the kings of Judah.

Chapter 36: Because the people of Judah often turned to worshiping idols, God allowed them to be defeated. They were taken as prisoners to a foreign country.

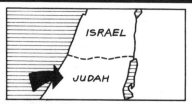

The Temple at Jerusalem was destroyed and the wall around the city was broken down.

The book ends by telling what the king of Persia did 70 years later. He gave permission for God's people to return and rebuild God's Temple in Jerusalem.

Discoveries from the Past

Hezekiah's Tunnel

Second Chronicles 32 tells us that Hezekiah wanted to be sure the people in Jerusalem would have water to drink in case of an attack. He had his men dig a tunnel that reached from inside the city to a spring outside the wall. When the enemy attacked, the people could reach the water supply without going outside the city wall. See pages 341, 353–355.

In 1880, the old tunnel was found by a young boy playing in the water. Writings on the wall of the tunnel told that it had been dug by Hezekiah's workers. The inscription said there were two groups of men working on the tunnel. One group started at one end and the other group started at the other end. When they got near the middle, they could hear each other's pickaxes. One group had to make a turn in the tunnel to meet the other group.

When Events Happened

See the time line on pages 102, 103.

Where It All Happened

See the map on page 76.

God's People

and the Land God Gave Them

The last chapter of Second Chronicles tells how God allowed His people to be taken away from the land He gave them. It also tells how, 70 years later, the king of Persia gave permission for God's people to return to their own land. This was all part of God's plan. For it was to be in this land (Palestine) and through this people (the Jewish people) that God would send the promised Savior—His Son, Jesus Christ.

The next two books, Ezra and Nehemiah, tell about God's people returning to the land He gave them.

Ezra

WRITER: Ezra was probably the author of this book. He is not named in the book as the writer but he most likely wrote this book along with the Chronicles.

TITLE: The title "Ezra" is the name of the main person in this book. Ezra was a godly man who trusted in the Lord.

LOCATION: Ezra is in the History division of the Old Testament. It is the tenth book of History and the fifteenth book of the Old Testament.

The Books of History

Joshua | Judges | Ruth | First Samuel | Second Samuel | First Kings | Second Kings | First Chronicles | Second Chronicles | Ezra | Nehemiah | Esther

MAIN PEOPLE: Sheshbazzar, Ezra

OUTLINE: ☐ The return under Sheshbazzar (Ezra 1—6)
- The decree of the Persian king (Ezra 1)
- The census of the people (Ezra 2)
- The rebuilding of the Temple (Ezra 3—6)

☐ The return under Ezra (Ezra 7—10)
- The return to Jerusalem (Ezra 7,8)
- Dealing with the people's sins (Ezra 9,10)

Main Events

■ God's People Return to Their Land

The book of Ezra begins where the book of Second Chronicles ends. In the book of Ezra we see God's promise coming true. The people returned to the Promised Land after being captives in Babylon for 70 years.

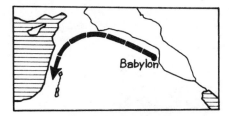

Chapter 1: Cyrus, king of Persia, made an announcement to the Jewish captives in Babylon. He said they could return to Jerusalem to rebuild the Temple.

Chapter 2: The people were counted as they were going back to Jerusalem. The number of men was 42,360.

Chapter 3: When the people arrived in Jerusalem, they rebuilt the altar for burnt offerings and offered sacrifices to God.

They also celebrated the Feast of Tabernacles.

When the building materials were ready, the workers began laying the foundation of the Temple.

Chapter 4: Because enemies of God's people sent messages to the two kings who followed Cyrus, work on the Temple was ordered stopped.

When Events Happened

540 BC

538 BC

KING CYRUS   ZERUBBABEL   HAGGAI, ZECHARIAH

Chapters 5,6: The prophets, Haggai and Zechariah, told the people to go back to work on the Temple.

King Darius was asked if the people had permission to finish the Temple. He found the announcement of Cyrus and said the people could finish the Temple.

Chapters 7,8: Artaxerxes, the king of Persia, allowed Ezra to return to Jerusalem to teach the people God's laws.

A group that included almost 2000 men returned with Ezra.

Chapters 9,10: At this time, God's people were living with people who worshiped idols. Some even married people who worshiped idols.

Ezra prayed, asking God to forgive His people. The people were sorry for their sins. They promised to obey God from then on.

458 BC   432 BC

KING DARIUS   EZRA   NEHEMIAH

Discoveries from the Past

Archaeologists who have been digging in the Temple area in Jerusalem have uncovered part of the Temple wall. Much of the wall is made from large, smooth stones from New Testament times. But suddenly those stones stop—and there are smaller, less-finished stones. Archaeologists believe these are the stones used to rebuild the Temple at the time we read about in Ezra!

Where It All Happened

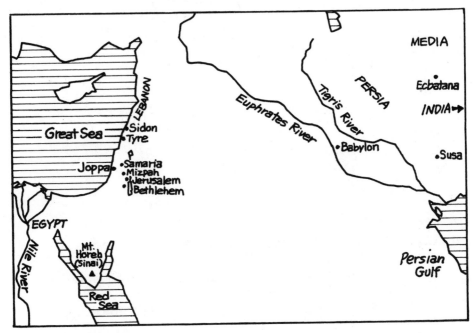

Nehemiah

WRITER: Nehemiah was probably the author of most of this book. Ezra may have had a part in putting the book together. Hundreds of years ago the books of Ezra and Nehemiah were in one book called the book of Ezra. Then they were divided into two books. The book we now call Ezra was called I Ezra. The book we now call Nehemiah was called II Ezra. Now these two books are named for important people in the books—Ezra and Nehemiah.

TITLE: "Nehemiah" means "the comfort of Jehovah (God)." The book is named after its main person—Nehemiah. Nehemiah was a cupbearer to the Persian king Artaxerxes I. This was a position of great responsibility. Nehemiah was trusted by the king. He was dedicated to God and His work. He was a man of prayer and gave God all the credit for the work that was done.

LOCATION: Nehemiah is in the History division of the Old Testament. It is the eleventh book of History and the sixteenth book of the Old Testament.

The Books of History

Joshua | Judges | Ruth | First Samuel | Second Samuel | First Kings | Second Kings | First Chronicles | Second Chronicles | Ezra | Nehemiah | Esther

MAIN PERSON: Nehemiah

OUTLINE:
☐ The rebuilding of the wall of Jerusalem (Nehemiah 1—7)
☐ The repairing of the agreement with God (Nehemiah 8—10)
☐ The reforming of the nation (Nehemiah 11—13)

Main Events

■ God's People Settle in Their Land

Chapters 1—13 God's people returned to Jerusalem from Babylon in three groups. The book of Ezra told about the first two groups. The first group rebuilt the Temple. The second group went back with Ezra who taught God's laws. Nehemiah tells about a third group that rebuilt the wall of Jerusalem.

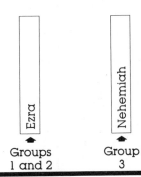

Ezra

Nehemiah

Groups 1 and 2

Group 3

Chapter 1: Nehemiah was a Hebrew servant to Artaxerxes, king of Persia. Nehemiah was sad when he learned the wall of Jerusalem was broken down.

Nehemiah prayed to God, asking Him to remember His promise to Moses to gather His people and bring them back to Jerusalem if they became scattered.

Chapter 2: The king allowed Nehemiah to go home to rebuild the wall. When Nehemiah got to Jerusalem, he inspected the wall to see what must be done.

Chapter 3: Nehemiah put the people to work rebuilding the wall. Each group of people had one section of the wall to repair.

Chapters 4,5: While the people were working on the wall, their enemies Sanballat and Tobiah made fun of them.

The people carried weapons in case they were attacked as they worked on the wall. Nehemiah helped the people solve problems that came up.

113

Chapters 6,7: Enemies tried to get Nehemiah to leave Jerusalem. They even threatened to report to the king that Nehemiah was planning to fight against the king.

The wall was completed in only 52 days! Even the enemies knew that God helped the people do this.

Chapters 8,9: After the wall was built, the people turned to Ezra to hear the words of the Lord. Ezra read the laws and the people shouted, "Amen! Amen!"

The people worshiped the Lord and asked God to forgive them for their sins.

Chapter 10: The people agreed to obey God. They would not marry people who worshiped idols. They would worship God on the Sabbath and give to God.

Chapter 11: The people decided who would live in the city of Jerusalem and protect it.

Chapter 12: The wall of Jerusalem was dedicated—given to God. All the men, women and children were full of joy!

Chapter 13: Nehemiah helped the people obey God's Word.

When Events Happened

See time line on pages 110, 111.

Where It All Happened

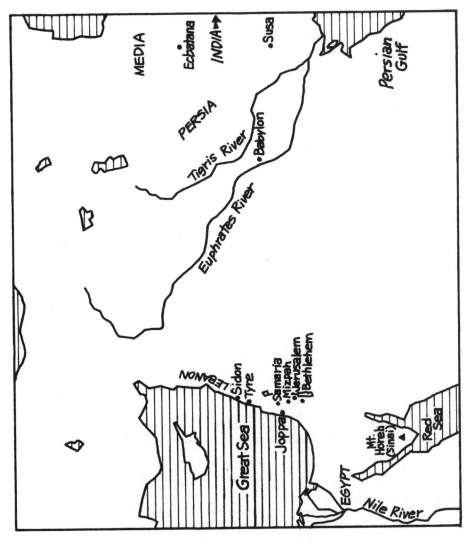

Esther

WRITER: The writer of this book is not known. He must have been a Jew living in Persia. He made use of records kept by Mordecai and could have used the records of the books of Chronicles.

TITLE: This book is named after its main person, Esther. It records the beginning of the Feast of Purim. The Jewish people celebrate this feast every year to remember how God saved His people from being destroyed.

LOCATION: Esther is in the History division of the Old Testament. It is the twelfth book of History and the seventeenth book of the Old Testament.

The Books of History

Joshua | Judges | Ruth | First Samuel | Second Samuel | First Kings | Second Kings | First Chronicles | Second Chronicles | Ezra | Nehemiah | Esther

MAIN PEOPLE: Vashti, Esther, Mordecai, Haman, Ahasuerus (Xerxes)

OUTLINE:
- [ ] The rejection of Vashti (Esther 1)
- [ ] The crowning of Esther (Esther 2)
- [ ] The plotting of Haman (Esther 3,4)
- [ ] The courage of Esther (Esther 5)
- [ ] The deliverance of the Jews (Esther 6—10)

When Events Happened

460 BC

VASHTI   ESTHER   HAMAN / MORDECAI

Main Events

■ God Saves His People

Chapters 1—10 The story of Esther happened sometime between chapters 6 and 7 of the book of Ezra. It happened sometime between the first return of the Jews from Babylon and the second return led by Ezra. This is a story of the Jews who stayed in Persia instead of going to Jerusalem.

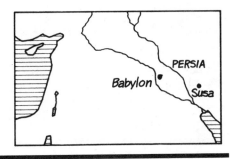

Chapter 1: The book begins in King Ahasuerus' (Xerxes') palace in Susa. The king wanted Queen Vashti to be part of a great celebration.

The queen would not come and was punished. She was sent away from the palace.

Chapter 2: When the king saw beautiful Esther, a Jew, he made her his new queen, in Vashti's place. Her uncle Mordecai told her not to say she was Jewish.

Mordecai was able to warn the king of a plot to kill the king. He told Esther who then told the king.

Chapter 3: Mordecai would not honor Haman, the prideful captain of the princes.

Haman learned that Mordecai was Jewish. He plotted to have the king order all Jewish people killed.

Chapters 4,5: Esther heard of the plot from Mordecai. She made plans of her own. She invited Haman and the king to a banquet. Haman was very happy.

Haman's anger at Mordecai kept growing. He decided to have Mordecai hanged. He had gallows built for the hanging.

Chapters 6: The king could not sleep. He asked that the book of records be read to him.

It was found that Mordecai had told the king of a plot to kill the king (see chapter 2). But Mordecai had never been rewarded for this.

The king ordered Haman to give honor to Mordecai.

Chapter 7: Esther told the king that Haman planned to have her and all of her people killed. Haman was hanged on the gallows that he built for Mordecai.

Chapter 8: The king could not change the command to kill the Jews. Instead, he gave a new order that the Jews could meet together and defend themselves.

Chapter 9: When the order to kill the Jews was put into action, the Jews and many other people joined together to defeat the enemies of the Jews.

The people celebrated God's care with feasting and joy (the Feast of Purim).

Chapter 10: Mordecai became second in importance only to the king. He was now a great man among the Jews. He wanted only good for his people.

Discoveries from the Past

The City of Susa

From finds by archaeologists we know that "Sushan the palace" refers to the Elamite city of Susa. The beautiful palace of the Persian kings was in Susa. Archaeologists found Xerxes' home. It was so large that it covered two and one-half acres.

Where It All Happened

See the map on page 111. The events in the book of Esther happened in the same time period as the events in Ezra.

Esther

and God's Plan to Send a Savior

In this book we see a danger to the line of the promised Savior. The Jewish people could have been killed and the line of the family of Jesus Christ ended. But God is all powerful. He can do anything. He kept the Jewish people safe and protected the family line of the promised Savior, Jesus Christ.

The same great God who loved and cared for the Jewish people loves and cares for you!

Let's Look at the Books of Poetry

There are five books included in the Poetry section of the Old Testament. They talk about the experiences of God's people in life and what it is like to trust Him and follow Him.

The Books of Poetry

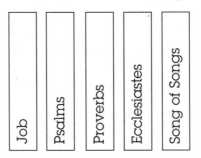

Job   Psalms   Proverbs   Ecclesiastes   Song of Songs

Why is this section called "poetry"?

These books were written in Hebrew, the language of Israel. Poems in Hebrew do not rhyme like poems in English. They are poems because of how they are written. Some Psalms are poems because they begin with different letters of the Hebrew alphabet. Others are poems because they can be chanted rhythmically or sung to music.

What does the New Testament say about these books?

Job—The book of James tells us that the suffering Job is an example of patience and God's kindness: "You have heard of Job's perseverance and have seen what the Lord finally brought about. The Lord is full of compassion and mercy" (James 5:11).

Psalms—We are to use these songs to express ourselves to God and to each other, just as Israel did. "Speak to one another with psalms, hymns and spiritual songs. Sing and make music in your heart to the Lord." (Ephesians 5:19).

Proverbs, Ecclesiastes. Song of Songs—We are to seek for wisdom as Solomon did and practice it in our daily lives. "Be very careful, then, how you live—not as unwise but as wise" (Ephesians 5:15).

Job

WRITER: The writer of this book is not known. There are no helps from the book itself as to the writer. However, the book is actual history and can be trusted as God's Word.

TITLE: The name "Job" (pronounced JOHB) means "persecuted one" (Hebrew) or "repent" (Arabic). The title is taken from the main person in the book—Job.

LOCATION: Job is in the Poetry division of the Old Testament. It is the first book of Poetry and the eighteenth book of the Old Testament.

The Books of Poetry

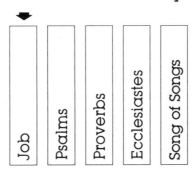

The five books of Poetry come after the five books of Law and the twelve books of History.

LAW   **HISTORY**   **POETRY**

MAIN PEOPLE: Job, his family, his friends (Eliphaz, Bildad, Zophar, Elihu)

OUTLINE: ☐ The disasters of Job (Job 1,2)
      ☐ The friends of Job (Job 3—37)
      ☐ Job's conversation with God (Job 38—42)
      ☐ The deliverance of Job (Job 42)

Main Events

■ God's Man Is Tested

Chapters 1—42 Job was a godly man who probably lived eastward of the land of Canaan in a place called Uz. Job was a real person and the events that you will read about really took place. The events probably happened around the time of Abraham.

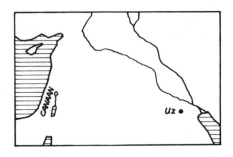

Chapters 1,2: Satan tested Job's love for God by causing the destruction of all of Job's family and belongings.

When Satan saw that Job still loved and trusted the Lord God, he made Job painfully sick. Three of Job's friends came to visit him.

Chapter 3: Job was so unhappy that he was sorry he was ever born.

Chapters 4—7: Job's friend Eliphaz said Job was being punished for some sin. He told Job to ask God's forgiveness. Job said he had done nothing wrong.

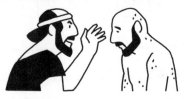

Chapters 8—10: Bildad, another friend, agreed that Job must have deserved the punishment. Again, Job said he did not deserve such trouble.

Chapters 11—14: The third friend, Zophar, like the others, warned Job to stop sinning and pray for forgiveness.

When Events Happened

SOMEWHERE BETWEEN 2000~1000 BC

JOB   ELIPHAZ, BILDAD, ZOPHAR

Job said he couldn't understand why he was being punished because he did not know what he had done wrong.

Chapters 15—31: Job and his friends continued debating the cause of Job's suffering.

Chapters 32—37: Elihu, another friend, told Job that God can have a reason to allow bad things to happen to a good person.

Chapters 38—42: God talked to Job. He helped Job see that no person can understand what God does and why He does it.

God told the first three friends that they were wrong in what they said.

Through all his sufferings Job never blamed God. God rewarded Job by giving him a new family and even more riches than he had before.

ELIHU

Discoveries from the Past

The name "Job" is not used very often today. In Job's time, however, it was popular enough to appear in several writings that have been discovered. The discovery of the name in old writings helps to show that this book is very, very old.

Job

and God's Plan to Send a Savior

In Job 19:25-27, Job in his suffering comforted himself because he knew that God was his helper. He looked ahead to the time that he would go to heaven to be with his Lord. Job calls his Lord "Redeemer." Our lives were bought (redeemed) by Jesus Christ on the cross. Jesus Christ is our Redeemer.

Psalms

WRITER: There were many writers of the book of Psalms. We do not know the writers for all the psalms. The chart at the bottom of the page shows the main people who wrote or collected groups of psalms.

TITLE: The title "Psalms" means "book of praises." Psalms is actually a book of 150 songs of praise to God. It is a final collection of several groups of psalms that had been collected over the years for use in worshiping God. The book of Psalms was the book of prayer and praise that God's people used after rebuilding the Temple at Jerusalem. The people also used it when they worshiped God in their synagogues.

LOCATION: Psalms is in the Poetry division of the Old Testament. It is the second book of Poetry and the nineteenth book of the Old Testament.

The Books of Poetry

Job | Psalms | Proverbs | Ecclesiastes | Song of Songs

OUTLINE: The Book of Psalms is divided into five books, or collections of psalms.

BOOK	PSALMS	MAIN AUTHOR OR COLLECTOR
1	1-41	David
2	42-72	David/sons of Korah
3	73-89	Asaph
4	90-106	Unknown
5	107-150	David/Unknown

Asaph was David's choir leader. The sons of Korah were a family of official musicians.

■ The Songbook of God's People

Psalms 1—150 There are many kinds of songs in the book of Psalms. Some are happy; others are sad. Some tell of great trouble; others tell of wonderful happenings. But all the psalms are sung to God—showing that His people can tell Him anything about their lives. And God cares and listens.

Where to find psalms of:
instruction: 1; 19; 39
praise: 8; 29; 93; 100
thanks: 30; 65; 103; 107; 116
repentance: 6; 32; 38; 51; 130
trust: 3; 27; 31; 46; 56; 62; 86
distress: 4; 13; 55; 64; 88
hope: 42; 63; 80; 84; 137
history: 78; 105; 106

Some Instruments Used in Bible Times

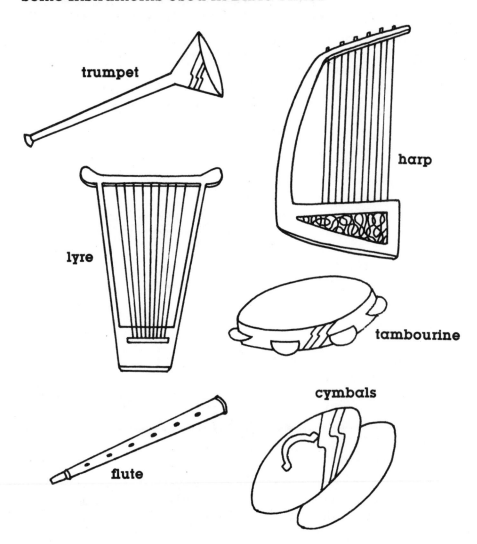

trumpet

harp

lyre

tambourine

cymbals

flute

Psalm 1: A person who loves God's Word is a well-watered tree which produces plenty of good fruit.

Psalm 19: God has shown us what He is like, both in creation and in His Word, the Bible.

Psalm 23: This psalm says the Lord is our shepherd. He cares for us as a shepherd cares for his sheep. David, who was a shepherd, wrote this psalm.

Psalm 27: In this prayer, David asks God for help because of people who seek to hurt him.

Psalm 34: This psalm thanks God for answering prayer.

Psalm 46: God protects His people when trouble comes.

Psalm 51: David wrote this psalm to humbly ask God's forgiveness and cleansing for his sin.

Psalm 56: David wrote this psalm to show his trust in God's care in times of danger.

Psalm 77: God has shown His power in many ways, such as when He led Israel through the sea.

Psalm 91: God protects His people, like a safe place shelters from a storm.

Psalm 100: This is a psalm for giving thanks to God. In verse 4, the gates and courts refer to the Temple gates and courts.

Psalm 119: All 22 sections of this chapter (one for each letter of the Hebrew alphabet) tell how wonderful the Word of God is. Different words are used over and over to refer to the Bible: "law," "statutes," "precepts," "commands," "commandments," "ordinances," "Word" and "decrees."

Psalm 119: God's Word is compared to many things: "great riches," "gold," "silver," "honey," "a shield" and "a lamp" (to guide in the way we should live).

Psalm 122: This is one of a group of psalms that were sung as people traveled to worship at the Temple in Jerusalem.

Psalm 136: When the Levites used this psalm at the Temple, the leader probably said the first part of each verse; and the choir said the last part of the verse.

Psalm 150: This psalm is a call to praise God. It tells many instruments that were used to praise the Lord in Bible times. See the pictures on page 126.

Psalms

and God's Plan to Send a Savior

Jesus Himself said that the book of Psalms tells about Him. In Luke 24:44, Jesus said, "Everything must be fulfilled that is written about me in...the Psalms."

The following psalms are called messianic psalms because they have references to the coming Messiah (another name for the promised Savior): Psalms 2; 16; 22; 24; 40; 45; 68; 69; 72; 97; 110; 118.

We read in the New Testament many quotations from the psalms. At least 20 of these are in direct reference to Christ and His life and death.

Psalm 22 gives a picture of Calvary. We see the crucifixion pictured here more clearly than in any other part of the Old Testament. The psalm opens with the cry of our Lord in the darkest hour of his life: "My God, my God, why have you forsaken me?"

Read and compare these verses:

Psalm 22:1	Matthew 27:46
Psalm 22:6,7	Luke 23:35,36
Psalm 22:6-8	Matthew 27:39,41,43
Psalm 22:12,13	Matthew 27:36,44
Psalm 22:28	1 Corinthians 15:23,24

Psalm 22:16 says, "They have pierced my hands and my feet." These words, written hundreds of years before Jesus' death, describe the way Jesus died—by crucifixion. Nailing hands and feet to a cross was the Roman method of death by crucifixion. The Jewish law did not know of this method.

Psalm 22:18 says, "They divide my garments among them and cast lots for my clothing." This verse describes what the soldiers would do at Jesus' crucifixion hundreds of years later! Read Matthew 27:35.

Proverbs

WRITER: 1 Kings 4:32 tells us that Solomon told 3,000 proverbs and 1,005 songs. Solomon was the writer or collector of most of the proverbs in this book. He was known as a wise man.

TITLE: The book of Proverbs can also be called the Book of Wisdom. A proverb is a wise saying that can help us decide what is the best thing to do.

LOCATION: Proverbs is in the Poetry division of the Old Testament. It is the third book of Poetry and the twentieth book of the Old Testament.

The Books of Poetry

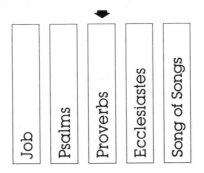

OUTLINE: Wise sayings to live by (Proverbs 1-31)
The book of Proverbs has wise sayings for everyone to read and follow. These sayings deal with many different problems and situations. Most of the proverbs are very short and easy to remember. The proverbs are not organized in a way that puts all the sayings on one topic together. Instead, almost every verse raises a new and important idea.

SOME PROVERBS TO MEMORIZE (choose from these):
Proverbs 1:8; 2:6; 3:5,6,11,12,27; 6:16-19; 10:12; 11:2,13,17,25,28; 12:22,25; 13:10; 14:21-23,29; 15:1,16,18,22; 16:7,8,16,18,20,32; 17:17,22; 18:9,10; 19:17,20,21; 20:3,11,19,22,24; 22:1,2,9; 23:12; 24:17,29; 25:21,22; 27:1,2; 28:13

AN IDEA TO TRY: Each week, copy one of the above proverbs on a piece of paper. Put it on a wall, mirror, refrigerator or notebook. Read it every day. Ask God to help you do what it says. Memorize the proverb.

Proverbs 1: A young person is encouraged to seek God's wisdom and is warned against being led into foolish, sinful ways.

Proverbs 3:5,6: Verses 5 and 6 teach that trusting God brings wisdom in making good choices.

Proverbs 10: Parents are made happy by a child who follows the wise advice of these proverbs.

Proverbs 14:21: Verse 21 is one of many proverbs which encourage us to be kind and generous with those in need.

Proverbs 17:17: Verse 17 says that following the guidance of these proverbs helps us build strong friendships.

Proverbs 20:11: Verse 11 tells that people of all ages, even children, should be careful about how they act.

Proverbs 22:9: Verse 9 helps us see how doing good for others is also good for us.

Proverbs 24:30-34: Verses 30-34 warn against being lazy.

■ Special Topics in Proverbs

Fear of the Lord

"The fear of the Lord is the beginning of wisdom, and knowledge of the Holy One is understanding." 9:10

"A wise man fears the Lord and shuns evil, but a fool is hotheaded and reckless." 14:16

"He who fears the Lord has a secure fortress, and for his children it will be a refuge." 14:26

Wisdom

"For the Lord gives wisdom, and from his mouth come knowledge and understanding." 2:6

"How much better to get wisdom than gold, to choose understanding rather than silver!" 16:16

"A wise man has great power, and a man of knowledge increases strength." 24:5

Anger

"Do not make friends with a hot-tempered man, do not associate with one easily angered, or you may learn his ways and get yourself ensnared." 22:24,25

"A fool gives full vent to his anger, but a wise man keeps himself under control." 29:11

"An angry man stirs up dissension, and a hot-tempered one commits many sins." 29:22

Honesty

"Truthful lips endure forever, but a lying tongue lasts only a moment." 12:19

"The Lord detests lying lips, but he delights in men who are truthful." 12:22

"Kings take pleasure in honest lips; they value a man who speaks the truth." 16:13

Money

"Do not wear yourself out to get rich; have the wisdom to show restraint." 23:4

"Cast but a glance at riches, and they are gone, for they will surely sprout wings and fly off to the sky like an eagle." 23:5

"He who gives to the poor will lack nothing, but he who closes his eyes to them receives many curses." 28:27

Foolishness

"The fear of the Lord is the beginning of knowledge, but fools despise wisdom and discipline." 1:7

"A wise son brings joy to his father, but a foolish son grief to his mother." 10:1

"The way of a fool seems right to him, but a wise man listens to advice." 12:15

Words

"Reckless words pierce like a sword, but the tongue of the wise brings healing." 12:18

"A gentle answer turns away wrath, but a harsh word stirs up anger." 15:1

"Pleasant words are a honeycomb, sweet to the soul and healing to the bones." 16:24

Patience

"A hot-tempered man stirs up dissension, but a patient man calms a quarrel." 15:18

"Better a patient man than a warrior, a man who controls his temper than one who takes a city." 16:32

"Through patience a ruler can be persuaded, and a gentle tongue can break a bone." 25:15

Ecclesiastes

WRITER: The writer tells about himself in chapter 1, verse 1: "son of David, king in Jerusalem." This reference, plus the mention of his riches, wisdom and building activities, all point to one man—Solomon.

TITLE: The title "Ecclesiastes" means "an assembly" or "preacher." The title can mean, "the speaker before an assembly."

LOCATION: Ecclesiastes is in the Poetry division of the Old Testament. It is the fourth book of Poetry and the twenty-first book of the Old Testament.

The Books of Poetry

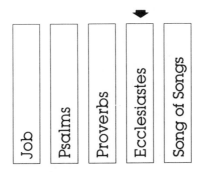

Job | Psalms | Proverbs | Ecclesiastes | Song of Songs

SUMMARY OF THE BOOK: Solomon explains to his readers what he has learned in his own life: How much you own or how smart you are is not important. The most important thing is loving and obeying God.

■ God Gives Meaning to Life

Chapters 1—12 The book of Ecclesiastes talks about the meaning of life. Why did God make people to live on the earth? What good is money or power? How should we behave? The writer of this book answers these questions.

A time for everything...

Chapters 1,2: The writer talks about having much wisdom and money. He had beautiful houses and enjoyed himself. But he knew none of that mattered very much.

Chapter 3: God is in charge of all things. He sets a time for everything that happens. Things that don't seem fair will be made right in the future.

Chapters 4,5: The writer warns us not to use power to hurt others or store up for ourselves things others need. He also gives instructions about worship.

Chapters 6—12: The best advice the writer gives is to obey God. Often we don't understand why things happen. The best thing to do is to obey God.

The Song of Songs

WRITER: The writer of the Song of Songs was Solomon. Chapter 1, verse 1 begins with "Solomon's Song of Songs."

TITLE: The title "Song of Songs" means that it is the best of all songs.

LOCATION: The Song of Songs is in the Poetry division of the Old Testament. It is the fifth book of Poetry and the twenty-second book of the Old Testament.

The Books of Poetry

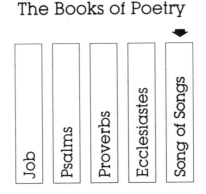

Job | Psalms | Proverbs | Ecclesiastes | Song of Songs

SUMMARY OF THE BOOK: The Song of Songs is Solomon's beautiful love song. It is a poem and a picture. It tells of the closeness of a husband and wife. It describes real love as the love that makes one person willing to give up everything for the one he or she loves.

Let's Look at the Books of Prophecy

The rest of the Old Testament is made up of 17 books of prophecy. The events in these 17 books happened at the same time as those in the 12 books of History.

Notice how the Old Testament books are arranged:

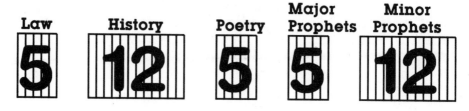

Law	History	Poetry	Major Prophets	Minor Prophets
5	12	5	5	12

The terms Major Prophets and Minor Prophets have to do with the length of the books, not the importance of the prophets.

MAJOR PROPHETS   **MINOR PROPHETS**

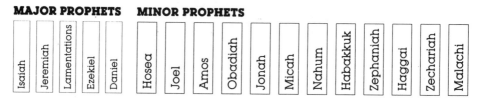

Isaiah · Jeremiah · Lamentations · Ezekiel · Daniel · Hosea · Joel · Amos · Obadiah · Jonah · Micah · Nahum · Habakkuk · Zephaniah · Haggai · Zechariah · Malachi

NOTE: Lamentations was a book that was probably written by Jeremiah. Lamentations is not the name of a prophet.

OLD TESTAMENT PROPHETS

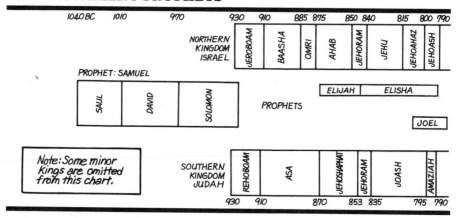

What Is a Prophet?

The prophets were people God used to give messages to His people. Read what God says about them in 2 Kings 17:13. The prophets spoke fearlessly to kings and common people alike. They told of the people's sins and failures.

Who Were the Prophets?

Samuel was the first of the prophets. The period of the prophets covered about 500 years. Then there were no prophets until the coming of John the Baptist in New Testament times.

To Whom Did the Prophets Speak?

God gave the prophets messages for specific nations.

God spoke to:	through these prophets:
Israel (10 northern tribes)	Amos, Hosea
Judah (2 southern tribes)	Joel, Isaiah, Micah, Jeremiah Habakkuk, Zephaniah
Jews returned to Jerusalem	Haggai, Zechariah, Malachi
Nineveh	Jonah, Nahum
Babylon	Daniel, Ezekiel
Edom	Obadiah

The map on the next page shows the locations of the nations to whom each prophet spoke.

Note: God gave some of the prophets messages for other nations in addition to the nations listed above. For example, many prophets included messages to Nineveh, Babylon, Edom, Egypt, Moab and other nations. But the above shows the prophet whose main message was to the countries listed.

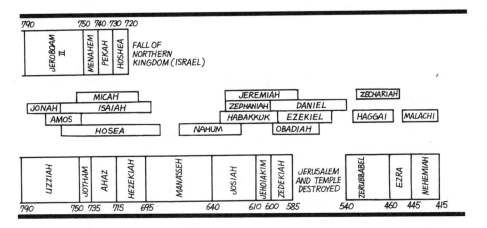

Nations to Whom the Prophets Spoke

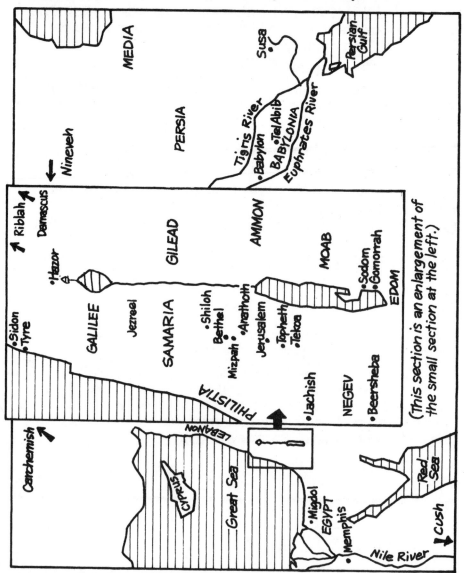

(This section is an enlargement of the small section at the left.)

The Message of the Prophets

God sent the prophets to tell people to turn from their sin. The prophets warned the people what would happen if they did not turn from their sin.

Prophets were never sent when the people were obeying God. They were sent to turn the people from their sin. And so they were not very popular with the people. Their job was not easy!

138

The prophets also told of events that would happen in the future. These were the future events they told about:

1. The Jews would be scattered among the nations of the world. (This did happen. Many of the Jewish people are still scattered among the nations today.)

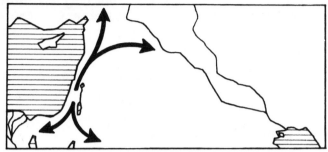

2. God would send a Messiah to save His people. (This did happen. God sent His Son Jesus to be our Savior. However, many of the Jews did not believe in Jesus. Today, many of the Jews are still looking for the Messiah.)

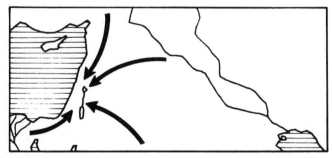

3. The Jews would return to their own land under the Messiah. (Many Jews have returned from all over the earth to live in their own land, Israel. They have a longing in their hearts to be part of the nation of Israel.)

4. The Messiah will rule over the whole earth. God wanted all people to know that the captivity of His people did not end His plans. There is yet to be a glorious future when Jesus Christ the Prince of Peace will rule over all the earth.

When you read the Gospels, you constantly find the phrase "this was to fulfill what was spoken." God was constantly unfolding His plan as prophecy after prophecy was fulfilled.

The prophets spoke of the earthly ministry of Christ. But they said nothing about the church—the believers in Christ. Jesus Christ Himself announced that He was building His church (Matthew 16:81). We read about the church in the New Testament.

God's Messages Are for Us

So important is prophecy in God's Word that it occupies about one third of the whole Bible. Through prophecy God tells His plans to His children.

The messages of the prophets contain these three things:
1. A message for the prophet's own time
2. A message of coming events
3. A message for us today—eternal principles of right and wrong.

The Spirit of God spoke by the prophets. Read 2 Peter 1:21; Jeremiah 1:9; Ezekiel 2:7 to find ways the message was given.

Read what Christ said of the prophets (Luke 24:25-27).

The prophecies about Christ Himself are so definite that it gives great assurance to us that the Bible is the Word of God.

The next 17 books of the Bible tell about the messages of God's prophets.

Isaiah

WRITER: The writer of this book was Isaiah, the prophet.

PROPHET OF: Judah—the southern kingdom. (Many of Isaiah's prophecies were about other nations as well as Judah.) Isaiah lived at the time the northern kingdom of Israel was destroyed by Assyria. He spoke God's words during the reigns of Uzziah, Jotham, Ahaz and Hezekiah, kings of Judah. Isaiah probably spent most of his life in Jerusalem.

OTHER PROPHETS OF THIS TIME: Amos and Hosea (to Israel); Micah (to Judah).

TITLE: "Isaiah" means "Yahweh (God) is salvation." This Hebrew title gives us a good summary of the book.

LOCATION: Isaiah is in the Prophecy division of the Old Testament. It is the first book of the Major Prophets (five larger books) and the twenty-third book of the Old Testament.

The Books of Major Prophets

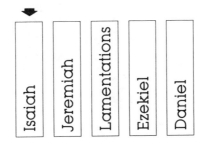

Isaiah | Jeremiah | Lamentations | Ezekiel | Daniel

NOTE: Lamentations was a book that was probably written by Jeremiah. Lamentations is not the name of a prophet.

OUTLINE: ☐ God's messages of judgment (Isaiah 1-39)
- Under Kings Uzziah and Jotham (Isaiah 1—6)
- Under King Ahaz (Isaiah 7—14)
- Under King Hezekiah (Isaiah 15—39)

☐ God's messages of Comfort (Isaiah 40—66)
- God's promise to free His people and bring them again to the land He gave them (Isaiah 40—52)
- The coming of God's Servant (Jesus Christ) to be the Messiah King (Isaiah 52,53)
- The future glory of God's people (Isaiah 54—66)

When Events Happened (See time line on pages 136, 137.)

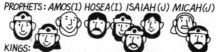

790 BC

722 BC

◻⊡ = KING
(I) = ISRAEL
(J) = JUDAH

PROPHETS: AMOS(I) HOSEA(I) ISAIAH(J) MICAH(J)

KINGS:

JEROBOAM II (I) AZARIAH(J)
(UZZIAH)

PEKAH(I)
JOTHAM(J)

HOSHEA(I)

END OF NORTHERN KINGDOM

Main Events
■ God's Messages of Judgment

Chapters 1—39 Isaiah lived when the northern kingdom of Israel was captured by the Assyrians. He saw God's protection of Judah, the southern kingdom, from the Assyrians. But he knew Judah would someday fall to the Babylonians. He wrote God's words about these events—and also of the coming Savior.

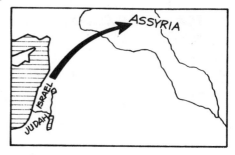

Chapters 1—5: Isaiah told Israel that their sinfulness was the cause of the enemy attacks on their country. He also told of terrible destruction yet to come.

Chapter 6: Isaiah told about his call to speak for God.

Chapters 7—12: Again Isaiah warned of God's judgment for sin. But he also included a wonderful promise of a coming Savior.

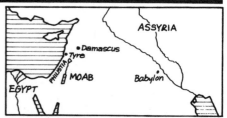

Chapters 13—23: Isaiah said God was angry not only with Israel, but also with the enemies of Israel. He told how these wicked nations would be destroyed.

The prophets Hosea, Isaiah and Micah continue their ministry.

700 BC

AHAZ(J)   HEZEKIAH(J)   ASSYRIAN ARMY DESTROYED   MANASSEH(J)

Chapters 24—35: The prophet explained that at some future time God will destroy all the forces of evil on earth and set up His own Kingdom.

Chapters 36—38: Isaiah reported events going on in Jerusalem. (These events are also recorded in Second Chronicles 29—32.)

The Assyrians had already carried off the people of Israel and made an attack on Judah. Isaiah told how God protected Judah by destroying the Assyrian army.

Chapter 39: King Hezekiah showed off his riches to some visiting Babylonians. Isaiah told him the Babylonians would return to capture Judah and its treasures.

■ God's Messages of Comfort

Chapters 40—66 Isaiah told God's promise of His people's return to their land and of the coming Savior. This was all part of God's plan. For it would be in the land of Palestine and through God's people, the Jews, that the promised Savior would be born. Isaiah also told of the future glory of Israel.

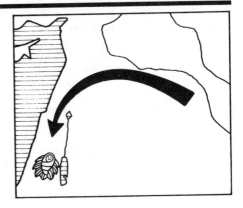

Chapters 40—48: Isaiah told the people that Israel's enemies were being used by God to teach them a lesson.

When God's people learned to obey, their enemies would be destroyed and the nation of Israel would be given back its strength.

Chapters 49—66: The prophet described in detail the Savior God promised to send.

He also said the time will come when God will show His power and glory to all the nations. God will judge the people and either reward or punish them.

Where It All Happened

See the map on page 138.

What Was Happening

in the Rest of the World?

Isaiah was born at about the time the great kingdoms of Rome and Greece were just beginning.

Discoveries from the Past

The Dead Sea Scrolls

The words in your copy of the Bible were first written down a long, long time ago. They were written by men through whom God chose to speak. We don't have the first copies of the books of the Bible. But other people who knew how important God's Word is made some extra copies.

God watched over this copying of His Word. As the years passed and the old copies got lost or hard to read, new copies were made. Some of the new copies were made in other languages so everyone could understand God's Word.

If you have ever tried to copy something word for word, you know that it is hard to do it correctly. Usually there are some mistakes. People began to worry that, over the years, some mistakes might have been made in copying God's Word.

In the 1940s a discovery was made which proved that those who copied the Bible had been very, very careful. A shepherd boy in the Bible lands found a cave that had been forgotten for a long time. The cave was near the Dead Sea. Inside the cave the boy found scrolls that had been hidden in jars. One of the scrolls turned out to be a copy of the book of Isaiah—copied by people who lived when Jesus lived on earth!

People who knew a lot about what is written in the Bible checked the Bible we have today with this very old copy. They found that God had truly protected His Word. We can know for sure that what we read in our Bible is the same message God gave to the first writers.

Babylon

Isaiah's prophecy concerning Babylon in Isaiah 13:19-22 is still true today. No one lives there. See photos on page 356.

Isaiah

and God's Plan to Send a Savior

Isaiah had a lot to say about the coming Savior. Here are some verses in which Isaiah told about the coming Messiah (Savior).

- Birth—Isaiah 7:14; 9:6
- Family—Isaiah 11:1
- Empowered by the Holy Spirit—Isaiah 11:2
- Characteristics (what He is like)—Isaiah 11:3-5; 42:1-4
- Suffering and death—Isaiah 53
- Resurrection—Isaiah 25:8
- Glorious reign—Isaiah 11:3-16; 32:1

In chapter 53 Isaiah explained the reason for the Messiah's death. He explained that the Messiah would take the punishment for our sins. Jesus, the Messiah, never sinned. He took on Himself the punishment for our sin. Make verse 5 personal to your own life by saying, "He was pierced for (my) transgressions, he was crushed for (my) iniquities; the punishment that brought (my) peace was upon him, and by his wounds (I am) healed." It is accepting this great fact that makes you a child of God. If you want to know more about this, read "Becoming God's Child" in this guidebook.

Jeremiah

WRITER: The writer of this book was Jeremiah, the prophet.

PROPHET OF: Judah—the southern kingdom. (Many of Jeremiah's prophecies were about other nations as well as Judah.) Jeremiah spoke God's words for over forty years, beginning in the reign of Josiah. He continued to speak God's words even in Egypt where some of God's people went after the fall of Jerusalem.

OTHER PROPHETS OF THIS TIME: Habbakuk and Zephaniah (to Judah), Ezekiel and Daniel (to Babylon) and perhaps Nahum (to Nineveh).

TITLE: "Jeremiah" means "Yahweh (God) establishes or sends."

LOCATION: Jeremiah is in the Prophecy division of the Old Testament. It is the second book of the Major Prophets and the twenty-fourth book of the Old Testament.

The Books of Major Prophets

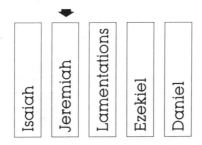

Isaiah | Jeremiah | Lamentations | Ezekiel | Daniel

NOTE: Lamentations was a book that was probably written by Jeremiah. Lamentations is not the name of a prophet.

OUTLINE: Before the fall of Jerusalem (Jeremiah 1—38)
After the fall of Jerusalem (Jeremiah 39—52)

NOTE: The book of Jeremiah does not follow the order in which things happened. Jeremiah and his assistant, Baruch, wrote Jeremiah's messages on a long scroll. Probably, while writing down one message, Jeremiah would be reminded of another message he had spoken before. The earlier message would then be added to the scroll where he had left off writing. This mixing of early and late messages makes it very difficult to know the order in which his messages were given.

When Events Happened (See time line on pages 136, 137.)

650 BC
PROPHETS:

HABAKKUK (J)
ZEPHANIAH (J)
JEREMIAH (J)

= KING
(J) = JUDAH
(B) = BABYLON

KINGS: JOSIAH (J)

Jeremiah's ministry continued past the fall of Jerusalem.

Main Events
■ God's Coming Judgment

Chapters 1—52 Jeremiah spoke to the nation of Judah during its hardest times. The people worshiped idols and lived lives that did not please God. God promised to judge the people because they did not obey. For forty years, God spoke to the people through Jeremiah, warning of coming destruction.

Jeremiah is called "the weeping prophet" because he was deeply sad for the people even though they got what they deserved. Jeremiah lived to see many of his words (prophecies) come true.

Chapter 1: God called Jeremiah to speak for Him. God told him that He would give Jeremiah the words to say. God promised to be faithful to His prophet.

Chapters 2—25: Jeremiah spoke twelve messages to the people about the coming judgment on the nation of Judah.

600 BC

DANIEL (B)

EZEKIEL (B)

586 BC

JEHOIAKIM (J)   ZEDEKIAH (J)   FALL OF JERUSALEM

The people's sin was very bad. Jeremiah told them they would be captured and taken to Babylon for many years.

Chapters 26—45: Jeremiah told his involvement in many events leading to the fall of Jerusalem. Because he did God's work, he was rejected and thrown into prison.

Finally, Jeremiah was taken to Egypt by a group of God's people who went there in disobedience to God. Jeremiah continued telling the people God's words.

Chapter 52: This chapter describes how the city of Jerusalem was taken and destroyed. All the leaders were killed and the people were carried off to Babylon.

Where It All Happened

See the map on page 138.

Discoveries from the Past

The Destruction of Lachish

In 1935, very old letters were found that tell us about the fall of Lachish (Jeremiah 34). The information in these letters, written by people who saw the destruction of the city, is the same as the information that Jeremiah wrote in the Bible.

The Destruction of Babylon

Compare Jeremiah's description (Jeremiah 51:37-43) with Isaiah's description (Isaiah 13:17-22).

By the time of Christ, Babylon's power was gone. In the first century after Christ the city was mostly in ruins. Its bricks have been used in building the city of Baghdad and in repairing canals. For centuries Babylon has lain desolate. Only the beasts of the deserts live there. The once-magnificent city of Babylon is today a heap of fallen bricks. What a remarkable fulfillment of prophecy! See photos on page 356.

The Destruction of Jerusalem

Archaeologists who have explored Jerusalem have found that the destruction was very complete when the city fell (Jeremiah 52).

We should remember that the truth of the Bible does not depend on archaeological discoveries. The prophet Isaiah wrote "The grass withers and the flowers fall, but the word of our God stands forever" (Isaiah 40:8). When places and things are found that prove that what was written in the Bible is true, it helps people trust God always to keep His promises.

Jeremiah

and God's Plan to Send a Savior

Jeremiah, in chapter 23, told of a coming Shepherd who will rule and help His people. Jeremiah even told His name. It is "the Lord Our Righteousness," another name for Jesus (Jeremiah 23:5,6).

Jeremiah said the coming Shepherd (Jesus) will bring a new agreement between God and His people (Jeremiah 31:31-34). These new words will complete the promises given to Abraham, Moses and David.

What wonderful news! The promise of a Savior can be found here in the Old Testament many years before He actually came to earth! God has a plan for His people. His promises always come true.

Lamentations

WRITER: The writer of this book was probably Jeremiah, the prophet. Jeremiah's name is not mentioned in the book but Lamentations is like the book of Jeremiah.

TITLE: "Lamentations" means "to lament or to cry out loud." Jeremiah cried out loud about the destruction of the Temple and the city of Jerusalem. After forty years of telling the people to turn from their evil ways, Jeremiah's words came true. He saw the defeat and destruction of the people and their city.

LOCATION: Lamentations is in the Prophecy division of the Old Testament. It is the third book of the Major Prophets and the twenty-fifth book of the Old Testament.

The Books of Major Prophets

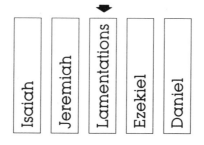

NOTE: Lamentations was a book that was probably written by Jeremiah. Lamentations is not the name of a prophet.

SUMMARY: The book of Lamentations is the saddest book of the entire Old Testament. Here, Jeremiah wrote his words of sorrow after the fall of the great city of Jerusalem. Even though he was sad, Jeremiah talked about God and His goodness. Everything seemed very sad, but in the future there would be joy. God will always be faithful to His people.

One of the most comforting and encouraging passages in the Bible is Lamentations 3:22,23: "Because of the Lord's great love we are not consumed, for his compassions never fail. They are new every morning; great is your faithfulness."

Ezekiel

WRITER: The writer of this book was Ezekiel, the prophet.

PROPHET TO: The Jewish captives (exiles) in Babylon. (Many of Ezekiel's prophesies were about other nations as well as the Jews.) Ezekiel's message to the Jewish captives was that their captivity was the result of their sin. Before they could hope to return to their land, they must return to their Lord.

OTHER PROPHETS OF THIS TIME: Jeremiah, who remained with the Jews in Jerusalem; Daniel, who lived in the court of the rulers in Babylon. Daniel was taken captive to Babylon nine years earlier than Ezekiel. Ezekiel and Daniel were probably about the same age. Jeremiah was older. He had been a prophet for about 30 years in Jerusalem when Ezekiel was taken to Babylon.

TITLE: "Ezekiel" means "God strengthens." Ezekiel was strengthened by God for the ministry God gave him.

LOCATION: Ezekiel is in the Prophecy division of the Old Testament. It is the fourth book of the Major Prophets and the twenty-sixth book of the Old Testament.

The Books of Major Prophets

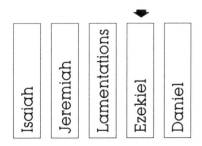

Isaiah | Jeremiah | Lamentations | Ezekiel | Daniel

NOTE: Lamentations was a book that was probably written by Jeremiah. Lamentations is not the name of a prophet.

OUTLINE: ☐ Ezekiel's call (Ezekiel 1—3)
☐ Ezekiel's prophecies
- against Judah and Jerusalem (Ezekiel 4—24)
- against the nations (Ezekiel 25—32)
- about Israel and the last days (Ezekiel 33—48)

When Events Happened (See time line on pages 136, 137.)

600BC
PROPHETS: JEREMIAH(J)   DANIEL(B)

⌐◉⌐ = KINGS
(J) = JUDAH
(B) = BABYLON

KINGS:

ZEDEKIAH(J)

Main Events
■ Ezekiel, a Prophet in Babylon

Chapters 1—48 Not all the people of Judah were taken to Babylon at the same time. For a while Jeremiah stayed in Jerusalem warning the people who remained there about the city's coming destruction. Ezekiel was one of the captives taken to Babylon.

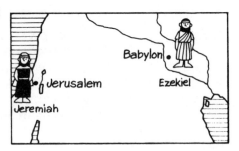

Ezekiel's job was to give God's Word to the prisoners in exile (away from their own country). Many of the events of this book are in visions that God showed to Ezekiel. These visions were pictures to Ezekiel so that he would know what to tell the people.

Chapters 1—3: God called Ezekiel and gave him a job to do. Ezekiel heard God's words and told them to the people.

Chapters 4—24: By using special stories and actions, the prophet taught the people why God would destroy their city, Jerusalem.

593 BC — EZEKIEL(B)

Ezekiel was one of the captives taken to Babylon. He spoke God's word to the captives there.

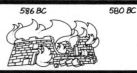

586 BC — 580 BC

JEWS EXILED
TO BABYLON

FALL OF JERUSALEM

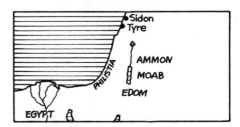

Some of the prisoners hoped they would be able to go home to Jerusalem soon. But Ezekiel told them this would not happen.

Chapters 25—32: Ezekiel said that other nations who did not listen to God would also be destroyed.

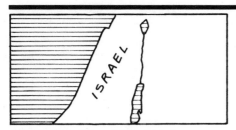

Chapters 33—48: Ezekiel gave the people God's good news. Someday the people of Israel will be gathered from wherever they are and made a great nation again.

Ezekiel told the people that they will be led by a wonderful Shepherd. (This Shepherd is Jesus.)

Where It All Happened

See the map on page 138.

Discoveries from the Past

Evidence from the Enemy

Among the old writings from the time of Ezekiel are records kept by a Babylonian priest named Berosus. He recorded that Nebuchadnezzar (the king of Babylon) had left Babylon to put down a revolt among the Jews in Palestine. Other writings from Babylon refer to Jehoiachin, king of Judah, who was king even while a prisoner.

The Greatness of Babylon

The Bible records how Nebuchadnezzar bragged about the greatness of his capital. Archaeologists have uncovered the ancient city. They agree that it was a city of many large buildings, wide streets and beautiful gardens. They have found clay tablets that list the names of many Israelite prisoners.

See information and photos on pages 342, 356.

Ezekiel

and God's Plan to Send a Savior

The people were very unhappy as prisoners far from home. Hearing the prophets tell them that their captivity was punishment for their sin did not cheer them up, either. Ezekiel told the people that they would be rescued by a King who would also be their Shepherd. The people hoped that it would happen very soon. It was hard for the people to wait. They could not understand that the promised King was not for only one nation and one time in history. He would be King for all people and for all time.

The promised King was Jesus. He would not lead an army against Israel's enemies as Israel expected. His Kingdom is a special kind of Kingdom. The people who heard Ezekiel's message never got to see it come true. Today we know that Jesus, the Prince of Peace, is the Shepherd in Ezekiel's message.

Daniel

WRITER: The writer of this book was Daniel, the prophet.

PROPHET IN: Babylon. Unlike the other prophets, Daniel dealt more with the Gentile (non-Jewish nations) than with his own Jewish nation.

OTHER PROPHETS OF THIS TIME: Jeremiah (in Jerusalem); Ezekiel (in Babylon). Look at the end of this chapter for more information about the prophets of this time.

TITLE: "Daniel" means "God is my judge." The book is named after its main person, Daniel. Through Daniel God revealed, more than through any prophet before him, the hidden things of the future. We are seeing more and more that Daniel's great prophecies are history written before it happened. A study of the book of Daniel helps us understand the book of Revelation, the great prophetic book at the end of the Bible.

LOCATION: Daniel is in the Prophecy division of the Old Testament. It is the fifth book of the Major Prophets and the twenty-seventh book of the Old Testament.

The Books of Major Prophets

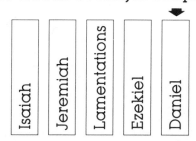

Isaiah | Jeremiah | Lamentations | Ezekiel | Daniel

NOTE: Lamentations was a book that was probably written by Jeremiah. Lamentations is not the name of a prophet.

OUTLINE: ☐ Daniel's life in Babylon (Daniel 1—6)
- Daniel, a young man in Babylon (Daniel 1)
- Nebuchadnezzar's dream: the great image (Daniel 2)
- The fiery furnace (Daniel 3)
- Nebuchadnezzar's dream: a great tree (Daniel 4)
- Belshazzar: the handwriting on the wall (Daniel 5)
- Daniel in the lion's den (Daniel 6)

☐ Daniel's visions (Daniel 7—12)

When Events Happened (See time line on pages 136, 137.)

650 BC
PROPHETS: JEREMIAH(J)

⬤ = KINGS
(J) = JUDAH
(B) = BABYLON

Daniel taken to
Babylon with
other captives.

DANIEL(B)

KINGS:

JEHOIAKIM(J)   ZEDEKIAH(J)

■ Daniel's Life in Babylon

Chapters 1—6 As a young man of about 16, Daniel was taken from Jerusalem to Babylon in the first group of captives. Even though he was a captive, he rose to be prime minister of Babylon. He was a man of faith, prayer and courage. He would not go against God or His commandments.

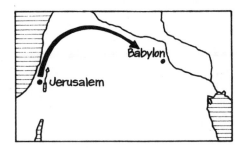

Daniel lived to be over 90 years of age. He saw the Babylonian kingdom fall and the Medo-Persian kingdom established. He held high positions under kings Nebuchadnezzar, Belshazzar, Darius and Cyrus.

Nebuchadnezzar   Belshazzar

Darius   Cyrus

Chapter 1: When Nebuchadnezzar conquered Jerusalem, he ordered the sharpest young men to be taken to Babylon. Daniel and his friends were in this group.

They were trained to serve in the king's palace. They were given food that was not prepared according to God's laws. Part of it was offered to idols.

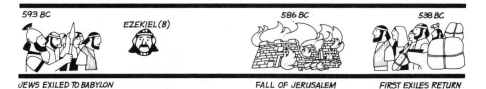

Daniel and his friends would not eat this food. They insisted on eating only vegetables and water.

When the time came to go before the king, they were healthier than the other young men. And they answered the king's questions better than anyone else.

Chapter 2: The king had a strange dream. He demanded that his wise men tell him what he dreamed and what it meant.

But they could not do this. God showed Daniel the dream and its meaning. Daniel told the king the meaning of his dream.

The dream was of a huge statue which was shattered. This was a picture of the future of Nebuchadnezzar's kingdom.

Because Daniel explained the dream, he was given an important job in the government.

Chapter 3: The king decided to build a golden statue of himself. Everyone had to bow down before the statue or be killed!

Daniel's three friends would not worship the statue and were thrown into a furnace to be burned alive. God protected the men in the furnace.

The king admitted there is no other god who could do that. The king gave Daniel's friends important jobs in his kingdom.

Chapter 4: The king had another dream. Daniel explained that the king would be sick in his mind and act like an animal.

At the end of his illness the king understood the power of God and worshiped Him.

Chapter 5: Belshazzar, the new king, threw a party. A mysterious handwriting appeared on the wall. Only Daniel knew what it meant.

Daniel warned Belshazzar that an enemy army would soon take away his kingdom. That very night Belshazzar was killed. Darius of Persia captured Babylon.

Chapter 6: Daniel worked hard for the new king. He became a very important person. Those who were jealous of Daniel tried to get him into trouble.

A law was passed that ordered all people to pray only to the king. Daniel went on praying to God.

Daniel was arrested and thrown into a den of lions!

The king was sorry that he made the law. He went early the next morning to find out what happened to Daniel. Daniel had been protected by God.

A new law was made that everyone must worship Daniel's mighty God.

■ Daniel's Visions

Chapters 7—12 Daniel, like Ezekiel, was shown the future in pictures called visions. He saw the end of Israel's enemies, and the end of other nations not yet formed. Many of the events Daniel said would happen came true during his life time. After Daniel died, more of these events came true. These are things that we read about in our history books. Some of Daniel's visions are yet to happen. We can be sure the rest of Daniel's prophecies will also come true.

Where It All Happened

See the map on page 138.

The Prophets at the Time of Daniel

Three prophets were giving God's messages at this time: Daniel, Ezekiel and Jeremiah. Daniel and Ezekiel were about the same age. Daniel was taken from Jerusalem to Babylon in the first group of captives; Ezekiel, in the second group. Daniel spent his life in the palace at Babylon and took part in the government. Ezekiel spent his life giving God's messages to the other captives in Babylon. Jeremiah was older than Daniel and Ezekiel. He remained in Jerusalem, giving God's messages to the small group of people the king allowed to stay in Jerusalem.

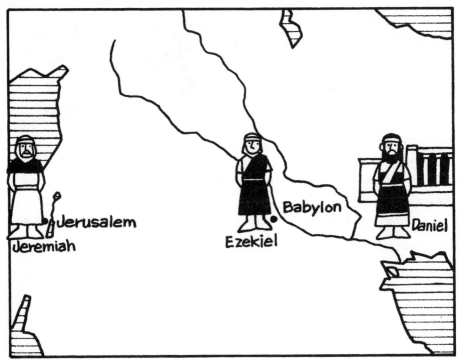

Daniel

and God's Plan to Send a Savior

Some of Daniel's visions (pictures) showed him facts about Jesus. Daniel told about the coming of the Messiah (Jesus) who would give His life in Jerusalem. Daniel was able to tell us that God would give Jesus a kingdom. All of the people of the earth will serve Him. His kingdom will never be destroyed (Daniel 7:13,14).

Hosea

WRITER: The writer was Hosea, the prophet. (See Hosea 1:1.)

PROPHET TO: The kingdom of Israel (the 10 northern tribes) during the reigns of King Jeroboam II and the six kings who followed (2 Kings 14—17). The people's sin was very great. About the middle of Hosea's ministry a great part of the northern kingdom of Israel was carried away by the Assyrians. At the end of Hosea's life the kingdom of Israel came to an end with the fall of Samaria. Hosea saw his prophecies fulfilled.

OTHER PROPHETS OF THIS TIME: Amos (to the northern kingdom of Israel—either at the same time or slightly before Hosea), Isaiah and Micah (to the southern kingdom of Judah).

TITLE: "Hosea" means "salvation." This name is almost the same as "Joshua" or "Jesus." However, "Joshua" and "Jesus" mean "Yahweh (God) is salvation." Hosea wrote about salvation, stressing that the nation of Israel will be saved only if it turns from the worship of idols to the worship of God.

LOCATION: Hosea is in the Prophecy division of the Old Testament. It is the first book of the Minor Prophets (twelve books that are shorter than the five books of Major Prophets). It is the twenty-eighth book of the Old Testament.

The Books of Minor Prophets

Hosea | Joel | Amos | Obadiah | Jonah | Micah | Nahum | Habakkuk | Zephaniah | Haggai | Zechariah | Malachi

OUTLINE: ☐ Hosea's wife (Hosea 1—3)
☐ Hosea's people (Hosea 4—14)
• The message of judgment (Hosea 4—10)
• The message of love (Hosea 11—14)

When Events Happened (See time line on pages 136, 137.)

790 BC

PROPHETS: AMOS(I) HOSEA(I) ISAIAH(J) MICAH(J)

722 BC

= KING
(I) = ISRAEL
(J) = JUDAH

KINGS:

JEROBOAM II (I) AZARIAH(J)   PEKAH(I)   HOSHEA(I)   END OF NORTHERN KINGDOM
              (UZZIAH)   JOTHAM(J)

Main Events
■ God's Love for His People

Chapters 1—14 God called Hosea to speak to the nation of Israel just before it was destroyed. In this book we see a story within a story. The nation of Israel had not been faithful to God. Israel had gone after false gods to worship.

Hosea's wife, Gomer, had not been faithful to him. Gomer had gone after other men to love. Hosea searched for Gomer—and bought her back from slavery. In the same way God promised to save His people because He still loves them.

Chapters 1—3: Hosea married Gomer. They had three children. Gomer left Hosea to go after other men.

As sinful as Gomer was, Hosea went after her to buy her back from slavery. He loved her in spite of everything.

Chapters 4—14: God was sad because Israel worshiped false gods. Hosea warned that the people would be taken captive and carried off to Assyria.

God will discipline you. But He loves you. He will care for you.

God is loving and kind but He must also discipline His children when they do not obey. Because of His love, He also promised to help His people.

Hosea

and God's Plan to Send a Savior

Hosea recorded in his book that God said, "Out of Egypt I called My son" (Hosea 11:1). God was talking about the time He brought Moses and the Israelites out of slavery in Egypt. Many years later, the writer Matthew told about Joseph and Mary bringing little Jesus back from Egypt, where they had gone to escape the evil King Herod. Matthew remembered Hosea's words (Matthew 2:15) and used them to show God's loving plan in sending Jesus.

Hosea bought his wife Gomer from slavery to save her and get her back. This is a picture of what Jesus Christ did for us. He bought us back and the price He paid was His own life. He died in our place. When we become part of God's family we are with Him forever.

Think about what Jesus Christ has done for you. Are you a member of God's family? (See "Becoming God's Child" in this guidebook.) Thank God for what Jesus did for you. Thank God that He cares for you every day!

Joel

WRITER: The writer was Joel, the prophet. (See Joel 1:1.)

PROPHET TO: Judah. Joel told the people of Judah that a terrible attack of locusts which had just taken place was God's judgment on them for their many sins. Joel told the people to turn to God and His love.

OTHER PROPHETS OF THIS TIME: Joel spoke to the southern kingdom of Judah a little before Hosea spoke to the northern kingdom of Israel.

TITLE: "Joel" means "Yahweh is God." It is the name of the man who wrote the book. It is also a good title because it tells about God loving and helping His people.

LOCATION: Joel is in the Prophecy division of the Old Testament. It is the second book of the Minor Prophets and the twenty-ninth book of the Old Testament.

The Books of Minor Prophets

Hosea	Joel	Amos	Obadiah	Jonah	Micah	Nahum	Habakkuk	Zephaniah	Haggai	Zechariah	Malachi

OUTLINE: ☐ Looking back at God's judgment (Joel 1)
☐ Looking toward the Day of the Lord (Joel 2,3)

When Events Happened

850 BC

800 BC

☐ = KING
(I) = ISRAEL
(J) = JUDAH

PROPHETS:

JOEL

KINGS:

JEHU (I)   JOASH

Main Events

■ Looking Back at God's Judgment

Chapter 1: Joel spoke to the people of Judah just after huge swarms of locusts (insects) had destroyed the land. They ate all the green plants needed for food. At the same time there was no rain, so there was no water to drink.

However, as terrible as this destruction was, Joel wrote that it would be nothing compared to what God was going to do because the people did not obey Him. Joel asked the people to turn to God and obey Him before it was too late.

■ Looking Toward the Day of the Lord

Chapters 2,3: Joel used the destruction by the locusts to show the people a picture of a worse time that was to come. He warned that the people's land would be taken over by an enemy army. Joel asked the people to turn to God and ask His forgiveness while there was still time. Because He is kind and merciful, God will not completely destroy His people, but will drive out the enemy and return Israel to times of goodness. The nations who mistreated Israel will be punished, but God will protect His people.

Where It All Happened

See the map on page 138.

Joel

and God's Promise to Send a Savior

Joel warned of God's judgment upon the people of Judah. Jesus Christ is the One who will come to judge all the nations some time in the future.

Joel told about something that was reported later on, in the New Testament. In Acts, chapter 2, the Holy Spirit came as Jesus had promised and as Joel had predicted. When it happened, Peter said, "This is what was spoken by the prophet Joel" (see Joel 2:28-32a and Acts 2:16-21).

God promised to send a Savior. Here in the book of Joel we see the time of His coming getting closer. God will make His promise come true in Jesus Christ.

Amos

WRITER: The writer was Amos, the prophet. (See Amos 1:1.)

PROPHET TO: Israel. (Some of the prophecies of Amos were about other nations as well as the Jews.) Amos was a shepherd who lived in Judah, but who preached to the people of Israel. He preached during the reigns of Uzziah (king of Judah) and Jeroboam II (king of Israel). Both of these kingdoms were very prosperous at this time. This was a time of great idolatry and luxurious living. Amos told the people the importance of living a life that pleases God. He told them not to rely on money, land or idols. They should worship the one, true God.

OTHER PROPHETS OF THIS TIME: Hosea (to Israel). When Amos's work was coming to a close, Isaiah and Micah began their ministry to the people of Judah.

TITLE: "Amos" means "to lift a burden" or "to carry a burden." The prophet Amos lived up to his name by caring about the burdens of the people and speaking about their evil ways.

LOCATION: Amos is in the Prophecy division of the Old Testament. It is the third book of the Minor Prophets and the thirtieth book of the Old Testament.

The Books of Minor Prophets

Hosea | Joel | Amos | Obadiah | Jonah | Micah | Nahum | Habakkuk | Zephaniah | Haggai | Zechariah | Malachi

OUTLINE: ☐ Amos's prophecies: warning the nations (Amos 1,2)
☐ Amos's sermons: speaking about Israel (Amos 3—6)
☐ Amos's visions: the future of Israel (Amos 7—9)

When Events Happened (See time line on pages 136, 137.)

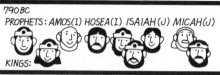

= KING
(I) = ISRAEL
(J) = JUDAH

790 BC
PROPHETS: AMOS(I) HOSEA(I) ISAIAH(J) MICAH(J)

722 BC

KINGS:

JEROBOAM II (I) AZARIAH(J)   PEKAH(I)   HOSHEA(I)   END OF NORTHERN KINGDOM
(UZZIAH)   JOTHAM(J)

Main Events
■ God's Justice and Righteousness

Chapters 1—9: Amos was a prophet to Israel during the time when everything seemed to be well with the people. They were making money and were very happy. No enemy nation was strong enough to attack them. However, many people only pretended to worship God. The people did not truly worship God. They were greedy. They were unfair to the poor. They were more interested in themselves than in God. No matter how many warnings they received, the people would not turn to God.

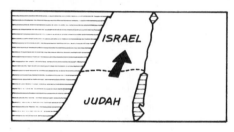

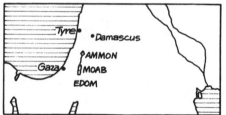

Chapters 1,2: God called Amos to leave his home in Judah to go and speak to the people in Israel about the coming judgment.

Amos warned other nations that God will send fire on them because they have sinned again and again.

Hear this word...

Then he listed many of the wrong things the people of Israel had done. He warned that Israel would not escape being punished.

Chapters 3—6: Amos spoke three sermons about Israel's sin. Each sermon began with, "Hear this word . . . ."

The prophets Hosea, Isaiah and Micah continue their ministry.

  700 BC

AHAZ (J) HEZEKIAH (J) ASSYRIAN ARMY DESTROYED MANASSEH (J)

Even though God loved and cared for the people, they had been dishonest and had cheated the weak and poor.

They pretended to worship God, but didn't obey Him. They should have asked God's forgiveness and stopped sinning. Times of easy living were over.

Chapters 7—9: Amos told five visions of coming judgment on Israel. These visions were pictures that helped Amos know what to tell the people.

The first two visions showed terrible punishment. After each vision Amos asked God to spare the people. God agreed to hold off the punishments.

But in the third vision God checked the people. They were obviously far out of line. God said He would not withhold punishment.

The fourth vision compared the people to a basket of fruit, once beautiful but soon to be rotten. The last vision showed terrible judgment on Israel.

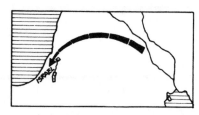

Chapter 9: Amos finished his book by telling the people of God's promise to restore the family line of David.

God promised that after the people's sin has been punished, He will return them to their land.

Where It All Happened

See the map on page 138.

Discoveries from the Past

Archaeologists (people who study very old buildings and objects) have found that what Amos said was true. The capital city of Israel was very beautiful. The city had a double wall around it that was thirty-three feet thick in some places. It took the Assyrian army three years to capture the city (2 Kings 17:5). With this kind of protection, the people Amos preached to thought they could trust in their own strength and not in the power of God.

Obadiah

WRITER: The writer of this very short book was Obadiah, the prophet. (See Obadiah, verse 1.)

PROPHET TO: The people of Edom, a longtime enemy of Judah.

OTHER PROPHETS OF THIS TIME: Jeremiah (to Judah); probably Daniel and Ezekiel (in Babylon).

TITLE: "Obadiah" means "Worshiper of Yahweh (God)" or "Servant of Yahweh." It is the name of the writer of the book.

LOCATION: Obadiah is in the Prophecy division of the Old Testament. It is the fourth book of the Minor Prophets and the thirty-first book of the Old Testament.

The Books of Minor Prophets

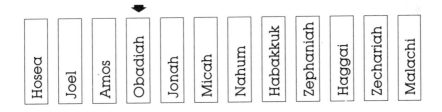

Hosea | Joel | Amos | Obadiah | Jonah | Micah | Nahum | Habakkuk | Zephaniah | Haggai | Zechariah | Malachi

SUMMARY: When the kingdom of Judah was attacked by the Babylonians, the people of Edom were happy. They helped the invading army of Babylon and then looted Jerusalem after its defeat. Obadiah said God would destroy Edom as punishment. Obadiah reported God's promise that He would someday bring the people of Israel back to their land. They would have not only their own land back again, but also the land of the Edomites.

When Events Happened   (See time line on pages 136, 137.)

⬭ = KING
(I) = ISRAEL
(J) = JUDAH
(E) = TO EDOM
(B) = BABYLON

NOTE: The events in verses 11-14 may refer to an invasion of Jerusalem at the time of King Jehoram and the prophet Elisha. Or they may refer to the Babylonian attacks on Jerusalem in 605-586 BC. Since many people who study the Bible believe it refers to the Babylonian attacks, this chapter uses those dates.

Who Were the Edomites?

To answer this question we need to go clear back to the time of Jacob and Esau. (You can read about these twin brothers in Genesis 27.) Jacob cheated Esau and then had to leave home because Esau wanted to kill him. Even after these brothers made peace—many years later—they decided to live apart.

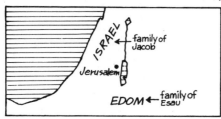

Jacob   Jacob   Esau   Jacob

The family of Jacob became the nation of Israel. The family of Esau became the nation of Edom. The Israelites and the Edomites, like Jacob and Esau, were longtime enemies.

Entrance to Petra

Discoveries from the Past

The Home of the Edomites

The capital of Edom was a place that is called Petra today. ("Petra" means "rock.") Petra is one of the wonders of the world. The only entrance to this great rock city is through a narrow passage more than a mile long. On both sides of the passage are cliffs hundreds of feet high. See photos on pages 357, 358.

600BC 605BC
PROPHETS: JEREMIAH (J)
DANIEL(B)
593BC
EZEKIEL(B) OBADIAH
586BC
KINGS:

JEHOIAKIM (J)   Daniel and others   ZEDEKIAH (J)   Ezekiel and others   FALL OF JERUSALEM
                     taken captive.   taken captive.

The city could easily be defended against attackers—and so the Edomites were very proud and self-confident.

Many temples were cut out of the walls of this great rock city. The homes were mostly caves cut out of the rock.

The Edomites would go on raiding expeditions and then retreat to their great fortress. They never forgot their bitter hatred toward the Jews—a hatred that began with Jacob and Esau. Because of this hatred, the Edomites were always ready to help any army that attacked the Jews. When the Babylonians attacked Jerusalem, the Edomites helped them catch the fleeing Jews.

What Happened to the Edomites?

History tells us what happened to the Edomites many years after Obadiah's prophecy.

What Obadiah Said About Edom

☐ "As you have done, it will be done to you; your deeds will return upon your own head" (Obadiah, verse 15).

☐ "There will be no survivors from the house of Esau" (Obadiah, verse 18).

What Happened to Edom

The Edomites were driven from their rocky home by King Nebuchadnezzar of Babylon five years after he destroyed Jerusalem. The Edomites fell before the same Babylonian kingdom they had helped five years before—when Jerusalem was attacked.

Hundreds of years later, after the crucifixion of Jesus, the Edomites completely disappeared from history.

Obadiah also promised that the nation of Israel would rise again and possess not only her own land but also Philistia and Edom. She will finally rejoice in the reign of the promised Messiah (Savior).

175

Jonah

WRITER: The writer was probably Jonah, the prophet. (See Jonah 1:1.)

PROPHET TO: The city of Nineveh. Jonah did not want the people of Nineveh to have a chance to hear God's word. He was very unhappy when they believed his message and obeyed God. Jonah was a prophet during the reign of Jeroboam II of Israel (2 Kings 14:25).

OTHER PROPHETS AT THIS TIME: Amos (to Israel).

TITLE: "Jonah" means "dove." It is the name of the main character in the book.

LOCATION: Jonah is in the Prophecy division of the Old Testament. It is the fifth book of the Minor Prophets and the thirty-second book of the Old Testament.

The Books of Minor Prophets

Hosea | Joel | Amos | Obadiah | Jonah | Micah | Nahum | Habakkuk | Zephaniah | Haggai | Zechariah | Malachi

OUTLINE:
☐ Jonah tried to run away (Jonah 1).
☐ Jonah prayed to God (Jonah 2).
☐ Jonah preached to the people in Nineveh (Jonah 3).
☐ Jonah learned God loves all people (Jonah 4).

When Events Happened (See time line on pages 136, 137.)

= KING
(I) = ISRAEL
(J) = JUDAH
(N) = NINEVEH

785 BC
PROPHETS:

KINGS:

JONAH (N)

775 BC

JEROBOAM II (I) AMAZIAH (J)
UZZIAH (J)

Main Events

■ God Speaks to Nineveh through Jonah

Chapters 1—4: Assyria was growing powerful. God's people, Israel, were afraid they would be conquered by Assyria. Nineveh was an evil city within the Assyrian empire. God called Jonah to go to Nineveh and warn them they would be destroyed for their wickedness. Jonah did not want to go. He wanted Nineveh to be crushed.

Chapter 1: God called Jonah to go to Nineveh to tell the people to stop doing wrong. Jonah did not want to go, because the Assyrians were enemies of Israel.

Jonah decided not to obey God. He set out by boat to Tarshish (Spain).

On the trip a great storm came up.

To save themselves, the sailors threw Jonah overboard. God sent a giant fish to swallow Jonah.

Chapter 2: Inside the fish, Jonah was sorry that he did not obey God. He prayed for God's help and was set free from the fish.

Chapter 3: Once again God called Jonah. This time Jonah obeyed God by going to Nineveh. He spoke to the people, they listened and obeyed.

They asked God for forgiveness. Because God loved the people, He did not bring disaster upon them.

Chapter 4: When God forgave the people and had mercy on the city, it made Jonah mad. God taught Jonah that He cares about all people.

Where It All Happened

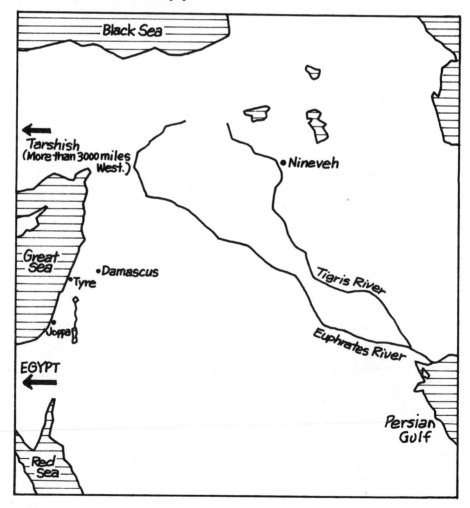

Discoveries from the Past

The Assyrian King Sennacherib was famous in the Bible as the one who attacked Jerusalem in the time of King Hezekiah. Sennacherib's capital city was Nineveh. The Bible calls Nineveh a great city. It was filled with temples and palaces. It was surrounded by a high wall. A water system brought water to the city from the mountains far away. The royal palace had 71 rooms. All of this has been found by archaeologists. No wonder Jonah did not want to warn such a powerful enemy that they were doomed!

See photo on page 359.

Jonah

and God's Plan to Send a Savior

Jesus said in Matthew 12:40,41 "For as Jonah was three days and three nights in the belly of a huge fish, so the Son of Man will be three days and three nights in the heart of the earth. The men of Nineveh will stand up at the judgment with this generation and condemn it; for they repented at the preaching of Jonah, and now one greater than Jonah is here."

Jonah was in the belly of the great fish for three days and three nights and then came up on the dry land. He then went to speak to the people in Nineveh. Jesus Christ, after His death, was buried in His tomb for three days and three nights. On the third day, Jesus rose from the dead. Jesus knew what was going to happen to Him. He used the story of Jonah to help His listeners understand.

Micah

WRITER: The writer of this book was Micah, the prophet. (See Micah 1:1.)

PROPHET TO: Judah during the reigns of Jotham, Ahaz and Hezekiah, kings of Judah. Micah spoke about Samaria, the capital of Israel, and Jerusalem, the capital of Judah. But his message was directed especially to Judah. The northern kingdom of Israel was taken into captivity during Micah's lifetime.

OTHER PROPHETS AT THIS TIME: Isaiah (to Judah) and Hosea (to Israel).

TITLE: "Micah" means "Who is like Yahweh (God)?" It is the name of the man who wrote the book.

LOCATION: Micah is in the Prophecy division of the Old Testament. It is the sixth book of the Minor Prophets and the thirty-third book of the Old Testament.

The Books of Minor Prophets

| Hosea | Joel | Amos | Obadiah | Jonah | Micah | Nahum | Habakkuk | Zephaniah | Haggai | Zechariah | Malachi |

OUTLINE:
- ☐ Micah warned that nations and rulers who do not obey God will be defeated (Micah 1—3).
- ☐ Micah promised that God will provide a new King (Micah 4,5).
- ☐ Micah gave the people God's promise that He will forgive them (Micah 6,7).

When Events Happened (See time line on pages 136,137.)

= KINGS
(J) = JUDAH
(I) = ISRAEL

750 BC
PROPHETS: ISAIAH(J) MICAH(J)
HOSEA(I)

722 BC

686 BC

KINGS:

PEKAH(I)
JOTHAM(J)

HOSHEA(I)
AHAZ(J)

End of Northern Kingdom

HEZEKIAH(J)

Main Events

■ God's Message of Judgment and Hope

Chapters 1—7: Before the nations of Israel and Judah were carried away by their enemies, Micah brought God's word to the sinful people. The prophet Micah spoke about false prophets, dishonest leaders and ungodly priests. He brought God's warning that these wrongs would have to be punished. He urged the people to change their ways and ask God's forgiveness. Then he told of God's great plan to restore peace and hope in His kingdom.

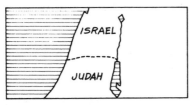

Chapters 1—3: Micah spoke against the kingdoms of Israel and Judah—they were living in sin and rebellion against God.

Both kingdoms would be captured because of their sinful ways.

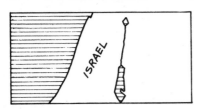

Chapters 4,5: Micah also told the people to look forward to the time when their nation would again be strong and powerful.

While they would have to suffer because of the things that they had done wrong, soon it would be their enemies' turn to suffer.

Israel will have a great King, born in Bethlehem, and who will bring strength and peace.

The Lord has a case against His people.

Chapters 6,7: Micah presented God's words as though he were in a courtroom.

God accused the people of doing wrong. Instead of just offering gifts and sacrifices to God, they are to act out of fairness and love and obedience to God.

The people deserved their punishment. But their punishment would not last forever. God loves them and will care for them as a shepherd cares for his sheep.

Where It All Happened

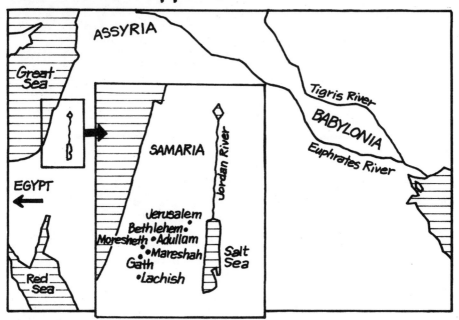

Micah

and God's Plan to Send a Savior

Micah gives us special information about Jesus the Ruler for Israel. He names Bethlehem as the town of Jesus' birth (Micah 5:2). He also tells us some of the qualities of this Ruler: strength, majesty, greatness, peace.

Seven hundred years before God sent His Son, He had already picked out the town where Jesus would be born. God plans ahead. He has a plan for your life, too. Exciting things can happen when you ask God to tell you what to do.

Nahum

WRITER: The writer was Nahum, the prophet. (See Nahum 1:1.) He lived during the reign of King Josiah of Judah. The northern kingdom of Israel had already been captured by the Assyrians.

PROPHET TO: Nineveh. There are some words spoken to Judah, but most are to, or about, Nineveh. This book about God's judgment on wicked Nineveh was meant as a comfort to the people of Judah, who suffered from the cruelty of the Assyrians. Nineveh was the capital city of Assyria. Nahum was written about 150 years after the time Jonah went to Nineveh telling the people to turn to God and stop sinning. The people turned from their sin after hearing Jonah's message. But we find that many years later, when the book of Nahum was written, the people in Nineveh were again very wicked, cruel people. Nahum told of God's judgment on these wicked people.

OTHER PROPHETS AT THIS TIME: Zephaniah, Habakkuk and young Jeremiah (to Judah).

TITLE: "Nahum" means "comfort" or "the comfort of Yahweh (God)." Nahum's words about God's judgment on Nineveh were a comfort to the people of Judah.

LOCATION: Nahum is in the Prophecy division of the Old Testament. It is the seventh book of the Minor Prophets and the thirty-fourth book of the Old Testament.

The Books of Minor Prophets

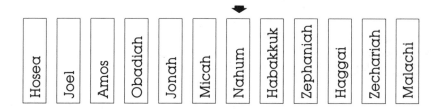

Hosea | Joel | Amos | Obadiah | Jonah | Micah | Nahum | Habakkuk | Zephaniah | Haggai | Zechariah | Malachi

SUMMARY: See "God's Justice and Love" on the next page.

When Events Happened (See time line on pages 136,137.)

⬭ = KING
(I) = ISRAEL
(J) = JUDAH
(N) = NINEVEH

780 BC
PROPHETS: JONAH

KINGS:

JEROBOAM II (I)   JONAH IN NINEVEH
AMAZIAH (J)

AMOS(I)   HOSEA(I)

UZZIAH(J) MENAHEM(I)

God's Justice and Love

Nahum told of God's justice and love. "The Lord takes vengeance on his foes and maintains his wrath against his enemies. The Lord is slow to anger and great in power; the Lord will not leave the guilty unpunished.... The Lord is good, a refuge in times of trouble" (Nahum 1:2,3,7).

Nahum warned that Nineveh will be destroyed because of the people's wickedness. He described the capture of Nineveh by the Babylonians. A great flood would destroy the walls of the city. Nineveh would be attacked, taken and burned. Nahum also said God will again restore His people Israel (Nahum 1:15; 2:2).

Where It All Happened

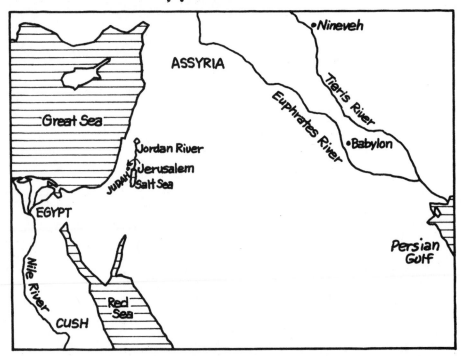

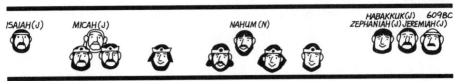

ISAIAH(J) MICAH(J) NAHUM (N) HABAKKUK(J) 609BC ZEPHANIAH(J) JEREMIAH(J)

PEKAH(I) HOSHEA(I) HEZEKIAH(J) MANASSEH(J) AMON(J) JOSIAH(J) FALL OF NINEVEH
JOTHAM(J) AHAZ(J)

Discoveries from the Past

Nineveh was captured by the Medes and Babylonians about six hundred years before Jesus was born. The capture of Nineveh happened exactly as Nahum had described. A sudden rise of the Tigris River carried away part of the wall, making it easier for the enemy troops to enter the city. The city was partly destroyed by fire.

The destruction of Nineveh was so complete that all traces of it disappeared. Then in 1845 archaeologists uncovered the ruins of the great city of Nineveh. They found ruins of magnificent palaces. They discovered thousands of inscriptions that tell us the story of Assyria as the Assyrians wrote it themselves!

The city of Nineveh had walls 100 feet high. These great walls were so thick that four chariots could ride on them side by side. There were hundreds of towers on the walls. A moat 140 feet wide and 60 feet deep surrounded the walls. The people of Nineveh thought nothing could destroy their city. But their great wealth and strength could not save them. God destroyed this great city because of the people's great wickedness. The city still lies in ruin today. See photo, page 359.

Habakkuk

WRITER: The writer was Habakkuk, the prophet. (See Habakkuk 1:1.)

PROPHET TO: Judah toward the end of Josiah's reign or the beginning of Jehoiakim's reign. The northern kingdom of Israel had been conquered by Assyria. Then Assyria had fallen, just as Nahum had prophesied. Egypt and Babylon fought for power and the Babylonians won. Now the southern kingdom Judah was being threatened by the strong but sinful nation of the Babylonians.

OTHER PROPHETS AT THIS TIME: Jeremiah and Zephaniah (in Judah) and Daniel (in Babylon).

TITLE: "Habakkuk" means "embrace," or "the one who embraces." Habakkuk chose to "embrace" or hold on to God no matter what happened to his nation.

LOCATION: Habakkuk is in the Prophecy division of the Old Testament. It is the eighth book of the Minor Prophets and the thirty-fifth book of the Old Testament.

The Books of Minor Prophets

Hosea	Joel	Amos	Obadiah	Jonah	Micah	Nahum	Habakkuk	Zephaniah	Haggai	Zechariah	Malachi

SUMMARY: See "Habakkuk's Conversation with God" on the next page.

When Events Happened (See time line on pages 136, 137.)

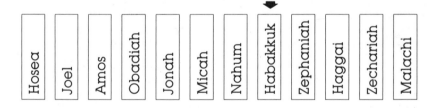

| = KING |
| (I) = ISRAEL |
| (J) = JUDAH |
| (N) = NINEVEH |

730 BC
PROPHETS: MICAH   NAHUM (N)   HABAKKUK(J)   609BC
ZEPHANIAH(J) JEREMIAH(J)

KINGS:

HEZEKIAH(J) MANASSEH(J) AMON(J) JOSIAH(J)   FALL OF NINEVEH

Habakkuk's Conversation with God

The book of Habakkuk is a book of questions and answers. It is a conversation between Habakkuk and God.

Habakkuk's First Question: Why aren't the people of Judah punished for the wicked things they are doing? **God's answer:** The Babylonians will punish Judah.

Habakkuk's Second Question: How can a just God use the wicked Babylonians to punish the people of Judah who are more righteous than the Babylonians? **God's Answer:** Babylon will also be punished—in God's time. God will reward the faith of His people.

Habakkuk's Prayer: When Habakkuk understood God's plan, he rejoiced in the Lord God. He praised God for His great power and holiness. The prophet saw God's plan in the punishment of Judah. At the end of his book Habakkuk said, "I will be joyful in God my Savior" (Habakkuk 3:18).

Where It All Happened

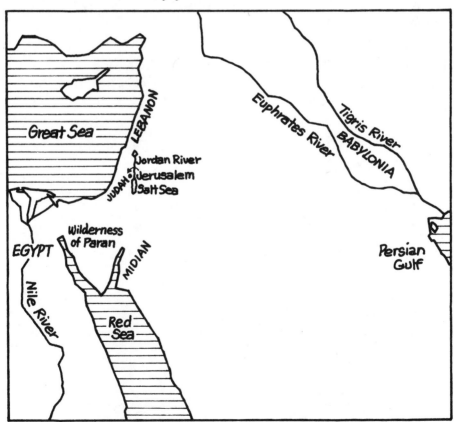

Zephaniah

WRITER: The writer was Zephaniah the prophet. (See Zephaniah 1:1.) He was a descendant of the great King Hezekiah.

PROPHET TO: Judah during the reign of King Josiah. Zephaniah was, no doubt, mainly responsible for the revival under Josiah. At the time 16-year-old Josiah was king, the situation in Judah was very bad. The rich people built great fortunes by treating the poor people unfairly. People worshiped idols. Young King Josiah tried to turn the people back to God. He cut down the idols and the altars used to worship them. Josiah became one of the most beloved kings of Judah. How encouraged he and other reformers must have been to hear the words of hope that Zephaniah gives at the end of this book!

OTHER PROPHETS AT THIS TIME: Jeremiah, Nahum and Habakkuk. All of these prophets had messages for Judah, although Nahum's message was mostly about Nineveh.

TITLE: "Zephaniah" means "Yahweh hides," or "Yahweh has hidden." (Yahweh is the Hebrew name of God.)

LOCATION: Zephaniah is in the Prophecy division of the Old Testament. It is the ninth book of the Minor Prophets and the thirty-sixth book of the Old Testament.

The Books of Minor Prophets

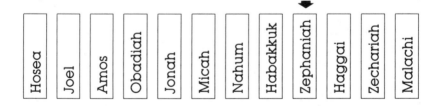

Hosea · Joel · Amos · Obadiah · Jonah · Micah · Nahum · Habakkuk · Zephaniah · Haggai · Zechariah · Malachi

SUMMARY: See "A Message of Sorrow and Singing" on the next page.

A Message of Sorrow and Singing

The book of Zephaniah begins with sorrow but ends with singing. The first part of the book is full of sadness and gloom. But the last part contains one of the sweetest songs of love in the Old Testament.

The "day of the Lord" is mentioned seven times in this prophecy. In the Bible, when the word "day" is used without a number in front of it, it usually means a period of time—not a 24-hour day. (For example, when we say "people who live in our day," we don't mean a 24-hour day—we mean the period of time in which we are living.)

When the Bible says "the day of the Lord," it means a time when the Lord will do a special thing. To the Jews in Zephaniah's day, it meant the time when God would deal with His people in punishment and captivity. The future day of the Lord is the period of the great tribulation and the millennium. The millennium is a thousand-year period of time when Jesus will rule over Jerusalem and all the nations. We read about this time in the book of Revelation at the end of the Bible.

Zephaniah tells of God's judgment not only on His people the Jews, but also on their enemies.

Zephaniah ends his book with some wonderful promises for God's people. His people will return to their own land. They will not only be blessed by God but they will also be a blessing to all the earth.

The last verse in Zephaniah says, "At that time I will gather you; at that time I will bring you home. I will give you honor and praise among all the peoples of the earth when I restore your fortunes before your very eyes.'"

There is great rejoicing ahead for God's people. Zephaniah 3:17 says, "The Lord your God is with you, he is mighty to save. He will take great delight in you, he will quiet you with his love, he will rejoice over you with singing.'"

When Events Happened (See time line on pages 136, 137.)

= KING
(I) = ISRAEL
(J) = JUDAH
(N) = NINEVEH

730 BC
PROPHETS: MICAH   NAHUM (N)   HABAKKUK(J) 609BC
ZEPHANIAH(J) JEREMIAH(J)

KINGS:

HEZEKIAH (J) MANASSEH(J) AMON(J) JOSIAH(J)   FALL OF NINEVEH

Zephaniah

and God's Plan to Send a Savior

Zephaniah said, "The Lord, the King of Israel, is with you; never again will you fear any harm" (Zephaniah 3:15). This King of Israel is Jesus Christ. What good news for the people of Zephaniah's day. What good news for you! Just think, even when the people were at their worst, God was planning to send Jesus Christ!

Sometimes God makes a promise that is misunderstood. God promised the people a new King, but He did not say when. It was easy to think that "the day of the Lord" would be the very next day. It was easy to wish that the new King would bring armies with Him to defeat Judah's enemies. In the New Testament we read how God's promise of a King came true in Jesus Christ.

Where It All Happened

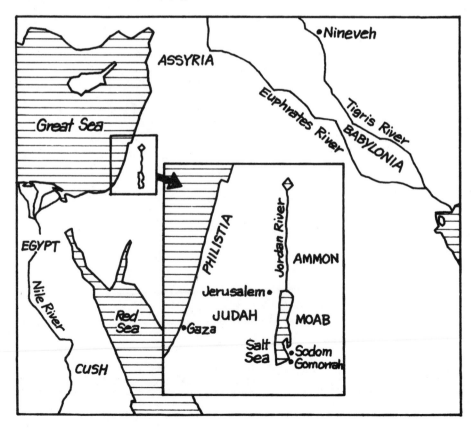

Haggai

WRITER: The writer was Haggai, the prophet. (See Haggai 1:1.)

PROPHET TO: The Jews who returned to Jerusalem after 70 years of captivity in Babylon.

OTHER PROPHETS AT THIS TIME: Zechariah. Haggai prophesied for four months. Zechariah, a younger prophet, prophesied for several years. Both of these prophets tried to persuade God's people to finish rebuilding the Temple.

TITLE: "Haggai" means "festival" or "the festival of Yahweh." (Yahweh is the Hebrew name for God.)

LOCATION: Haggai is in the Prophecy division of the Old Testament. It is the tenth book of the Minor Prophets and the thirty-seventh book of the Old Testament.

The Books of Minor Prophets

Hosea	Joel	Amos	Obadiah	Jonah	Micah	Nahum	Habakkuk	Zephaniah	Haggai	Zechariah	Malachi

OUTLINE:
- ☐ The Temple must be rebuilt (Haggai 1).
- ☐ A new Temple will be greater than the rebuilt one (Haggai 2:1-9).
- ☐ God's blessings will come as the Temple is rebuilt (Haggai 2:10-19).
- ☐ The Lord God will overthrow the nations and will bless Zerubbabel (Haggai 2:20-23).

Where It All Happened

See the map on page 115.

When Events Happened (See time line on pages 136, 137.)

540 BC   538 BC

KING CYRUS   ZERUBBABEL   HAGGAI, ZECHARIAH

Main Events
■ Rebuild the Temple in Jerusalem

Chapters 1,2: The 70-year Babylonian captivity was over. A group of Jewish people came back to Jerusalem under the leadership of Zerubbabel. They began rebuilding the Temple. However, 16 years later, the Temple was still not finished. Haggai urged the people to finish the work they started.

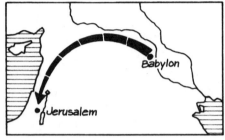

Chapter 1: The people started to rebuild the Temple. The work stopped and the people made excuses why they could not finish the Temple.

God took away His blessings. He held back the rain needed for crops and animals.

God spoke to the people through His prophet Haggai. In a little more than three weeks, they began rebuilding the Temple again.

Chapter 2: One month after the work began again, it was obvious the rebuilt Temple would be much smaller than Solomon's great Temple.

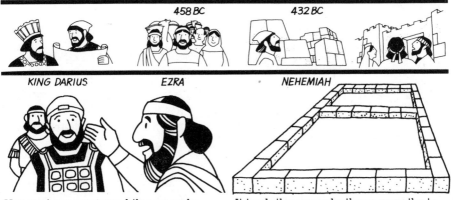

458 BC   432 BC

KING DARIUS   EZRA   NEHEMIAH

Haggai encouraged the people by telling them God was still with them and would someday cause a great new Temple to be built.

It took the people three months to complete the Temple foundation. Haggai said that their past troubles were over because now they were obeying God.

Haggai also said that in the future God will judge the nations and reward those who have been faithful.

Zerubbabel, who led the first return to the city, will be honored.

Haggai

and God's Plan to Send a Savior

The leader Zerubbabel is part of the line of David, the family line of the Savior—Jesus Christ. God took care of the family line of Jesus all of these years to provide you with a Savior. Thank God for His love and care!

Zechariah

WRITER: Zechariah, the prophet. (See Zechariah 1:1.)

PROPHET TO: The Jews who returned to Jerusalem after 70 years of captivity in Babylon.

OTHER PROPHETS AT THIS TIME: Haggai. Haggai was older than Zechariah. He prophesied for four months. Zechariah prophesied for several years. Both prophets tried to persuade God's people to finish rebuilding the Temple.

TITLE: "Zechariah" means "God remembers" or "God has remembered." The nation of Israel will be blessed because God remembers the agreement He made with His people.

LOCATION: Zechariah is in the Prophecy division of the Old Testament. It is the eleventh book of the Minor Prophets and the thirty-eighth book of the Old Testament.

The Books of Minor Prophets

Hosea | Joel | Amos | Obadiah | Jonah | Micah | Nahum | Habakkuk | Zephaniah | Haggai | Zechariah | Malachi

OUTLINE:
- [ ] The call to turn back to God (Zechariah 1:1-6).
- [ ] The eight visions of Zechariah (Zechariah 1:7—6:8).
- [ ] The crowning of Joshua, the high priest (Zechariah 6:9-15).
- [ ] The question of fasting (not eating) (Zechariah 7:1-3).
- [ ] The four messages of Zechariah (Zechariah 7:4—8:23).
- [ ] The two burdens of Zechariah (Zechariah 9—14).

Main Events

■ Rebuild the Temple. The Messiah Is Coming

Chapters 1—14: Some of God's people left Babylon and returned to Jerusalem. They were to rebuild the Temple. But they got side-tracked. God called Zechariah and Haggai to encourage the people to finish rebuilding the Temple. They told the people about the future of the Temple and the coming Messiah (Savior).

Haggai Zechariah

Chapters 1—6: One night God sent Zechariah eight visions. The visions told of the restoring of Jerusalem and the coming of good times for God's people.

The visions also told of the future times when God's Servant (Jesus Christ) will rule.

Chapters 7,8: The people asked questions about their ceremonies. Zechariah said the people would please God more if they simply were kind to one another.

Chapters 9—14: Zechariah spoke of the coming of a great King. But he told of two very different ways the King would be seen.

Zechariah referred to two different comings of Jesus Christ. The first coming would be to live as a man and die on the cross for our sake.

The second coming, which is in the future, will be to judge the nations and rule over the whole world.

Zechariah

and God's Plan to Send a Savior

The book of Zechariah is very clear about the coming of the Savior. The prophet sees Jesus Christ coming the first time as the SERVANT—to die for the sins of the world. He sees Him coming the second time as the GLORIOUS KING—to rule over the heaven and the earth!

The book of Zechariah has more promises about the coming of Jesus than any other book, except for Isaiah. There are many things that are told about His first coming: Zechariah 3:8; 9:9; 9:16; 11:11-13; 12:10; 13:1,6. There are many things that are told about His second coming: Zechariah 6:12; 14:1-21.

As you read this book, look for the times when Zechariah refers to Jesus' first coming to earth and His second coming in glory.

Where It All Happened

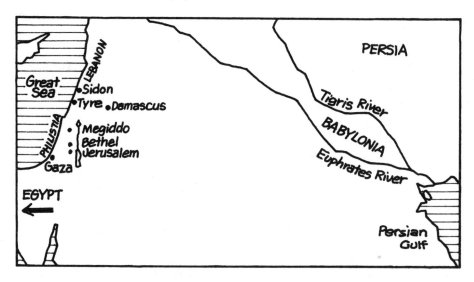

When Events Happened

See time line on pages 192, 193.

Malachi

WRITER: The writer was Malachi, the prophet.
(See Malachi 1:1.)

PROPHET TO: The Jews who returned to Jerusalem after their captivity. Malachi probably prophesied during the time of Nehemiah. Malachi is probably the last prophet to speak to Israel in Old Testament times. (Israel here means all the people of Israel and Judah who returned after the Babylonian captivity.)

TITLE: "Malachi" means "My messenger" or "the messenger of Yahweh." (Yahweh is the Hebrew name of God.)

LOCATION: Malachi is in the Prophecy division of the Old Testament. It is the twelfth book of the Minor Prophets and the thirty-ninth book of the Old Testament. This book is the bridge between the Old Testament and the New Testament.

The Books of Minor Prophets

Hosea	Joel	Amos	Obadiah	Jonah	Micah	Nahum	Habakkuk	Zephaniah	Haggai	Zechariah	Malachi

OUTLINE:
☐ God's love for the people of Israel (Malachi 1:1-5).
☐ God's complaint against the people of Israel (Malachi 1:6—2:15).
☐ The Lord's coming announced (Malachi 3:1—4:6).

When Events Happened (See time line on pages 136, 137.)

450 BC	444 BC			430 BC	420 BC
EZRA	NEHEMIAH			MALACHI	

Main Events

■ Trust and Obey God. The Savior Is Coming

Chapters 1—4: When God's people returned from their Babylonian captivity, they again fell into sin. They worshiped idols and married people who worshiped idols. Malachi told the people to turn to God. He promised that the Savior (Messiah) would come to bring hope to all people.

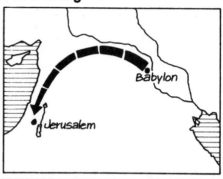

Chapter 1: The Lord reminded the people of Israel about His great love for them.

Chapters 1-3: The religious leaders and people went through the forms of worship, but didn't really try to please God. And so God kept His blessings from them.

God told of the coming Savior and warned about the judgment He will bring. God promised to bless His people if they put Him first in their lives.

Chapters 3,4: God said the wicked will be judged and those who love God will be rewarded. God's plan for a Savior will come true in New Testament times.

Where It All Happened

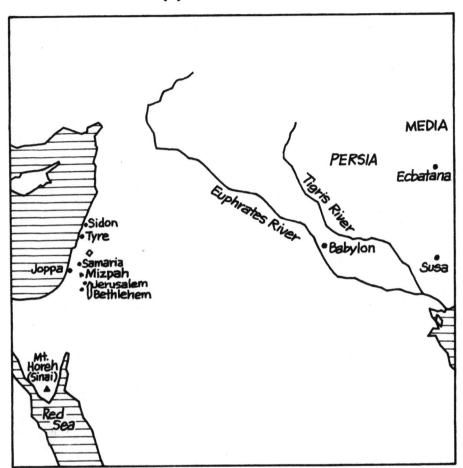

Malachi

and God's Plan to Send a Savior

Malachi told of the person who will prepare the way for the Savior (Messiah). Four hundred years passed between the time Malachi said a messenger would be sent and the arrival of that messenger, John the Baptist. John had the job of "preparing the way" for Jesus by telling people to be sorry for their sins.

Malachi spoke not only of Jesus' first coming, but also of the second time He will come to earth.

In the New Testament you will read about the Savior in the books of Matthew, Mark, Luke and John.

Let's Look at the Time Between

THE OLD TESTAMENT
THE NEW TESTAMENT

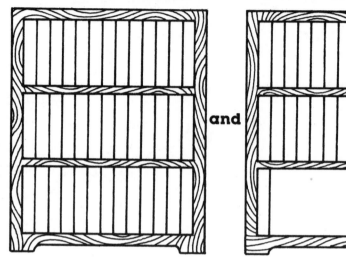

and

The Last 100 Years of Old Testament History

The books of Ezra, Nehemiah and Esther tell us what happened in the last 100 years of Old Testament history. Ezra and Nehemiah tell of the return of some of the Jewish captives to their own land. They tell how the people rebuilt the Temple and then the wall of Jerusalem. The book of Esther tells events that happened to Jews who remained in Persia during this period of time. Some of the prophets also tell events that happened at this time. Malachi was the last of the Old Testament prophets.

Four Hundred Years of Silence

Then, from Nehemiah and Malachi to the beginning of New Testament times, 400 years passed by. During this time, no biblical prophet spoke or wrote. These years are often called "the years of silence." But they were far from silent! A lot of changes were going on.

What Happened During Those 400 Years?

We can understand the New Testament better if we know some of the things that happened during the 400 years before the New Testament begins.

Palestine—A Land Bridge

If you look at the map, you'll see that Palestine is like a bridge of land that connects three continents: Europe, Asia and Africa. Because of the important location of this little piece of land, every world empire that came to power wanted to control it. And so Palestine was conquered first by one and then another and then another world power.

- Alexander the Great from Greece conquered Palestine and the lands around it. He introduced the Greek language and customs to Palestine.

- When Alexander died, his empire went to his four generals. The kingdom founded in Egypt conquered Palestine first. Then this kingdom was overpowered by the kingdom founded in Syria and Mesopotamia.

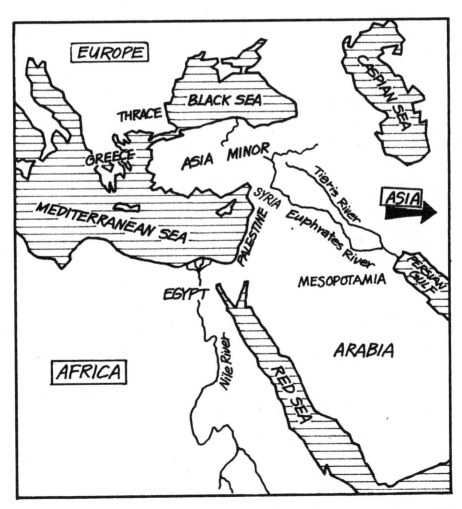

Worship in Palestine

Some of the conquerors of Palestine allowed the Jews to worship as they wished, but one of the rulers, Antiochus (an-tee-OK-us), tried to force the Jews to adopt Greek customs and worship.

- Antiochus tried to stop the Jews from worshiping the one true God.
- He tried to get rid of all copies of the Torah—the five books of Law.
- He commanded the Jews to worship the Greek god Zeus (zoose).
- He set up a statue of Zeus in the Temple at Jerusalem and sacrificed a pig in the Temple.

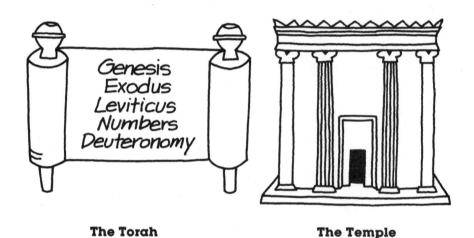

The Torah   **The Temple**

The Jews Revolt

Because of the terrible things Antiochus was doing, the Jews revolted and fought victoriously for their independence. The Maccabee (MACK-a-bee) family who led the revolt became the new rulers.

Roman Rule

The Jews' independence did not last long. Palestine was soon conquered by the expanding Roman empire. The conquering Romans killed the Jewish priests as they were ministering at the Temple. This and other acts made the Jews hate their Roman conquerors. They hoped their promised Messiah would come soon and free them from Roman rule.

The Stage Is Set

At last the stage was set for the coming of the Messiah. God chose a time when the wonderful message of the coming of the Savior could be spread quickly throughout the entire world. When the Greeks were in power, they had established Greek as a common language for the lands they conquered. When the Romans were in power, they built a great network of roads. The good news about Jesus could be sent throughout the world.

Through the years, God had told His people many things about the promised Savior. He told them the promised Savior would be born in David's family line. He told them many things the promised Savior would do. He even told them WHERE the promised Savior would be born (Micah 5:2)—but He didn't say WHEN.

And now—after 400 years without any new messages from God's prophets—the time had come! The stage was set. The Son of God was about to leave His home in heaven and be born as a baby in Bethlehem. He was about to come to earth to be our Savior—just as God had promised over and over again in Old Testament times.

The New Testament opens with this wonderful event!

Let's Look at the Gospels

What Are the Gospels?

The word "gospel" means "good news." The four Gospels are four books that tell the good news that Jesus came to be our Savior. They are the first four books of the New Testament. They were written by four men: Matthew, Mark, Luke and John.

Similarities and Differences

The diagram below shows some similarities and differences in the four Gospels. The first three Gospels are the most alike. They tell mainly about Jesus' ministry in Galilee (although they tell about His ministry in Judea, too). They focus on Jesus' actions—His miracles, parables and messages to the crowds. The Gospel of John tells some of these events, too—but John focuses more on Jesus' deeper conversations and prayers. John tells mainly about Jesus' ministry in Judea (although he includes some events in Galilee).

The Gospels

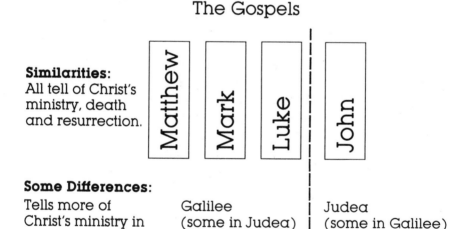

Similarities:
All tell of Christ's ministry, death and resurrection.

Matthew   Mark   Luke   John

Some Differences:

Tells more of Christ's ministry in	Galilee (some in Judea)	Judea (some in Galilee)
Tells more of Christ's	actions	deeper conversations and prayers

All of the Gospels deal with Christ's earthly ministry, His teachings, miracles, death and resurrection. But each Gospel has its differences, too. Each writer is trying to present a different picture of Jesus Christ.

Writer:	Presents Jesus as:
Matthew	King
Mark	Servant
Luke	Son of Man
John	Son of God

When we read all the Gospels, we get a more complete picture of Jesus than if we read only one.

Old Testament Pictures of Jesus

The Old Testament prophets also described the four pictures of Jesus that we find in the Gospels. You might like to look up what the prophets said about Jesus as:

- **King:** Isaiah 9:6,7; 32:1; Jeremiah 23:5; Zechariah 9:9; 14:9
- **Servant of Yahweh (God):** Isaiah 42:1-7; 52:13-15; 53
- **Man, Son of Man:** Isaiah 7:14-16; 9:6
- **God:** Isaiah 9:6; 40:3-5; 47:4; Jeremiah 23:6

The Gospels—The Beginning of the New Testament

Remember that the **Old Testament** is the story of a PROMISE. The **New Testament** reports how that PROMISE CAME TRUE.

Jesus Christ quotes from 22 Old Testament books: in Matthew—19 times, in Mark—15 times, in Luke—25 times, in John—11 times.

In the New Testament, men who saw the promise come true wrote down exactly how it happened. They wrote many important things about what God's promise can mean to everyone.

The four Gospels are the first group of books in the New Testament. We will look at them next.

THE GOSPELS

Matthew

Mark

Luke

John

HISTORY

Acts

LETTERS BY PAUL

Romans

1 Corinthians

2 Corinthians

Galatians

Ephesians

Philippians

Colossians

1 Thessalonians

2 Thessalonians

1 Timothy

2 Timothy

Titus

Philemon

GENERAL LETTERS

Hebrews

James

1 Peter

2 Peter

1 John

2 John

3 John

Jude

PROPHECY

Revelation

Matthew

WRITER: The writer was Matthew, a tax collector in Capernaum for the Roman government. He was not liked by the Jewish people. Jesus called Matthew to follow Him. Matthew quickly went with Jesus and became one of Jesus' twelve disciples. Matthew is sometimes called Levi in the Bible.

TITLE: "Matthew" means "the gift of the Lord." The Gospel of Matthew was written to the Jewish people to answer questions they had about Jesus. The Old Testament closed with God's people looking for their long-promised King, their Messiah. Matthew's Gospel shows that Jesus was that King. Matthew quotes from the Old Testament more than any of the other Gospel writers. He wanted to show the Jews that Jesus fulfilled the Old Testament prophecies about the Messiah.

LOCATION: Matthew is the first of the four Gospels and the first book of the New Testament.

The Gospels

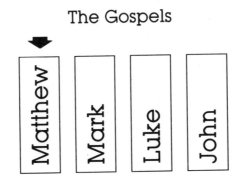

MAIN PEOPLE: Jesus, the disciples

OUTLINE: ☐ Jesus' birth and boyhood (Matthew 1,2)
☐ Jesus' teaching and healing ministry (Matthew 3—20)
☐ Jesus' crucifixion and resurrection (Matthew 21—28)

When Events Happened

BC / AD   26

Main Events
■ The Book of Matthew

The Savior is coming.

The Savior has come.

Chapters 1—28 In the **Old Testament,** the prophets told of God's promise to send a Messiah (Savior). The Messiah would save people from their sins. In **Matthew,** the Messiah's arrival is announced! Jesus Christ is here! This is Matthew's story of Jesus— His life and ministry.

Old Testament Prophets   Matthew

■ Jesus' Birth and Boyhood

Chapters 1,2 The first two chapters of Matthew tell how God kept His promise to send the Messiah (Savior).

Chapter 1: Matthew tells about the family line of Jesus Christ. It included Abraham, Jacob, David and Solomon. Hundreds of years later Jesus was born.

Chapter 2: Led by a star, wise men came to worship Jesus. King Herod tried to find little Jesus to kill Him, but Joseph took Jesus and Mary to Egypt.

■ Jesus' Teaching and Healing Ministry

Chapters 3—20 When Jesus grew up, He traveled to different cities doing the work God sent Him to do. He healed many people and taught them about God.

Chapter 3: Jesus was baptized by John the Baptist in the Jordan River.

This is my Son, whom I love.

At the baptism of His Son, God the Father spoke and the Holy Spirit was present.

Chapter 4: Alone in the desert, Jesus was tempted by Satan (the devil) three times. Jesus did not sin by obeying Satan.

Jesus left the desert and went to Galilee. He began to preach and heal people.

Chapters 5—7: Jesus went up on a mountain. He taught the people about the kind of life that pleases God.

Jesus taught about prayer. He gave an example of how we should pray. This is called the Lord's prayer.

Chapters 8,9: Jesus did eleven miracles. These miracles show that He has power over everything—sickness, Satan, nature, death.

Chapters 10—12: Jesus chose twelve men to be His disciples (followers). He had special teachings for His disciples.

Jesus' disciples were Peter, Andrew, James, John, Philip, Bartholomew, Thomas, Matthew, James, Thaddaeus, Simon and Judas Iscariot.

Chapters 13,14: Jesus taught about faith as He used picture stories called parables.

Jesus fed more than 5,000 people.

He showed power over nature by walking on the sea.

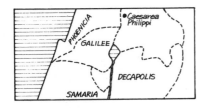

Chapter 15: After Jesus left Galilee, He traveled to the regions of Phoenicia, Decapolis and Caesarea Philippi.

Jesus healed the daughter of a Canaanite woman. He fed 4,000 people with a little fish and bread.

Chapters 16—18: Jesus asked His disciples, "Who do people say the Son of Man is?" Peter said, "You are the Christ, the Son of the living God."

Jesus and His disciples traveled back to Galilee. Jesus told them that He would soon die and come back to life. They were very sad because Jesus would soon die.

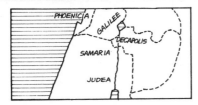

Chapters 19,20: Later Jesus and His disciples traveled into Judea.

Jesus told them that He would soon be betrayed and crucified. On the third day He would come back to life.

■ Jesus' Crucifixion and Resurrection

Chapters 21—28 Part of God's plan to send a Savior meant that Jesus, who never sinned, had to die for our sin. It was also God's plan to raise Jesus from the dead and to receive into His family all who trust Jesus as their Savior.

Chapters 21—23: The people welcomed Jesus into Jerusalem.

The religious leaders argued with Jesus. He explained that the greatest commandment is to love God.

Chapter 24: Jesus would soon leave His disciples. He warned them about what would happen in the future. They should always be ready for His return.

Chapter 25: Jesus told His disciples that, while they waited for His return, they should show kindness and tell others of God's love.

Chapter 26: Jesus ate the Passover meal with His disciples. He tried to prepare them for what was about to happen.

The Passover meal was a time for remembering how God saved His people from slavery in Egypt.

Jesus took two of the elements from the Passover meal—the bread and the fruit of the vine—and told His disciples to celebrate a new time of remembering.

We continue to celebrate this new time of remembering in our communion service. We remember that Jesus died for us and came back to life.

Judas turned Jesus over to the religious council leaders. Peter was afraid and said that he did not know Jesus.

Chapter 27: Jesus was put on trial before the governor, Pilate. The people demanded Jesus' death and He was crucified. His body was buried in a tomb.

Chapter 28: Three days after Jesus' death, women came to visit His grave. The tomb was empty and an angel told them that Jesus was alive again.

When they ran to tell Jesus' disciples, they met Jesus on the way. Jesus told them to have His friends meet Him in Galilee.

Jesus met His disciples on a mountaintop in Galilee. He told them to go everywhere in the world and teach people about God's love.

It was time for Jesus to return to His father in heaven, but He told His friends that He would always be with them.

Discoveries from the Past

The land of Palestine was ruled by a line of kings who took the name "Herod." It seemed unlikely to many people that Jesus would be tried by a Roman named Pontius Pilate. Archaeologists, digging up an old theater in the city of Caesarea, found the name "Pontius Pilate" written in the ruins. The writing also gives the name of Tiberius, the Emperor who sent Pilate to Palestine as his governor.

Where It All Happened

Below is a map that shows Palestine at the time of Jesus Christ and His ministry. As you read the Gospel of Matthew, find on the map the places where Jesus went. Also read what He did and said in each place.

To begin, find Bethlehem, where Jesus was born. Find Capernaum, where Jesus healed the centurion's servant. Find Caesarea Philippi, where Jesus asked His disciples, "Who do people say the Son of Man is?" (Matthew 16:13). Now read the Gospel of Matthew and look for other places on the map.

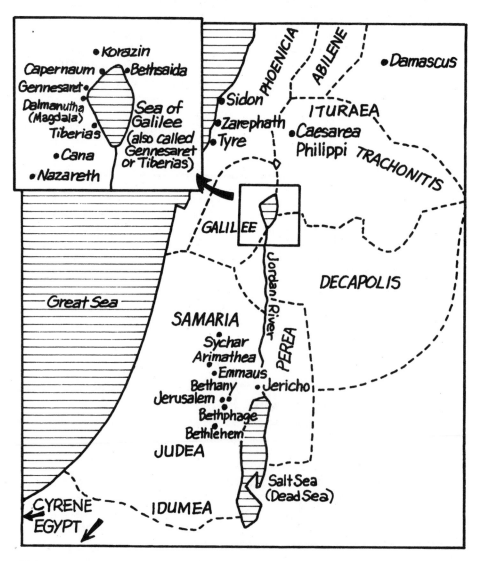

Christist

in the Book of Matthew

God promised Abraham (in Genesis 12:2,3) that in him all of the people on the earth would be blessed. Jesus Christ is "the son of Abraham" (Matthew 1:1). Jesus is also called "the son of David" (Matthew 1:1). God's promises all came true in Jesus Christ.

Jesus is the KING in the Gospel of Matthew. He has power over everything. He can forgive sin, heal the sick and get rid of demons in people. He even has power over death. The grave could not hold Him.

Remember what Jesus Christ did for you! He died for you. If you would like to know more about this, please turn to "Becoming God's Child" in this guidebook. There you will learn how to become a member of God's family.

Mark

WRITER: The writer was Mark, a relative of Barnabas. Mark traveled with Barnabas and Paul. He also worked closely with Peter. Peter told Mark much of the information for this book. The reference to "a young man" in Mark 14:51,52 may refer to Mark.

TITLE: Mark is the name of the man who wrote this Gospel. Mark probably wrote it to readers who were Roman. They were more interested in what Jesus DID than in fulfilled prophecies. And so Mark's Gospel is a book of action—it tells what Jesus DID in His ministry. It is a short Gospel, in which the events move very quickly. Mark sees Jesus as "the Servant."

LOCATION: Mark is the second of the four Gospels and the second book of the New Testament.

The Gospels

Matthew | Mark | Luke | John

MAIN PEOPLE: Jesus, the disciples

KEY VERSE: "For even the Son of Man did not come to be served, but to serve, and to give His life as a ransom for many" (Mark 10:45).

OUTLINE: ☐ Jesus, the Servant—serving people (Mark 1—10)
☐ Jesus, the Servant—giving His life to save others (Mark 11—16)

When Events Happened

See time line on pages 208, 209.

Main Events

■ Jesus Came to Serve

Chapters 1—10 The key verse of Mark's Gospel is 10:45, "For even the Son of Man did not come to be served, but to serve, and to give His life as a ransom for many." (See "Son of Man" on page 329.) Chapters 1—10 show Jesus serving others.

Chapter 1: Jesus came to John, Jesus' cousin, to be baptized in the Jordan River.

Jesus went into the wilderness. There Satan (the devil) tempted Jesus to sin. Jesus would not obey Satan.

Chapters 2,3: Jesus began His work. He healed many who were sick. He called His twelve disciples together to learn from Him.

Chapters 4,5: Jesus told picture stories, called parables, that taught about faith. He healed many who were sick and brought to life a girl who had died.

Chapter 6: John the Baptist was killed by King Herod. Jesus fed over 5,000 people with a little fish and bread. His disciples saw Him walk on the sea.

Chapters 7,8: Jesus told some of the religious leaders to be more concerned with the law of love than with their own traditions. Jesus fed another large crowd.

This is my Son, whom I love.

Chapters 9,10: Three of Jesus' disciples saw Him with Elijah and Moses on the mountain. God's voice from heaven called Jesus His Son.

Jesus taught that a truly great person is one who serves others. Jesus also showed His love for children.

■ Jesus Came to Give His Life

Chapters 11—16 Jesus came to earth not only to serve but also to give. He gave His life so that we can live forever with Him. Jesus told His disciples what was going to happen to Him in Jerusalem, and to the world in the future.

Chapters 11,12: The people welcomed Jesus into Jerusalem. Jesus showed the people that He was the promised Savior.

Chapter 13: The disciples asked Jesus about the future. Jesus told them that He would one day return.

Chapter 14: Jesus ate with His disciples. Jesus prayed in a garden where He was arrested by the religious leaders. The leaders said Jesus deserved to die.

Chapter 15: The Roman governor tried Jesus and found Him not guilty. But the people demanded His death. Jesus was crucified and buried.

Chapter 16: Women who came to visit Jesus' tomb found it empty. An angel told the women that Jesus is alive!

Jesus gave His disciples a job to do. He said, "Go into all the world and preach the good news to all creation" (Mark 16:15).

Discoveries from the Past

Jerusalem, the city in which many of the events in the Gospels took place, is a modern city. Much of the Jerusalem of Jesus' time is covered with newer buildings. See page 362.

It is hard to find the exact location of some of the most important places mentioned in this story of Jesus' life. For example, we can't be sure of the exact place of Jesus' tomb. We can be sure that the kind of tomb described in the Bible was very common at the time of Jesus' death. Tombs have been found with a round stone that rolled in front of the opening. These stones are large and heavy. No wonder the women thought they would need help moving the stone! See page 361.

Where It All Happened

See the map on page 214. As you read the Gospel of Mark, find on that map the places where Jesus went. Also read about what He did and said in each place.

Christ

in the Book of Mark

Christ is pictured as "the Servant." He served by giving His life that you might live again. He was obedient to His heavenly Father in everything that He did.

If you want to know how to become a member of God's family by trusting Jesus as your Savior, read "Becoming God's Child" in this guidebook.

Luke

WRITER: The writer was Luke, a doctor who loved Jesus and told people about Him. Luke traveled with Paul. Luke wrote this Gospel and the book of Acts (also called the Acts of the Apostles).

TITLE: Luke is the name of the man who wrote this Gospel. Luke wrote to a man named Theophilus to help him—and all people—know what is true about Jesus. He told what Jesus did in His ministry. Luke called Jesus "the Son of Man."

LOCATION: Luke is the third of the four Gospels and the third book of the New Testament.

The Gospels

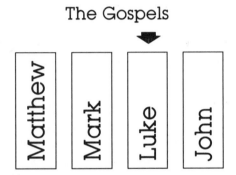

MAIN PEOPLE: Jesus, the disciples

OUTLINE: ☐ Jesus, the Son of Man, grows up (Luke 1—4:13)
☐ Jesus, the Son of Man, has power over everything (Luke 4:14—9:50)
☐ Jesus, the Son of Man, teaches His disciples (Luke 9:51—19:17)
☐ Jesus, the Son of Man, suffers and dies (Luke 19:28—23:56)
☐ Jesus, the Son of Man, lives again forever (Luke 24)

When Events Happened

See time line on pages 208, 209.

Main Events

■ The Book of Luke

Chapters 1—24 Doctor Luke tells us much about the life of Jesus. We learn details about His birth and something about His childhood. Like the other Gospel writers, Luke tells of Jesus' ministry, His death and His return to life.

■ Jesus Grows Up

Chapters 1—4: God sent John the Baptist to prepare people for Jesus' arrival. Jesus was born in Bethlehem and grew up in Nazareth. When Jesus was ready to begin His work, He went to John to be baptized. God said of Jesus, "You are my Son, whom I love" (Luke 3:22).

You are my Son, whom I love.

Chapters 1: An angel prophesied the birth of John, Jesus' cousin. Soon afterwards, an angel told Mary that she would give birth to Jesus.

Chapters 2: Jesus was born in Bethlehem. When Jesus was a boy, He talked with the teachers in the Temple. They were surprised at His understanding.

Chapter 3: John baptized people in preparation for the coming of Jesus. Jesus came to John for baptism before beginning His work.

Chapters 4: Verses 1-13 tell about when Jesus was tempted by the devil in the desert. Jesus did not do what the devil wanted.

221

■ Jesus Has Power Over Everything

Chapters 4—9 After being in the desert, Jesus began His work of healing and teaching the people. He gathered His 12 disciples together. Jesus showed His power over demons, death and nature.

Chapters 4—6: Jesus began telling people who He is and gathering His disciples. He showed His power over demons and disease.

Jesus told people the reasons they should be happy. He taught them how to act in loving ways.

Chapters 7-9: Jesus taught the people many things and healed many of their illnesses.

Jesus showed His love to people who had done bad things. Jesus explained who He was and what He was about to do.

■ Jesus Teaches His Disciples

Chapters 10—19 Jesus taught His disciples many things about God's love and how they should share it with other people.

Chapters 10—19: Jesus used picture stories, called parables, to tell people about God's love. Many leaders did not believe that Jesus is the Son of God.

Jesus taught how to live a life that pleases God. Jesus wanted people to know that God is willing to forgive their sins.

■ Jesus Dies and Lives Again

Chapters 19—24 The leaders of the Council wanted to have Jesus killed. After He said good-bye to His disciples, Jesus was arrested and tried by the Council. They demanded that the Romans crucify Jesus. But after Jesus died, He came back to life.

Chapters 19—22: The people welcomed Jesus into Jerusalem.

He ate a last supper with His disciples.

Jesus and His disciples went to a garden to pray. The religious leaders arrested Jesus.

Chapter 23: Even though Jesus was not guilty of a crime, the crowd demanded His death. Jesus died on a cross and was buried in a tomb.

Chapter 24: Jesus' friends found His tomb empty. Angels said Jesus was alive. Jesus' friends remembered what He had said about His death.

Jesus explained to two friends why He died. Before going to heaven, He gave His disciples special work to do.

Discoveries from the Past

Joseph and Mary lived in Nazareth. The Old Testament said that Jesus would be born in Bethlehem. No one would choose to go on a long trip just before the birth of a baby. Why was Jesus born in Bethlehem?

People who study very old writings have found reports that the Romans liked to count the number of people who lived in their empire. In order to get a true count, the Romans sent people back to the town in which they were born. Joseph's family came from Bethlehem. Mary and Joseph made the trip from Nazareth to Bethlehem just in time for Jesus to be born there.

Where It All Happened

See the map on page 214. As you read the Gospel of Luke, find on that map the places where Jesus went. Also read about what He did and said in each place.

Christ

in the Book of Luke

Luke pictures Jesus Christ as the "Son of Man." The events recorded by Luke show that Jesus was MAN as well as GOD. He was born, grew up and died. He had to suffer temptation and pain just as we do. He knows what it is like to be human. He is the One who can help us in every way.

If you would like to know more about becoming a member of God's family by trusting Christ as your Savior, see "Becoming God's Child" in this guidebook.

John

WRITER: The writer was John, one of Jesus' 12 disciples. John is called "the disciple whom Jesus loved" (John 21:20). John saw the things Jesus did and knew Him very well (John 21:24).

TITLE: John is the name of the man who wrote this Gospel. John wrote this book so that people might BELIEVE in Jesus (John 20:31). John sees Jesus as "the Son of God."

LOCATION: John is the last of the four Gospels and the fourth book of the New Testament.

The Gospels

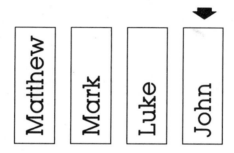

MAIN PEOPLE: Jesus, the disciples

KEY VERSE: "These are written that you may believe that Jesus is the Christ, the Son of God, and that by believing you may have life in his name" (John 20:31).

OUTLINE: ☐ Jesus God's Son's healing and teaching ministry (John 1:1-12)
☐ Jesus God's Son's death and resurrection (John 13-21)

When Events Happened

See time line on pages 208, 209.

Main Events

■ God the Son Comes to Earth

Chapter 1 John begins his Gospel with Jesus Christ BEFORE His birth as a baby in Bethlehem. Jesus is eternal—He has no beginning and no ending. God the Son was in the beginning with God the Father and God the Holy Spirit. He is the Creator of all things. God is one God who exists in three special ways: as God the Father, as God the Son (Jesus) and as God the Holy Spirit. Jesus is God born as a man, but He is still God.

John does not give the details of Jesus' birth, as Matthew and Luke do. John establishes the fact that Jesus, God's Son, came to earth. Then he tells how people responded when Jesus began His ministry (when He was about 30 years old).

When Jesus came to earth, some people believed in Him and some did not. "Yet to all who received him, to those who believed in his name, he gave the right to become children of God" (John 1:12). The purpose of John's Gospel is to help people BELIEVE in Jesus.

John the Baptist prepared the way for Jesus. He preached to the people and told them to turn from their sin.

When John the Baptist began preaching, some people thought he might be the promised Messiah. But John said, "No, I am not the Christ (the Messiah)."

Then he introduced Jesus as the promised Messiah. He said, "Look, the Lamb of God, who takes away the sin of the world!" (John 1:29)

Just as lambs were used as sacrifices for sin, so Jesus came to be the one perfect sacrifice for sin.

Hundreds of years earlier the prophet Isaiah had described Jesus, the Lamb of God. (See Isaiah 53.)

John the Baptist introduced Jesus as the Lamb of God that Isaiah was talking about.

Jesus asked John the Baptist to baptize Him. When Jesus was baptized, God the Holy Spirit came as a dove and remained on Jesus.

Then John the Baptist knew who Jesus was. He said, "I have seen and I testify that this is the Son of God" (John 1:34).

John, the writer of this Gospel, was a disciple (follower) of John the Baptist. He was probably one of the two disciples John 1:35 tells about.

John tells how he and several others came to believe in and follow Jesus.

■ Jesus' Healing and Teaching Ministry

Chapters 2—12 Jesus said and did many things that show He is God's Son. Some people believed in Him and some did not.

Chapters 2: Jesus performed miracles—He did things that only God can do. He also drove out of the Temple people who were not using it for worship.

Chapter 3: A Pharisee, Nicodemus, came to talk to Jesus. Jesus told him he needed to be born again—to become a member of God's family.

When Jesus was explaining the need to believe in Him, He reminded Nicodemus of the time Moses held up a bronze snake on a pole.

People who looked at the bronze snake were cured of their snake bites. (See Numbers 21:9.)

Jesus said He came so that people who believe He died for them will be saved from their sin. They will have eternal life. Read John 3:16.

Chapter 4: By talking to a woman who was known as a sinner, Jesus showed that God's love is for everyone. She found He was the promised Messiah.

A father asked Jesus to come heal his son. Jesus healed the boy without even going to the boy's home.

Chapter 5: Jesus healed a man who was lame for 38 years. The religious leaders criticized Jesus for doing this on the Sabbath (Jewish day of worship).

Chapters 6—10: Over 5,000 people came to hear Jesus teach and to be healed by Him. Jesus fed them all from one boy's lunch.

That night Jesus' disciples were caught in a storm on the Sea of Galilee. Jesus walked on the water and calmed the storm.

Jesus taught the people who He was and who had sent Him. This angered many of the religious leaders. They did not believe Jesus is God's Son.

Chapters 11,12: Jesus brought Lazarus back to life. He said those who believe in Him will have life that lasts forever.

■ Jesus' Death and Resurrection

Chapters 13—21 Jesus knew that His death would permit God to forgive people for their sins. He was willing to be tried by His enemies and to die on the cross. When He rose again, He gave His disciples the work of telling others the good news of salvation through trusting Christ as Savior.

Chapters 13—16: Jesus taught His disciples to love and serve one another. He said, "If you love me, you will obey what I command" (John 14:15).

Jesus told His disciples that He would die—but would rise again. He ate a last meal with His disciples.

Chapter 17: Jesus asked His Father, God, to protect those who believe in Him.

Chapters 18,19: Jesus was arrested and tried by Pilate. Pilate found Jesus innocent. The people demanded His death. Jesus was crucified and buried.

Chapter 20: Jesus' friends found His tomb empty. Jesus met with His friends to show them that He had come back to life.

Chapter 21: The disciples saw Jesus again when they were out fishing. Jesus told Peter to tell others about Him.

Where It All Happened

See the map on page 214. As you read the Gospel of John, find on that map the places where Jesus went. Also read about what He did and said in each place.

Christ

in the Book of John

John pictures Jesus as the Son of God. Jesus is both man and God. Jesus is the Savior of the world. In this Gospel, seven people state that Jesus is God or God's Son:

- John the Baptist: "This is the Son of God" (John 1:34).
- Nathanael (to Jesus): "You are the Son of God" (John 1:49).
- Peter (to Jesus): "You are the Holy One of God" (John 6:69).
- Martha (to Jesus): "You are the Christ, the Son of God" (John 11:27).
- Thomas (to Jesus): "My Lord and my God!" (John 20:28).
- John the disciple: "Jesus is the Christ, the Son of God" (John 20:31).
- Christ Himself: "I am God's Son" (John 10:36).

Acts

WRITER: The writer was Luke, a doctor who traveled with Paul on his missionary journeys. Luke used the words "we" and "us" to show that he was there with Paul. Luke also wrote the Gospel of Luke, which shows what Christ **began** to do on earth. Acts shows what He **continued** to do by the Holy Spirit.

TITLE: This book is called Acts (or The Acts of the Apostles) because it tells the **acts** of the Holy Spirit through the apostles. (See "apostle" in the dictionary that begins on page 293.) The book of Acts covers the period from the coming of the Holy Spirit to Paul's imprisonment in Rome.

LOCATION: The book of Acts is the history of the early Church. It is the fifth book of the New Testament.

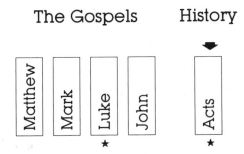

The Gospels   History

Matthew   Mark   Luke   John   Acts

Luke wrote the books marked ★.

MAIN PEOPLE: ☐ Chapters 1-12—Peter, Stephen, Philip, Barnabas, James
☐ Chapters 13—28—Paul, Barnabas, Silas

KEY VERSE: "But you will receive power when the Holy Spirit comes on you; and you will be my witnesses in Jerusalem, and in all Judea and Samaria, and to the ends of the earth" (Acts 1:8).

OUTLINE: The gospel is preached
☐ in Jerusalem (Acts 1—7)
☐ in Judea and Samaria (Acts 8—12)
☐ to the world (Acts 13—28)

When Events Happened

30 AD			35 AD	
ASCENSION	PENTECOST	PERSECUTION OF APOSTLES	SAUL (PAUL)	PETER

Main Events
■ The Book of Acts

Chapters 1—28 Luke starts the book of Acts where his first book, Luke, ends. The Gospel of Luke closes with Jesus going back to heaven. This is the opening scene in Acts (see Luke 24:49-51; Acts 1:10,11).

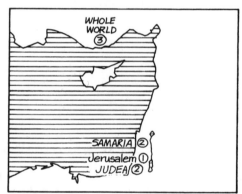

The action of the book follows the plan Jesus gave in Acts 1:8. The book divides into three sections. (1) The Church began in Jerusalem. (2) Then the action moved to Judea and Samaria. (3) Then it spread to the whole world.

■ The Gospel Is Preached in Jerusalem

Chapters 1—7 After Jesus went back to heaven, the Holy Spirit came just as Jesus promised. He gave Jesus' followers power to tell others the good news of the gospel. Jesus' followers preached the gospel first in Jerusalem.

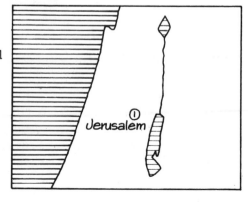

45 AD   48 AD   50 AD   52 AD   53 AD   57 AD   60 AD

PAUL: FIRST MISSIONARY
JOURNEY

SECOND MISSIONARY
JOURNEY

THIRD MISSIONARY
JOURNEY

Chapter 1: Forty days had passed since Jesus rose from the dead. It was time for Jesus to return to His Father.

Jesus told His disciples to wait in Jerusalem for the promised Holy Spirit.

You will receive power when the Holy Spirit comes on you.

Jesus told His disciples they would receive the power of the Holy Spirit to preach the gospel—the good news about Jesus.

Then Jesus went back to heaven. Two angels told Jesus' disciples that someday Jesus will return to earth—just as they saw Him go into heaven.

Jesus' friends and followers gathered together in Jerusalem and prayed. They chose a person to take Judas' place as the twelfth disciple.

Chapter 2: In Jerusalem, on the day of Pentecost, the Holy Spirit came upon the disciples. (See "Pentecost" on the chart on page 43.)

The Holy Spirit caused the believers to speak in many different languages.

Both Jews and converts to Judaism from many different countries heard God's message in their own languages. They were amazed.

Peter preached to thousands of people. His message was "Jesus is the Messiah. Repent—turn from your sin. Be baptized in the name of Jesus."

Three thousand people believed on Jesus as the promised Messiah (Savior). The believers met together for food, fellowship, prayer and hearing God's Word.

Chapters 3—5: Peter healed a lame man in the name of Jesus Christ. Then he preached to many people. The number of believers grew to about 5,000.

Men of the religious council, the Sanhedrin, made trouble for Peter and John. They ordered Peter and John not to preach the gospel. But Peter and John continued preaching.

The council had Peter and John put into prison. An angel of God freed them. They continued to preach the gospel by the power of the Holy Spirit.

Chapters 6,7: Seven deacons were chosen to care for the needy. Stephen, one of the deacons, did many miracles and preached about Jesus.

Stephen's enemies took him before the religious council. False witnesses told lies about him.

Stephen preached about Jesus to the religious council. The men became angry and Stephen was killed.

■ The Gospel Is Preached in Judea and Samaria

Chapters 8—12 In Acts 1:8 Jesus said to preach not only in Jerusalem, but also in Judea and Samaria and the remotest parts of the earth. The believers continued preaching in Jerusalem until persecution drove them out into other places. Chapters 8—12 tell about their witness in Judea and Samaria.

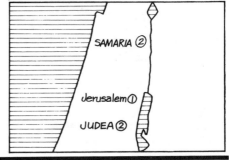

SAMARIA ②

Jerusalem①

JUDEA ②

Chapter 8: Saul, a religious leader, watched as Stephen was killed. Saul was determined to stop Jesus' followers.

Saul began putting believers in prison. Many believers escaped from Jerusalem and went to other parts of the country.

In Samaria, a magician tried to buy the disciples' power. Peter told the man he needed to repent of his wickedness and ask God's forgiveness.

Philip used the writings of the Old Testament prophet Isaiah to help a man from Ethiopia believe in Jesus.

Chapter 9: As Saul was going to Damascus, Jesus made him blind. Jesus spoke to Saul and told him what to do.

The man sent to heal Saul taught him about Jesus. Saul became a follower of Jesus.

Saul preached in the Jewish synagogues (places of worship) in Damascus. He said, "Jesus is God's Son." The people were amazed to hear Saul say this.

The religious leaders plotted to kill Saul. The believers helped him escape through an opening in the Damascus wall. They let Saul down in a basket.

When Saul tried to join the believers in Jerusalem, they were afraid of him. But Barnabas told them what had happened to Saul when he went to Damascus.

Saul preached boldly about Jesus in Jerusalem. His enemies plotted to kill him. The believers in Jerusalem helped Saul escape to Tarsus.

God used Peter to tell the people at Lydda about Jesus. When Peter healed a paralyzed man in Jesus' name, many people believed in Jesus.

A lady in Joppa made clothing for people who needed it. When she died, God used Peter to bring her back to life. Many people in Joppa believed in Jesus.

Chapter 10: God sent Peter a vision that the news about Jesus is for everyone—both Jews and Gentiles (people who are not Jews).

The next day, Peter taught a Roman soldier—and the people in his home—about Jesus. These Gentiles believed in Jesus and became His followers.

Chapter 11: Barnabas was sent to guide the new church in Antioch. The church grew. The people in Antioch sent money to help needy Christians in Judea.

Chapter 12: King Herod had James killed and Peter put into prison. The believers prayed for Peter.

An angel freed Peter from prison.

Peter went to the believers' prayer meeting. The people were excited to see how God answered their prayers.

■ The Gospel Spreads Out to the World

Chapters 13—28 In just a short time, the preaching of the gospel spread from Jerusalem, the center of the Jewish nation, to Rome, the center of a world empire.

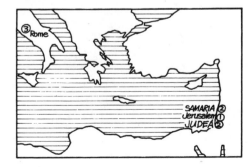

Up through Acts 12 we have seen the beginning of the church, with Peter as its leader, in Jerusalem. In Acts 13-28 we will see Paul and the church at Antioch. Paul's three missionary journeys start from Antioch—not Jerusalem.

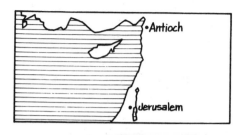

Chapters 13,14: Paul's First Missionary Journey—During a prayer meeting the Holy Spirit gave the church (believers) at Antioch a special message.

He told them to send Paul (Saul's new name) and Barnabas to preach the gospel to people in many other countries. The church at Antioch did this.

Paul and Barnabas visited many cities and helped people learn to love Jesus.

At Lystra, Paul healed a lame man. The people thought Paul and Barnabas were gods. Believing that he taught lies against God, enemies of Paul from other cities tried to kill him.

Paul and Barnabas went on to other cities to preach the gospel. Then they returned to Antioch and told the believers there all that God had done.

They told how Gentiles (non-Jews) from many countries had become followers of Jesus. Some men came and said that these new believers must obey all the Mosaic Laws.

Chapter 15: The apostles decided that a person does not have to obey all the Mosaic laws in order to be right with God.

Chapters 15:36—18:22: Paul's Second Missionary Journey— Paul wanted to visit the believers from his first journey. This time Silas went with him.

In Macedonia, Paul and Silas were beaten and put in prison. They prayed and sang praises to God.

An earthquake opened the prison doors. When Paul and Silas didn't run away, the jailer believed in Jesus.

In Thessalonica, many people believed in Jesus after hearing Paul. But some jealous people stirred up an angry mob and started a riot.

In Berea, Paul and Silas taught eager listeners who studied God's Word daily.

In Athens, Paul talked with interested listeners. Some believed and some did not.

When the Jews wouldn't believe in Jesus, Paul wanted to stop preaching to them and teach only Gentiles. God told Paul the good news is for everybody!

When Paul felt discouraged, God gave him new friends and a new vision of the work He had for Paul to do. God promised to take care of Paul.

Chapters 18:23—20:38: Paul's Third Missionary Journey— Paul again decided to visit the believers in the cities he had preached in before.

Paul encouraged the believers in many cities (see the maps on page 243.)

When Paul preached in Ephesus, he got in trouble with the makers of silver idols. When the trouble was over, Paul went on to other cities.

On the way back, Paul asked the leaders at Ephesus to come and meet with him.

He said good-bye to them and gave them advice. He did not know whether or not he would see them again.

Chapter 21: Paul returned to Jerusalem. Some of the people thought Paul was teaching Jews to turn away from Moses. They wanted to kill him.

Chapter 22: Paul tried to explain his faith in Jesus Christ. What he said angered the crowd. Soldiers took him to jail.

Chapter 23: God told Paul that he would preach in Rome. Soldiers took Paul to Caesarea to keep him from being murdered by an angry mob.

Chapter 24: Paul defended himself before Felix, the governor. But for two years Felix would not make a decision—and Paul was kept a prisoner.

Chapter 25: Felix was replaced by Festus, a new governor. When Festus put Paul on trial, Paul demanded to see Caesar, the Roman emperor.

Chapter 26: Paul told his story to Festus' visitor, King Agrippa. His listeners found Paul innocent of any crime. But they still had to send him to Rome.

Chapter 27: On the way to Rome, Paul's ship was wrecked in a storm. Everyone was safely washed ashore on an island.

Chapter 28: On the island, Paul was bitten by a snake. But God kept him from being harmed by the snake. God used Paul to heal many who were sick.

Paul was then taken to Rome. In Rome Paul was kept a prisoner in his own rented house for two years.

Even as a prisoner, Paul used every opportunity to preach the gospel. Many people became Christians.

■ Letters Paul Wrote from Rome

While Paul was a prisoner, he wrote many of his letters: Philemon, Colossians, Ephesians, Philippians. Paul was in a dungeon in Rome, waiting to be killed, when he wrote his second letter to Timothy.

■ After the Book of Acts

The acts of the Holy Spirit are still going on today. Believers in Jesus are still called to be His witnesses (Acts 1:8). We are called to tell others the good news about Jesus through the power of the Holy Spirit. Who will YOU tell about Jesus?

Christ

in the Book of Acts

The apostles taught about Jesus at every opportunity. Whenever they taught, they told of Jesus' death and resurrection. Often they reminded their listeners of the words of the prophets who told of Jesus' coming.

In chapter 1, Jesus spoke with His disciples and told them to be witnesses of all He had said and done. Then Jesus returned to heaven. The Holy Spirit gave Jesus' followers the power to tell people about Jesus.

In chapter 9, Jesus spoke to Saul from heaven. Shortly after this, Paul (Saul) became a believer. At that time Ananias said to Paul, "The God of our fathers has chosen you to know his will and to see the Righteous One (Jesus) and to hear words from his mouth. You will be his witness to all men of what you have seen and heard" (Acts 22:14,15). Paul traveled all over the world telling people about Jesus Christ.

Where It All Happened

Luke wrote his second book, Acts, from Rome where he was with Paul. Find Rome on the map.

Luke recorded Paul's three missionary journeys and his trip to Rome. Read the four stories as they are listed here. Find each city where Paul stopped on his four trips. Also read what Paul did and said at these places.

① Paul's first missionary journey: Acts 13:1—14:28
② Paul's second missionary journey: Acts 15:36—18:22
③ Paul's third missionary journey: Acts 18:23—21:26
④ Paul's trip to Rome: Acts 21:27—28:31

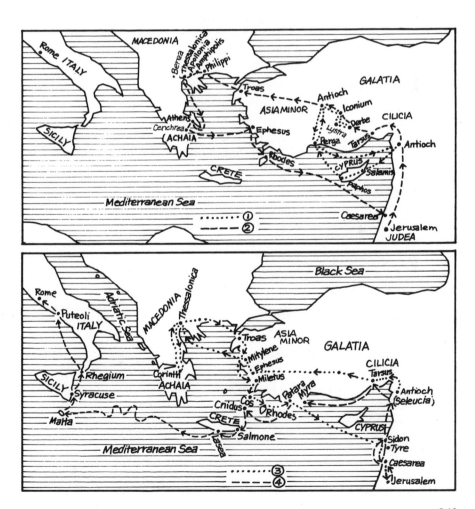

Discoveries from the Past

Acts 18:12 refers to the time when Gallio was proconsul (ruler) of Achaia (a district in Greece ruled by the Romans). An inscription (writing) found in Delphi (a Greek city) states that Gallio was proconsul of Achaia in A.D. 51 (about 50 years after the birth of Jesus).

Many of the cities of the apostles' time have grown into great modern cities. Other places mentioned in the book of Acts were deserted and lost. Most of these lost cities have been discovered by archaeologists.

The City of Ephesus

Archaeologists dug for over six years before finding the ruins of Ephesus. Twenty feet down they hit the white marble floor of the temple of the goddess Diana (a false god). Great treasure was uncovered under a statue of the goddess. Archaeologists have also found the ruins of a theater and silversmith shops (see Acts 19).

The City of Athens

Archaeologists have identified the Areopagus, the hill on which Paul spoke to the men of Athens (see Acts 17:19). Paul mentioned seeing altars on which stood objects of worship. Statues of their gods and goddesses fill museums today and show that the Greeks had many stone idols.

The City of Rome

God sent Paul to Rome (see Acts 28). It was the biggest city in the world of that time. It was the center of the great Roman Empire. Millions of people lived in the Rome that Paul knew. Even though Rome is now a modern capital, enough of the old city can be seen to show its greatness. Old monuments and coins have Roman names from Bible times.

Let's Look at the Letters of Paul and Others

After the book of Acts there are 21 books that were written as letters to early followers of Jesus. Thirteen of these were written by the apostle Paul. Eight were written by other people. We will look first at the 13 letters of Paul.

The Gospels

Matthew | Mark | Luke | John

History

Acts

Letters by Paul

Romans | 1 Corinthians | 2 Corinthians | Galatians | Ephesians | Philippians | Colossians | 1 Thessalonians | 2 Thessalonians | 1 Timothy | 2 Timothy | Titus | Philemon

General Letters

Hebrews | James | 1 Peter | 2 Peter | 1 John | 2 John | 3 John | Jude

Prophecy

Revelation

PAUL'S LETTERS

The first nine of Paul's letters were written to groups of believers (churches). The last four were written to three individuals: Timothy, Titus and Philemon.

Letters to: Churches

Romans | 1 Corinthians | 2 Corinthians | Galatians | Ephesians | Philippians | Colossians | 1 Thessalonians | 2 Thessalonians

Individuals

1 Timothy | 2 Timothy | Titus | Philemon

Timothy | Titus | Philemon

Where Were Paul's Letters Sent?

Can you match these books with the names on the map? Example: The book of Romans was written to the people who lived in Rome. They were called Romans.

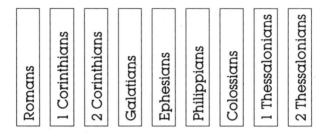

Romans | 1 Corinthians | 2 Corinthians | Galatians | Ephesians | Philippians | Colossians | 1 Thessalonians | 2 Thessalonians

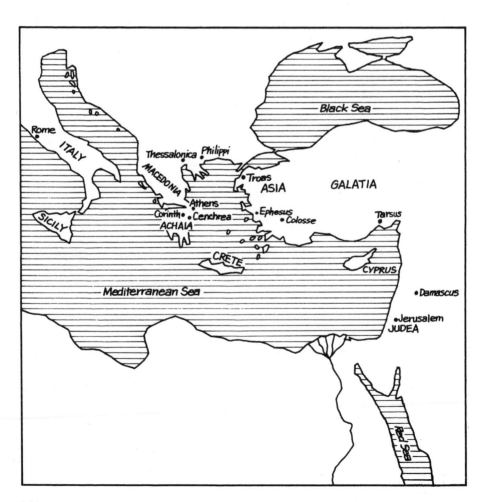

When Did Paul Write His Letters?

☐ The letters marked ⋆ were written when Paul was traveling on his missionary journeys.

☐ The letters marked ● were written when Paul was a prisoner in Rome at the time of Acts 28.

☐ The letters marked ▲ were written after Paul was freed from the imprisonment we read about in Acts 28. (He was later imprisoned again and killed for preaching about Jesus. Second Timothy was written during this later imprisonment.)

⋆	⋆	⋆	⋆	●	●	●	⋆	⋆	▲	▲	▲	●
Romans	1 Corinthians	2 Corinthians	Galatians	Ephesians	Philippians	Colossians	1 Thessalonians	2 Thessalonians	1 Timothy	2 Timothy	Titus	Philemon

LETTERS BY OTHER WRITERS

Pages 274-288 in this guidebook give information about these letters and their writers.

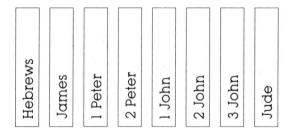

Hebrews	James	1 Peter	2 Peter	1 John	2 John	3 John	Jude

Romans

WRITER: The writer was Paul (Romans 1:1).

WRITTEN TO: The church (group of believers) at Rome. Paul was eager to visit this church. He sent them this letter from Corinth, the home of Gaius, a wealthy Corinthian Christian. (See Romans 16:23; 1 Corinthians 1:14.) Paul probably wrote this letter while he was on his third missionary journey.

BACKGROUND: We do not know who started the church at Rome. After Jesus' resurrection, visitors from Rome—in Jerusalem for the Passover and converted at Pentecost—must have gone back to Rome with the gospel message. (See Acts 2.) In the 28 years that followed, other believers probably moved to Rome. At the time this letter was written Nero was emperor of Rome.

LOCATION: Romans is the first book in the section of letters by Paul. It is the sixth book of the New Testament.

Letters by Paul

Letters to: Churches | Individuals

Romans | 1 Corinthians | 2 Corinthians | Galatians | Ephesians | Philippians | Colossians | 1 Thessalonians | 2 Thessalonians | 1 Timothy | 2 Timothy | Titus | Philemon

MESSAGE: ☐ Everyone is a sinner and needs God's salvation. God sent His Son Jesus to be our Savior from sin. Those who trust Christ as Savior have their sins forgiven and enjoy eternal life with God.

☐ Israel turned away from Jesus, the Messiah (Savior) God sent. God will still be faithful to the nation of Israel. He will restore Israel in the future.

☐ When we belong to God's family we should live our lives to please Him. We should obey God because we love Him.

BIBLE VERSES TO KNOW: Romans 1:16; 3:23,24; 5:1,2; 6:23; 8:28; 8:38,39; 10:13; 12:4,5,9-21

Where It All Happened

Find the city of Corinth from which Paul wrote this letter. Then find Rome, the home of the church (group of believers) that received this letter.

Christio

in the Book of Romans

In this book, Jesus Christ is the second Adam. The first Adam caused sin to come into the world. Jesus Christ brought forgiveness for sin. Everyone who believes in Him receives God's gift of forgiveness and everlasting life. Because Jesus Christ died and rose again from the grave we know that we can have eternal life.

When Events Happened

First Corinthians

WRITER: The writer was Paul (1 Corinthians 1:1).

WRITTEN TO: The church (group of believers) at Corinth. Paul probably wrote this letter to the Corinthians toward the end of his three-year stay in Ephesus.

BACKGROUND: Corinth was a very important city in Greece. It was a crossroads for travelers and merchants. The people built many temples for worshiping idols. They were interested in wealth and pleasure and did many sinful things.

The Christians in Corinth had many problems. Paul wrote to them about problems such as divisions in the Church, married people, food, worship, and believing in the resurrection of Jesus Christ.

LOCATION: First Corinthians is the second letter in the section Letters by Paul. It is the seventh book of the New Testament.

Letters by Paul

Letters to: Churches | **Individuals**

| Romans | 1 Corinthians | 2 Corinthians | Galatians | Ephesians | Philippians | Colossians | 1 Thessalonians | 2 Thessalonians | 1 Timothy | 2 Timothy | Titus | Philemon |

MESSAGE: ☐ The Corinthian believers were dividing into groups. Some favored Paul; some favored other leaders. Paul said to pay more attention to Jesus Christ than to which person is teaching about Him.

☐ Paul taught about the importance of marriage and how couples should live together.

☐ Paul told the people to think about whether or not what you do will hurt other people.

☐ A person who believes in Jesus Christ receives the Holy Spirit and one or more gifts. Some of these gifts are teaching, preaching, helping. The important thing is to do everything in love.

☐ Jesus Christ rose from the dead, just as He said He would. It is very important to believe in the Resurrection. We don't have to be afraid of death. If we believe in Jesus, we have everlasting life.

BIBLE VERSES TO KNOW: 1 Corinthians 12:27; 13:4-7; 15:3,4; 15:58; 16:13,14

Where It All Happened

Look at the map on page 249. Find Ephesus, the city from which Paul wrote this letter. Then find Corinth, the home of the church (group of believers) that received this letter.

Discoveries from the Past

There was a Jewish synagogue in Corinth. A piece of the synagogue that had writing on it has been found and put in the museum at Corinth.

Some writing on part of the theater in Corinth includes the name Erastus. This was probably the friend Paul wrote about in Romans 16:23.

Christ

in the book of First Corinthians

"For what I received I passed on to you as of first importance: that Christ died for our sins according to the Scriptures, that he was buried, that he was raised on the third day according to the Scriptures" (1 Corinthians 15:3,4).

When Events Happened

▲ = PROBABLE DATE OF WRITING	45AD	57 58 59	61 66	90 95
	PAUL'S MISSIONARY JOURNEYS ▲(55)	PRISONER IN ROME (ACTS 28)	SECOND IMPRISONMENT	JOHN

Second Corinthians

WRITER: The writer was Paul (2 Corinthians 1:1).

WRITTEN TO: The church (group of believers) at Corinth, Greece. Paul probably wrote his first letter to the Corinthians in the spring and this second one before winter the same year. This letter was probably written from Macedonia. Second Corinthians 1:1 indicates that this letter was to be shared with other believers in the Roman province of Achaia.

BACKGROUND: After Paul wrote First Corinthians, the Church had been given wrong teachings. The false teachers also tried to turn the people against Paul. Paul told the people of Corinth about his ministry and gave them words of advice.

LOCATION: Second Corinthians is the third book in the section Letters by Paul. It is the eighth book of the New Testament.

Letters by Paul

Letters to: Churches | **Individuals**

Romans | 1 Corinthians | 2 Corinthians | Galatians | Ephesians | Philippians | Colossians | 1 Thessalonians | 2 Thessalonians | 1 Timothy | 2 Timothy | Titus | Philemon

MESSAGE: ☐ Paul assured the Corinthian church that God had gven him the job of telling people the truth about Jesus. Paul did everything to give glory to God and not to bring attention to himself.

☐ Paul urged the people to help others in need by cheerfully sharing what they had. He said that those who give generously will be rewarded generously.

☐ Paul warned the people about false teachers who would turn them away from Jesus.

BIBLE VERSES TO KNOW: 2 Corinthians 1:3,4; 3:18; 5:7,10,17; 9:6,7

Where It All Happened

Paul probably wrote this letter from somewhere in Macedonia. Find Macedonia on the map. Then find Corinth, the home of the church (group of believers) that received this letter.

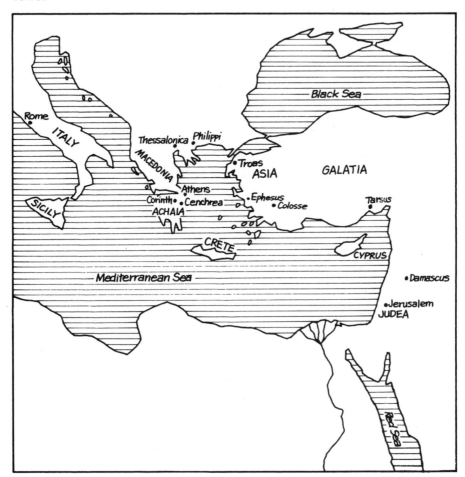

Christh

in the Book of Second Corinthians

Jesus Christ is the One who called Paul to his ministry. He also watched over Paul in his task. Jesus is shown to be the Lord (2 Corinthians 4:5) and the Christian's comfort (2 Corinthians 1:5). He gives power to the Christian (2 Corinthians 12:9).

Galatians

WRITER: The writer was Paul (Galatians 1:1; 5:2).

WRITTEN TO: The churches (groups of believers) in the area of Galatia. It is the only letter of Paul that was addressed to various churches.

BACKGROUND: During Paul's second missionary journey, he was delayed in Galatia by sickness (Galatians 4:13). Though he was ill, he kept on preaching the gospel. During this time he started a number of churches in Galatia.

LOCATION: Galatians is the fourth letter in the section Letters by Paul. It is the ninth book of the New Testament.

Letters by Paul

Letters to: Churches | **Individuals**

| Romans | 1 Corinthians | 2 Corinthians | Galatians | Ephesians | Philippians | Colossians | 1 Thessalonians | 2 Thessalonians | | 1 Timothy | 2 Timothy | Titus | Philemon |

MESSAGE: ☐ Paul explained that we are not saved from our sins by obeying God's laws. We are saved only by faith in Jesus Christ.

☐ When a Christian is saved by faith in Jesus Christ, the Holy Spirit lives within him or her to help that person avoid sinning.

☐ When a Christian does good things instead of sinning, others will see God's love.

☐ Christians are to help one another do what pleases God.

BIBLE VERSES TO KNOW: Galatians 3:26; 5:13; 6:2,9,10

Where It All Happened

This letter was written to the churches in the area called Galatia. Find this area on the map.

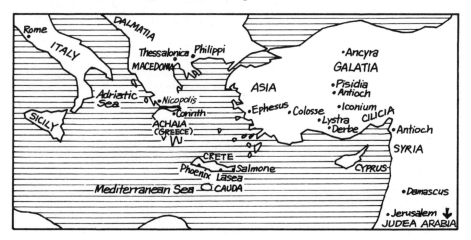

Christ

in the Book of Galatians

Christ is shown as the One who can make people right with God. Only He could give Himself for our sins to free us from the evil in the world. We must trust Christ and what He did for us as the way to have our sins forgiven. We must not trust our own attempts to do good. We can never be good enough to become perfect. When we trust Christ to take away our sin, He does just that.

All people, including Christians, can feel like doing something they know is wrong. This is called temptation. Jesus gives Christians special strength. Christians can use this strength to choose to do the right thing whenever they are tempted. Christians are free not to give in to sin.

When Events Happened

Ephesians

WRITER: The writer was Paul (Ephesians 1:1; 3:1).

WRITTEN TO: The church (group of believers) at Ephesus. This letter was written while Paul was a prisoner in Rome. It was probably passed around to other churches so that many people could read it.

BACKGROUND: Ephesus was the most important city in the area that is now called Turkey. It was at the crossroads of many trade routes. There was in Ephesus a temple for worshiping the Roman goddess Diana.

Paul had preached in Ephesus for about three years (Acts 20:31). He had a very special time of farewell with the Ephesian church leaders the last time he saw them (Acts 20:17-38).

LOCATION: Ephesians is called a "prison letter" because Paul wrote it while a prisoner in Rome. It is the fifth letter in the section Letters by Paul and the tenth book of the New Testament.

Letters by Paul

Letters to: Churches | **Individuals**

| Romans | 1 Corinthians | 2 Corinthians | Galatians | Ephesians | Philippians | Colossians | 1 Thessalonians | 2 Thessalonians | | 1 Timothy | 2 Timothy | Titus | Philemon |

MESSAGE: ☐ Because of the salvation Jesus provides, every Christian is blessed with a new life and power over sin. All Christians are part of Jesus' body, the Church.

☐ Because of what God has done for us, we love Him. Because we love Him, we want to obey Him and live in ways that please Him. We want to bring praise and glory to God.

☐ Christians are to be kind to each other, not trying to outdo each other.

☐ God has promised to help and protect us. God has given us a special "armor" to wear.

BIBLE VERSES TO KNOW: Ephesians 1:22,23; 2:8-10; 3:20,21; 4:2,16,25,29-32; 5:15,19,20; 6:1,7,10-17

Where It All Happened

Paul was a prisoner in Rome when he wrote this letter. Find Rome on the map below. Then find the city of Ephesus, the home of the church (group of believers) that received this letter.

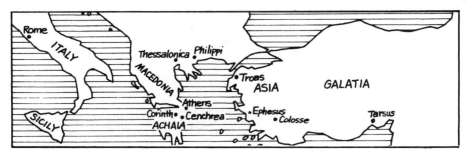

Christ

in the Book of Ephesians

As believers, we are "in Christ" (Ephesians 1:1), chosen by Him (Ephesians 1:4), saved by Him (Ephesians 1:7), given a great hope (Ephesians 1:12), and growing in Him as His children (Ephesians 2:21).

God makes available to us the same power that raised Jesus from the dead, for He has brought real life to those who were dead in their sins. All who believe in Jesus are part of His Body, the Church.

Jesus Christ has made it possible for us to live a life that is both exciting and pleasing to God, our heavenly Father.

When Events Happened

▲ = PROBABLE DATE OF WRITING

45 AD   57 58 59   61   66   90   95

PAUL'S MISSIONARY JOURNEYS   PRISONER IN ROME (ACTS 28) ▲ (60)   SECOND IMPRISONMENT   JOHN

Philippians

WRITER: The writer was Paul (Philippians 1:1).

WRITTEN TO: The church (group of believers) at Philippi. Paul wrote this letter while a prisoner—probably during the two years he was imprisoned in his own rented house in Rome (Acts 28). During this time he was free to tell the gospel message to everyone who came to him.

BACKGROUND: The city of Philippi was named after King Philip II, the father of Alexander the Great. At the time of Paul, Philippi was a prosperous Roman colony. There were probably not many Jews in Philippi.

Paul wrote this letter as a thank-you note to the believers in Philippi for the money and encouragement they had sent him. Paul was a prisoner, but he took time to tell his friends to be happy as Christians.

LOCATION: Philippians is called a "prison letter" because Paul wrote it while he was a prisoner. It is the sixth letter in the section Letters by Paul and the eleventh book in the New Testament.

Letters by Paul

Letters to: Churches | **Individuals**

Romans | 1 Corinthians | 2 Corinthians | Galatians | Ephesians | Philippians | Colossians | 1 Thessalonians | 2 Thessalonians | 1 Timothy | 2 Timothy | Titus | Philemon

MESSAGE: ☐ Paul knew that no matter what happened he could be happy with his circumstances. If he was killed, he would be with Jesus. If not, he would keep telling others about Jesus.

☐ Paul asked his friends to work together and to be as unselfish as Jesus was. Being like Jesus is more important than who you are or what you have done.

☐ Paul warned his friends to watch out for teachers who did not teach the truth about Jesus. He urged the Philippians to be strong in their faith and to do good—following Jesus in everything.

☐ Paul told the Philippians to rejoice, to pray and to be thankful to God. He urged them to think and do things that please God. He promised that God would give them peace, help them think and do what is right, and supply their needs.

BIBLE VERSES TO KNOW: Philippians 1:6,20,21; 2:3-8,14; 4:4-8,13,19

Where It All Happened

Look at the map below. Find Rome, where Paul was a prisoner. Then find Philippi, the home of the church (group of believers) that received this letter.

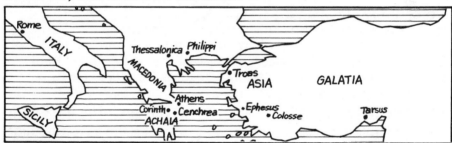

Christz

in the Book of Philippians

Paul told the Philippians that his one goal in life was to serve His Lord, Jesus Christ (Philippians 1:21). In his letter he used Christ as the example we should follow (Philippians 2:5). Paul gave Jesus credit for anything Paul was able to do (Philippians 4:13).

When Events Happened

Colossians

WRITER: The writer was Paul (Colossians 1:1,23; 4:18).

WRITTEN TO: The church (group of believers) at Colosse. Paul probably wrote this letter as a prisoner in his own rented house in Rome (see Acts 28).

BACKGROUND: Several hundred years before the time of Paul, Colosse had been one of the main cities in the area that is now called Turkey. It was located on a trading route. By the time of Paul, however, Colosse had become a second-rate market town. Neighboring towns such as Laodicea had become more important than Colosse.

The gospel message was taken to Colosse by Epaphras who had become a Christian through Paul's ministry in Ephesus. Colosse was about 100 miles from Ephesus. The church at Colosse was a Gentile (non-Jewish) church. Philemon was a member of this church.

False teachers had come into the church at Colosse. They were falsely teaching the people to worship angels and to closely observe Jewish ceremonies. Epaphras went to Rome to tell Paul what was happening. Paul wrote this letter to the Colossians and sent it back with Epaphras. In this letter Paul strongly emphasized the fact that Jesus is God. We are to worship and serve Jesus, our Lord.

LOCATION: Colossians is called a "prison letter" because Paul wrote it while he was a prisoner in Rome. It is the seventh letter in the section Letters by Paul and the twelfth book of the New Testament.

Letters by Paul

Letters to: Churches | **Individuals**

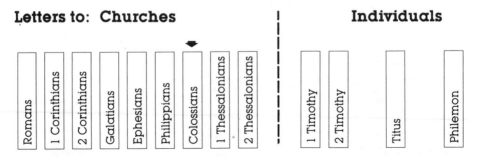

Romans | 1 Corinthians | 2 Corinthians | Galatians | Ephesians | Philippians | Colossians | 1 Thessalonians | 2 Thessalonians | 1 Timothy | 2 Timothy | Titus | Philemon

MESSAGE: ☐ Paul told the people in the church of Colosse that they need to know who Jesus is and what power He has. He is the Lord over all things.

☐ We are to live holy lives, turning away from evil and doing what pleases God. Jesus must be Lord over our lives.

☐ We are to work to the best of our ability, doing things as gifts for God.

BIBLE VERSES TO KNOW: Colossians 1:16-20; 2:6,7,9,10; 3:12-14,16,17,20,23,24; 4:2

Where It All Happened

Paul wrote this letter as a prisoner in Rome. Find Rome on the map. Then find Colosse, the home of the church (group of believers) that received this letter.

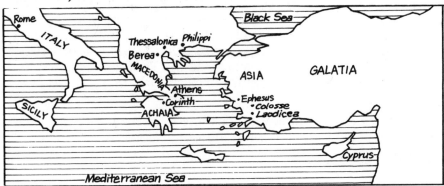

Christ

in the Book of Colossians

This book tells us that Christ is Lord over all things. He is the Lord of creation (Colossians 1:16,17), He helps us do right (Colossians 1:10) and He is the Head of the Church (Colossians 1:18).

When Events Happened

First Thessalonians

WRITER: The writer was Paul (1 Thessalonians 1:1).

WRITTEN TO: The church (group of believers) at Thessalonica. Paul wrote his two letters to the Thessalonians while he was in Corinth.

BACKGROUND: Thessalonica was a busy seaport city located at the junction of two main roads. It was the largest city in Macedonia.

Paul started the church at Thessalonica when he stayed there for a few weeks during his second missionary journey. In the short time Paul was there, he caused a lot of excitement. His enemies accused him of "turning the world upside down" (Acts 17:6, *KJV*). From Thessalonica Paul went on to Berea, Athens and Corinth. At Athens Paul sent Timothy back to Thessalonica to see how the new Christians were doing. Timothy brought back a favorable report. But he also mentioned that the church had some concerns and false ideas about Christ's return. And so, in Corinth, Paul wrote this letter to the Thessalonians. It focuses especially on the return of Christ, which is mentioned at the end of every chapter.

LOCATION: First Thessalonians is the eighth letter in the section Letters by Paul. It is the thirteenth book in the New Testament.

Letters by Paul

Letters to: Churches   **Individuals**

Romans | 1 Corinthians | 2 Corinthians | Galatians | Ephesians | Philippians | Colossians | 1 Thessalonians | 2 Thessalonians | 1 Timothy | 2 Timothy | Titus | Philemon

MESSAGE: ☐ Paul thanked God for the believers at Thessalonica. Their lives of faith, service and joy were an example to other Christians.

☐ Paul wanted to go back to see the Thessalonians again. He prayed that their love for other people would grow.

☐ Paul told his friends that when Jesus returns from heaven, Christians who are already dead will be taken with the living Christians to live with God in heaven.

☐ The actual time when Jesus returns will be a surprise. But God's people can know for sure that it definitely will happen.

☐ Paul told the people that while they waited for Jesus' return they should be joyful, pray, and thank God for everything.

BIBLE VERSES TO KNOW: First Thessalonians 3:12,13; 4:7,16-18; 5:2,11,15-18

Where It All Happened

Look at the map below. Find Corinth, the city from which Paul wrote this letter. Then find Thessalonica, the home of the church (group of believers) that received this letter.

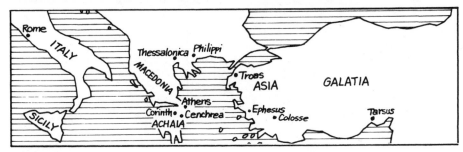

Christ

in the Book of First Thessalonians

Paul taught that Jesus Christ is our hope for the future. Jesus Christ is coming back. For those who trust in Him that will be a joyful day!

When Events Happened

263

Second Thessalonians

WRITER: The writer was Paul (2 Thessalonians 1:1; 3:17).

WRITTEN TO: The church (group of believers) at Thessalonica. This second letter was probably written in Corinth about six months after the first letter.

BACKGROUND: Paul wrote this second letter to encourage the church and to respond to some additional questions and concerns they had about the coming of Christ.

LOCATION: Second Thessalonians is the ninth letter in the section Letters by Paul. It is the fourteenth book of the New Testament.

Letters by Paul

Letters to: Churches

Individuals

| Romans | 1 Corinthians | 2 Corinthians | Galatians | Ephesians | Philippians | Colossians | 1 Thessalonians | 2 Thessalonians | 1 Timothy | 2 Timothy | Titus | Philemon |

MESSAGE: ☐ Some people made life hard for the Christians. Paul encouraged them to keep growing in Jesus Christ, even when it was hard to do.

☐ Some false teachers said that the Lord had already returned. Paul explained that the second coming of Jesus Christ will not happen until after a man of great evil appears and claims to be God.

☐ Paul asked people to pray for him and for the spread of the good news about Jesus. He also instructed all the people to work to take care of themselves and not to get tired of doing good.

BIBLE VERSES TO KNOW: 2 Thessalonians 1:6; 2:16,17; 3:1,3,13

Where It All Happened

Find Corinth, the city from which Paul wrote this letter. Then find Thessalonica, home of the church (group of believers) that received this letter.

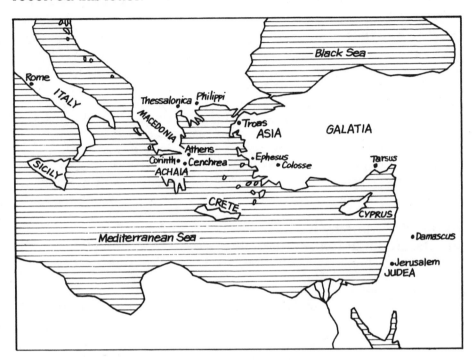

Christ

in the Book of Second Thessalonians

Paul taught about Jesus Christ's second coming. It is a joyful thought for those who believe. If you are not sure you are a Christian, please turn to "Becoming God's Child" in this guidebook. There you will find help with how to become a member of God's family.

When Events Happened

First Timothy

WRITER: The writer was Paul (1 Timothy 1:1).

WRITTEN TO: Timothy, a young man in charge of the church at Ephesus.

BACKGROUND: Timothy's family lived in Lystra. His father was a Greek; his mother a Jewish believer in Jesus. From his childhood he had been taught the Scriptures. Timothy probably first saw Paul when Paul came to Lystra on his first missionary journey. Timothy must have heard Paul preach the gospel and seen him heal the lame man. He may have even seen Paul stoned and left for dead. When Paul came back to Lystra on his second missionary journey, he asked Timothy to travel with him. Timothy helped Paul as Paul preached the gospel in Macedonia and Achaia. He was with Paul during much of his three-year ministry at Ephesus. Timothy traveled with Paul from Ephesus to Macedonia, to Corinth, back to Macedonia, and to Asia Minor. Timothy was with Paul during Paul's first imprisonment at Rome. When Paul was freed, Timothy traveled with him again. But eventually Timothy stayed at Ephesus to care for the church there.

Paul spoke very highly of Timothy. He wrote to the Philippians: "I have no one else like him, who takes a genuine interest in your welfare.... But you know that Timothy has proved himself." (Philippians 2:20,22).

Paul wanted to visit Timothy but could not at the time. He sent this letter to Timothy to help him be a good leader.

LOCATION: First Timothy is the tenth letter in the section Letters by Paul and the fifteenth book of the New Testament.

Letters by Paul

Letters to: Churches   **Individuals**

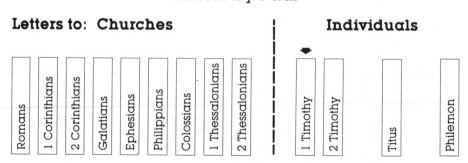

Romans | 1 Corinthians | 2 Corinthians | Galatians | Ephesians | Philippians | Colossians | 1 Thessalonians | 2 Thessalonians | 1 Timothy | 2 Timothy | Titus | Philemon

MESSAGE: ☐ Paul warned Timothy about false teachers. Timothy was called to the ministry by God and must teach the truth, that Jesus came into the world to save sinners.

☐ Paul taught Timothy about church worship.

☐ Paul showed Timothy how to choose good church leaders. They must be wise and self-controlled, worthy of respect.

☐ Paul challenged Timothy to be a good example for others to follow.

☐ Paul gave Timothy advice about how to treat people in the church.

☐ Paul told Timothy to turn away from what is false and do what is right.

BIBLE VERSES TO KNOW: First Timothy 1:15-17; 2:5,6,8; 4:12; 6:6-8,11

Where It All Happened

Look at the map on page 265. Find Macedonia, the area where Paul was when he wrote to Timothy. Then find Ephesus, the city where Timothy was when he received the letter.

Christie

in the Book of First Timothy

Paul told Timothy that Jesus Christ is the "one mediator between God and men" (1 Timothy 2:5). A mediator is a person who goes between two other persons to settle an argument. Jesus Christ is the One who makes everything right between us and God.

When Events Happened

▲ = PROBABLE DATE OF WRITING	45AD	57 58 59	61 66	90	95
	PAUL'S MISSIONARY JOURNEYS	PRISONER IN ROME (ACTS 28)	SECOND IMPRISONMENT	JOHN	
			▲ (BETWEEN IMPRISONMENTS)		

Second Timothy

WRITER: The writer was Paul (2 Timothy 1:1).

WRITTEN TO: Timothy, a young man in charge of the church at Ephesus.

BACKGROUND: See "Background" section on page 266 of this guidebook. Paul was again arrested and sent to Rome. This time Paul was not kept as a prisoner in his own rented house as he had been the first time (see Acts 28). This time Paul was thrown into a cold dungeon—and he knew that he would soon die (see 2 Timothy 4:6). Paul had already appeared once before the wicked Roman emperor Nero—and he expected to be tried again. He knew that God was with him and was using him to spread the good news about Jesus (see 2 Timothy 4:17,18).

Paul felt very lonely. Many of his friends had deserted him. At this time, only Luke was with him. In this, his last letter, Paul asked Timothy to come right away and bring Mark with him. He also asked Timothy to bring the cloak and scrolls he left behind. Paul was not sure Timothy would get to Rome before Paul was killed. This letter contains Paul's last words of warning and encouragement to Timothy.

LOCATION: Second Timothy is the eleventh letter in the section Letters by Paul and the sixteenth book of the New Testament. Three of Paul's letters (see below) are called "pastoral letters." They were written to help Timothy and Titus care for God's people in the churches they supervised.

Letters by Paul

Letters to: Churches | **Individuals**

Romans | 1 Corinthians | 2 Corinthians | Galatians | Ephesians | Philippians | Colossians | 1 Thessalonians | 2 Thessalonians | | 1 Timothy | 2 Timothy | | Titus | | Philemon

P   **P**   **P**

P = Pastoral letters

MESSAGE: ☐ FOLLOW THE TRUTH: Paul reminded Timothy of the teaching he had received as a child. The truth is the good news of Jesus Christ.

☐ BE A GOOD WORKER: Paul encouraged Timothy to be like a soldier, an athlete and a farmer—doing his best to teach the truth to others.

☐ BE FAITHFUL IN HARD TIMES: There will be many troubles in the last days and many people will turn from God's ways. Just as Paul was persecuted, anyone who follows Jesus will be mistreated. The Bible is the source of truth worthy of our trust.

☐ TEACH OTHERS: Paul urged Timothy to tell people the good news and to be a real servant of God. Then Paul gave some personal messages about his own needs and his friends.

BIBLE VERSES TO KNOW: Second Timothy 1:12; 2:3,15,23,24; 3:14-17; 4:5,7,8

Where It All Happened

Look at the map on page 265. Find Rome, the city where Paul was imprisoned when he wrote this letter. Then find Ephesus, the city where Timothy was when he received the letter.

Christo

in the Book of Second Timothy

Paul told Timothy that Jesus Christ is our Savior and Lord. He gave us salvation, He rose from the dead and He gives us eternal life. We are to look for Him to come in the future.

When Events Happened

▲ = PROBABLE DATE OF WRITING	45 AD	57 58 59	61 66	90 95
	PAUL'S MISSIONARY JOURNEYS	PRISONER IN ROME (ACTS 28)	SECOND IMPRISONMENT ▲ (67 OR 68 BEFORE EXECUTED)	JOHN

Titus

WRITER: The writer was Paul (Titus 1:1).

WRITTEN TO: Titus, a Greek who had trusted Jesus Christ through the ministry of Paul.

BACKGROUND: Titus had traveled with Paul and Barnabas. He probably worked with Paul at Ephesus during Paul's third missionary journey. From there Paul sent him to Corinth to help the church there. After Paul was freed from his first imprisonment in Rome, he and Titus worked together on the island of Crete. They found many people were rebellious, liars and lazy (see Titus 1:12). Paul left Titus at Crete to complete the work there and to appoint church leaders. Paul wrote this letter to tell him what he must do to carry on his ministry.

Paul asked Titus to meet him in Nicopolis (on the west coast of Greece) as soon as someone came to replace him in Crete. Later, Titus served the Lord in Dalmatia (modern Yugoslavia). See 2 Timothy 4:10.

LOCATION: Titus is the twelfth letter in the section Letters by Paul and the seventeenth book of the New Testament. Three of Paul's letters (see below) are called "pastoral letters." They were written to help Timothy and Titus care for God's people in the churches they supervised.

Letters by Paul

Letters to: Churches   **Individuals**

Romans	1 Corinthians	2 Corinthians	Galatians	Ephesians	Philippians	Colossians	1 Thessalonians	2 Thessalonians		1 Timothy	2 Timothy	Titus	Philemon
										P	**P**	**P**	

P = Pastoral letters

MESSAGE: ☐ Titus was to choose church leaders who would do what is right and who wanted to help others. The leaders must also teach what is true.

☐ Paul told Titus to teach both older and younger men and women to do what is right.

☐ Arguing and hating others should stop when people come to know God's kindness and love.

BIBLE VERSES TO KNOW: Titus 2:11; 3:1,2

Where It All Happened

Find the island of Crete, where Titus was serving the Lord at the time he received this letter. We do not know where Paul was at the time he wrote the letter.

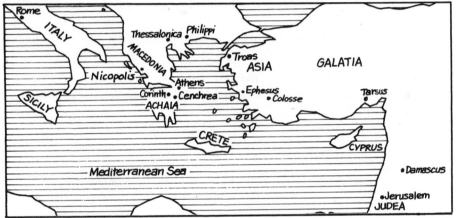

Christus

in the Book of Titus

Paul told Titus that Jesus Christ is our Savior and our Lord. Christ died for us so that we can have everlasting life. This should make us very thankful and very excited about working for Him.

When Events Happened

Philemon

WRITER: The writer of this short letter was Paul (Philemon, verse 1).

WRITTEN TO: Philemon, Paul's dear friend who lived in Colosse. Paul wrote this little "postcard" to Philemon about his runaway slave, Onesimus (oh-NEHS-i-muhs).

BACKGROUND: Paul probably wrote this letter while he was a prisoner in Rome (during the time Luke told about in Acts 28). He probably wrote it at the same time he wrote his letter to the Colossians—and sent it to Colosse with the same travelers, Onesimus and Tychicus (see Colossians 4:7-9).

Onesimus had run away from his master, Philemon. While he was away, he met Paul in prison. Through Paul Onesimus became a Christian. Paul now writes asking Philemon to take Onesimus back as "a dear brother"—a fellow Christian.

LOCATION: Philemon is the thirteenth letter in the section Letters by Paul and the eighteenth book of the New Testament. It is called a "prison letter" because Paul wrote it while he was a prisoner in Rome.

Letters by Paul

Letters to: Churches   **Individuals**

Romans	1 Corinthians	2 Corinthians	Galatians	Ephesians	Philippians	Colossians	1 Thessalonians	2 Thessalonians	1 Timothy	2 Timothy	Titus	Philemon

MESSAGE: ☐ Paul asked Philemon to forgive Onesimus, Philemon's runaway slave. He asked that Philemon accept Onesimus as a brother, not as a criminal, because Onesimus and Philemon were both Christians now.

☐ Paul offered to pay for anything Onesimus owed or had stolen from Philemon.

☐ Paul hinted that he would like Philemon to do more than forgive Onesimus—Paul wanted to visit Philemon and perhaps have Onesimus help him in his work.

☐ This letter teaches us about the change Jesus Christ makes in a person.

BIBLE VERSE TO KNOW: Philemon, verse 6

Where It All Happened

Find Rome, the city where Paul was imprisoned when he wrote this letter. Then find Colosse, the city where Philemon lived.

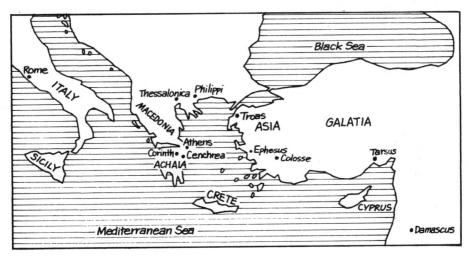

Christb

in the Book of Philemon

The story of Philemon, Paul and Onesimus reminds us of how God is able to forgive us for our sins. Onesimus committed a wrong act that separated him from his master. Onesimus was able to return home only because Paul was willing to pay for his crime. Our sins separate us from God. We are able to return to Him only because Jesus was willing to pay for our sin.

When Events Happened

Hebrews

WRITER: The writer of Hebrews is not known. For centuries people have wondered if the writer could have been Paul, Barnabas, Apollos or some friend of Timothy (see Hebrews 13:23). Even though we do not know who wrote it, we can trust this letter to give a true picture of Jesus Christ and the Christian faith.

WRITTEN TO: Jewish (Hebrew) people who trusted Jesus as their Messiah (Savior).

BACKGROUND: Jews who believed in Jesus as their Messiah and who loved their traditions were sometimes tempted to think that just believing in Jesus was not good enough. They wondered if they also needed to obey the Mosaic laws. Some were tempted to return to Judaism and to believe that Jesus was just another prophet. The book of Hebrews was written to prove that Jesus Christ is the perfect fulfillment of Judaism and that He is greater than the Law and greater than all the prophets.

LOCATION: Hebrews is the first letter in the section called General Letters and the nineteenth book in the New Testament. General Letters were usually not sent to specific individuals or churches. They were passed on from church to church.

General Letters

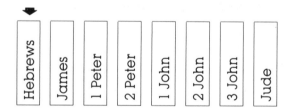

MESSAGE: Jesus Christ is greater!
- ☐ GREATER THAN THE PROPHETS: In the Old Testament, God spoke through messengers called prophets. Now God has spoken to us by His Son, Jesus Christ, through whom He made the universe.
- ☐ GREATER THAN THE ANGELS: Jesus is God's Son. Angels worship Him.

☐ GREATER THAN MOSES: Moses was a faithful servant of God. Jesus is God's Son.

☐ GREATER THAN JOSHUA: Joshua was a great leader who led God's people into the Promised Land. But he didn't lead them into rest. Jesus alone gives real rest. Those who trust Him as Savior stop trying to save themselves and put everything into His hand.

☐ GREATER THAN THE HIGH PRIESTS BEFORE HIM: The high priests offered animal sacrifices for the people's sins. They had to offer these sacrifices over and over again. These animal sacrifices could not take away sin—they were a picture of what God would one day do through His Son, Jesus, the Lamb of God. Jesus Christ never sinned. He offered Himself as a perfect sacrifice for our sin. Jesus' sacrifice never has to be made again.

Jesus is the Lamb of God and our High Priest. In the Old Testament the high priest could come into God's presence only once a year. Jesus, our High Priest is at the right hand of God the Father right now. Believers in Christ can come boldly into God's presence, through prayer, at any time. We can do this because of what Jesus did for us on the cross.

Hebrews tells about many Old Testament people who had strong faith. Noah, Abraham, Isaac, Jacob, Joseph, Moses, Rahab, Gideon, David and Samuel are some examples of people who had strong faith in God.

Noah

Abraham

Isaac

Jacob

Joseph

Moses

Rahab

Gideon

David

Samuel

We should have a strong faith in Jesus Christ, God's Son, because God's power is greater than any other power. We should never give up, because Jesus will help us live the Christian life. Our lives should be an example of obedience to Jesus.

BIBLE VERSES TO KNOW: Hebrews 1:1,2; 4:14-16; 7:27; 10:10,23,24; 11:1; 13:1,6,16,17

Christit

in the Book of Hebrews

Because this letter was written to Hebrews (Jews) who had just believed in Jesus, the writer talked about Old Testament people and customs. These new believers were familiar with the sacrifices the priests made for people's sins. The letter to the Hebrews talks about Jesus as our everlasting High Priest. He offered the best sacrifice—Himself. Jesus, the perfect Lamb of God, died for us. His sacrifice never has to be repeated. Because Jesus died for us and then came back to life again, we can have life that lasts forever. And we can go into the presence of God the Father in prayer at any time.

When Events Happened

PROBABLY WRITTEN BEFORE A.D. 70	45 AD	57	58 59	61	66	90	95
	PAUL'S MISSIONARY JOURNEYS			PRISONER IN ROME (ACTS 28)	SECOND IMPRISONMENT	JOHN	

James

WRITER: The writer was James (James 1:1). This James was probably the half brother of Jesus. He did not become a follower of Jesus until after Jesus rose from the dead. James was one of the people who saw Jesus after He rose from the dead. (See 1 Corinthians 15:7.) Later James became a leader in the church in Jerusalem. He met with Paul at least two times (Galatians 1:19; Acts 21:18).

WRITTEN TO: Jewish believers in Jesus who were scattered across many countries.

BACKGROUND: Many of the Jewish believers were being persecuted for their faith in Christ. James wrote to them about how to face their difficulties and live the Christian life.

LOCATION: James is the second of the General Letters and the twentieth book of the New Testament.

General Letters

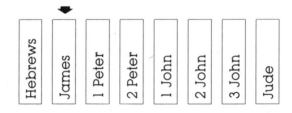

Hebrews | James | 1 Peter | 2 Peter | 1 John | 2 John | 3 John | Jude

MESSAGE: ☐ The book of James is the most practical of all the letters. A key verse is James 1:22: "Do not merely listen to the word.... Do what it says."

☐ James begins and ends his letter with a strong encouragement to pray.

☐ James teaches about faith. When a person's faith is tested, he or she can turn to God. God will make believers strong and help them through hard times.

☐ James also teaches that faith without a life of works is a dead faith. Faith in Christ should make Christians want to act in good and loving ways toward others.

☐ James includes practical instructions on how to live a life that pleases God. James teaches us to control our tongues—to use them to tell about Jesus and praise His name instead of saying unkind things about other people. He also tells us to control our anger, obey God and care for people who need help. We are not to treat some people better than we treat others.

☐ We are to be patient in hard times. We can trust God in whatever happens and be confident that our faith will be rewarded when Jesus returns.

BIBLE VERSES TO KNOW: James 1:2-8,12,22-25; 2:8; 3:17; 5:8,9,16

Where It All Happened

It is possible that James wrote this letter from Jerusalem. He was probably the leader in the Jerusalem church at the time. Find Jerusalem on the map on page 265.

Christist

in the Book of James

James knew Jesus very well. He teaches us about the Christian *faith* and our Christian *life*. All that James says teaches us to obey Christ's commands in everything we do.

When Events Happened

PROBABLY WRITTEN BEFORE A.D. 60	45 AD	57 58 59	61 66	90 95
	PAUL'S MISSIONARY JOURNEYS	PRISONER IN ROME (ACTS 28)	SECOND IMPRISONMENT	JOHN

First Peter

WRITER: The writer was Peter (1 Peter 1:1). Peter was one of Jesus' twelve disciples. The first 12 chapters of Acts center around Peter and his ministry.

There was a big difference in Peter before and after Pentecost. Before Pentecost Peter was sometimes fearful and undependable. By the time he wrote this letter, he was bold, courageous and faithful to Jesus Christ. What a wonderful example of what the Holy Spirit can do in the life of a believer!

WRITTEN TO: Christians who were suffering because they believed in Jesus. They could take courage from what Peter said, because he, too, was going through suffering. Peter's letter was probably passed from church to church.

BACKGROUND: Peter wrote this letter near the end of his life. He and other believers were suffering because of their faith in Christ. They were hated because they would not worship idols and do other sinful things. Persecution of Christians under the Roman emperor Nero was making it very difficult to live the Christian life. Peter encouraged the Christians and reminded them of the hope they had because Jesus will some day return. Peter has been called the "apostle of hope."

LOCATION: First Peter is the third of the General Letters and the twenty-first book of the New Testament.

General Letters

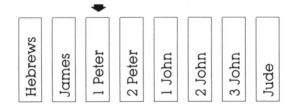

| Hebrews | James | 1 Peter | 2 Peter | 1 John | 2 John | 3 John | Jude |

MESSAGE: ☐ THE BELIEVER HAS NEW LIFE: The Christian receives new life because of what Jesus Christ did on the cross. Christians enjoy many blessings from God, even during hard times. They can look forward to the time when Jesus returns.

☐ THE BELIEVER IS TO BE HOLY: The Christian is to live a life that is holy in everything. At all times and in all places, a Christian's life must show that he or she belongs to Jesus Christ.

☐ THE BELIEVER OBEYS: The Christian is like a visitor in the world—someone who belongs to God, not to the evil in the world. However, the Christian is to obey those in authority, even to the point of suffering. This is one way to follow Jesus' example.

☐ THE BELIEVER LIVES IN A NON-CHRISTIAN WORLD. Peter knew that the Roman government would be punishing Christians. As the hard times got worse, many believers would have to explain why they were Christians and lived as they did. Peter tells his readers to be strong in their faith in Jesus and their love for one another. Peter knew that suffering for what you believe can help you grow stronger.

BIBLE VERSES TO KNOW: 1 Peter 1:3,6-9; 2:1,2,9,17,24; 3:15; 4:19

Where It All Happened

Peter wrote this letter to the Jews who believed in Jesus. They lived in areas that are now part of modern Turkey. He probably wrote from the city of Rome. Find Rome on the map on page 265.

Christq

in the Book of First Peter

Peter tells us that Jesus is our example. If you are having good times or bad times, look to Jesus Christ for help. You can have joy in Jesus even during times of suffering. The wonderful hope that Christians have is that someday Jesus will return— just as He said He would!

When Events Happened

PROBABLY WRITTEN IN EARLY 60'S	45 AD	57 58 59	61	66	90	95
	PAUL'S MISSIONARY JOURNEYS	PRISONER IN ROME (ACTS 28)	SECOND IMPRISONMENT		JOHN	

Second Peter

WRITER: The writer was Peter (2 Peter 1:1). Peter was one of Jesus' twelve disciples. The first 12 chapters of Acts center around Peter and his ministry.

There was a big difference in Peter before and after Pentecost. Before Pentecost Peter was sometimes fearful and undependable. By the time he wrote this letter, he was bold, courageous and faithful to Jesus Christ. What a wonderful example of what the Holy Spirit can do in the life of a believer!

WRITTEN TO: Believers. The letter was probably passed from church to church.

BACKGROUND: Peter wrote this letter just before his death. He was probably in the city of Rome. In his first letter, Peter taught his readers how to deal with persecution from outside the church. In this second letter, he warned believers about people within the church who were teaching false things about Jesus and His return.

LOCATION: Second Peter is the fourth of the General Letters and the twenty-second book of the New Testament.

General Letters

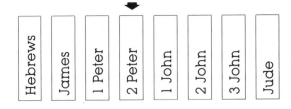

| Hebrews | James | 1 Peter | 2 Peter | 1 John | 2 John | 3 John | Jude |

MESSAGE: ☐ GROW AS GOD'S PEOPLE: The Christian has received everything he or she needs to live for Jesus Christ. With God's power and goodness, the Christian is to show real faith by acts of love and goodness.

☐ WATCH OUT FOR FALSE TEACHERS: Peter warns believers to be careful of false teachers in the church. They can lead newer Christians away from the truth. Peter explains that God will judge and destroy these teachers when Jesus returns.

☐ BE WATCHING FOR JESUS TO COME BACK:
Peter reminds his readers that Jesus will return.
Christians should live life as if Jesus will come
back today. They should be examples to others.

BIBLE VERSES TO KNOW: Second Peter 1:3-7; 3:9,18

Where It All Happened

Peter wrote this letter just before his death. He was probably
in the city of Rome. Find Rome on the map.

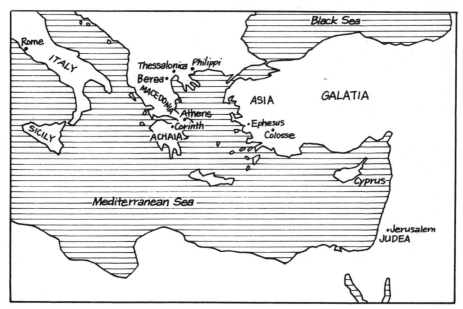

Christus

in the Book of Second Peter

Peter looked forward to the second coming of the Lord Jesus
Christ. At that time all people will see Him in His power and
glory. Jesus Christ is the coming Lord.

When Events Happened

	45 AD	57 58 59	61	66		90	95
PROBABLY WRITTEN BETWEEN 65-68							
	PAUL'S MISSIONARY JOURNEYS	PRISONER IN ROME (ACTS 28)	SECOND IMPRISONMENT			JOHN	

First John

WRITER: The writer of this letter was John, an apostle of Jesus Christ. John also wrote the Gospel of John and three other books (see diagram under "Location" below).

WRITTEN TO: Christians, young and old. John was an old man when he wrote this letter. He called his readers "dear children," even though they were grown up, because they had not been Christians as long as he had. This letter was probably passed from church to church in Asia Minor.

BACKGROUND: John was a fisherman when Jesus called him to be one of His followers. John was also probably a cousin of Jesus—his mother Salome (sa-LO-me) was probably a sister of Mary, Jesus' mother. Peter, James and John were special friends of Jesus. They knew Jesus well. John wrote this letter to help believers (1) KNOW they have eternal life in Christ and to (2) LIVE as Christ commanded.

LOCATION: First John is the fifth of the General Letters and the twenty-third book of the New Testament.

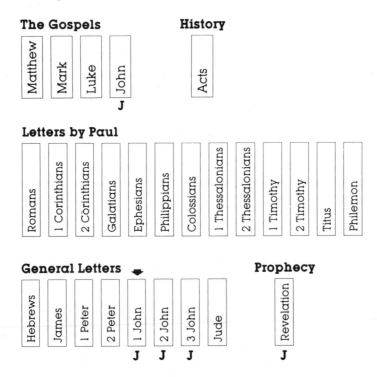

The Gospels

Matthew | Mark | Luke | John
J

History

Acts

Letters by Paul

Romans | 1 Corinthians | 2 Corinthians | Galatians | Ephesians | Philippians | Colossians | 1 Thessalonians | 2 Thessalonians | 1 Timothy | 2 Timothy | Titus | Philemon

General Letters

Hebrews | James | 1 Peter | 2 Peter | 1 John | 2 John | 3 John | Jude
J **J** **J**

Prophecy

Revelation
J

J = Books Written by John

KEY VERSES: (1 John 5:13).

MESSAGE: ☐ FRIENDSHIP WITH GOD: Because God is holy, He cannot be friends with sinners. Because Christians have been forgiven and made clean, they can have friendship with God. Friendship with God also means that Christians are children of God—members of God's family.

☐ FRIENDSHIP WITH OTHERS: Because God loves us, we should show our love for one another. One way we can do this is to pray for one another.

BIBLE VERSES TO KNOW: 1 John 1:3,9; 3:1,2,16-18,23,24; 4:7-15,18-21; 5:3,11-15

Where It All Happened

John probably wrote this letter from the city of Ephesus to the Christians who were scattered all over Asia Minor. Find Ephesus and Asia Minor on the map on page 243.

Christint

in the Book of First John

Jesus Christ is the Son of God. He is also the Son of Man. He is both man and God at the same time. John wrote this in his letter because false teachers were telling Christians that this was impossible. John wrote: "We know also that the Son of God has come and has given us understanding, so that we may know him who is true. And we are in him who is true—even in his Son Jesus Christ. He is the true God and eternal life (1 John 5:20).

When Events Happened

| ▲ = PROBABLE DATE OF WRITING | 45 AD | 57 58 59 | 61 | 66 | | 90 | 95 |

| PAUL'S MISSIONARY JOURNEYS | PRISONER IN ROME (ACTS 28) | SECOND IMPRISONMENT | ▲ | JOHN |

Second John

WRITER: The writer of this letter was John, an apostle of Jesus. John also wrote the Gospel of John and three other books.

WRITTEN TO: "the chosen lady," which could be a person or a church (group of believers).

BACKGROUND: John wrote at a time when there were only a few teachers left who had walked with Jesus and heard Him teach. These teachers had many churches to care for. Sometimes a new church would be left without a teacher. Sometimes a false teacher would come to a church and pretend to teach the truth. Because they were new Christians, the church members could not tell which teachers were false and which were true. John wrote this letter so that the people would have the truth in writing.

Believers usually took traveling preachers into their homes and gave them food and lodging. John told the believers to do this only for people who taught the truth about Jesus.

LOCATION: Second John is the sixth of the General Letters and the twenty-fourth book of the New Testament.

General Letters

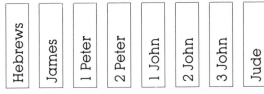

Hebrews | James | 1 Peter | 2 Peter | 1 John | 2 John | 3 John | Jude

MESSAGE: ☐ FOLLOW GOD'S COMMANDS: John told his readers how glad he was to hear that they had been following God's commands. Loving God, John said, includes loving others.
☐ DO NOT LISTEN TO FALSE TEACHERS: John said to watch out for teachers who did not tell the truth about Jesus. Believers were not to encourage false teachers by giving them food and a place to stay.

Third John

WRITER: The writer of this letter was John, an apostle of Jesus Christ. John also wrote the Gospel of John and three other books.

WRITTEN TO: John's very good friend Gaius (GAY-us).

BACKGROUND: John was getting older and could not visit all of the churches who needed his teaching. He chose helpers who would travel from church to church teaching the truth. John's friend Gaius had helped these travelers by letting them stay in his home and providing for their needs.

LOCATION: Third John is the seventh of the General Letters and the twenty-fifth book of the New Testament. See page 286.

MESSAGE: ☐ John told Gaius he was glad to hear that Gaius was faithful to the truth about Jesus. He also heard that Gaius continued to obey Jesus' commands. John thanked Gaius for being kind to the teachers he had sent. He asked Gaius to help them again.

☐ John warned Gaius to imitate only those who do good—not selfish people like Diotrephes (di-OT-re-feez) who wanted to be the boss in his church. Diotrephes would not listen to John's teaching.

When Events Happened

Second and Third John were written about the same time as First John.

Where It All Happened

Second and Third John were probably written from Ephesus. Find Ephesus on the map on page 265.

Jude

WRITER: Jude (Jude, verse 1). (Jude is another form of the Hebrew name "Judah" and the Greek name "Judas.") Jude was the brother of James and a half brother of Jesus.

WRITTEN TO: Believers. Jude's letter was probably passed around from church to church.

BACKGROUND: Jude wrote to warn about false teachers. All believers should believe only the truth about Jesus.

LOCATION: Jude is the eighth of the General Letters and the twenty-sixth book of the New Testament.

General Letters

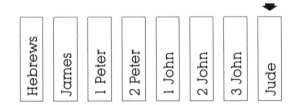

MESSAGE: ☐ Jude wrote that awful punishment is in store for anyone who teaches lies about Jesus.

☐ Jude warned the believers to defend the true teachings about Jesus. They should hate the lies but help those who have become confused.

When and Where Events Happened

This letter was probably written a little before Second Peter. We don't know where it was written.

Christ

in the Book of Jude

Jude, the half brother of Jesus, told his readers that they can trust Jesus Christ to take care of them and keep them from making mistakes.

Revelation

WRITER: The writer of this letter was John, an apostle of Jesus Christ. John also wrote the Gospel of John and three letters (see diagram under "Location" on the next page).

WRITTEN TO: Seven churches: Ephesus, Smyrna, Pergamum, Thyatira, Sardis, Philadelphia and Laodicea. The title "Revelation" tells us that this book reveals or shows us about Jesus and how He will triumph in the end times.

BACKGROUND: The Romans tried to make everyone worship the Roman emperor. Since Christians worshiped God, rather than the emperor, the Romans made their lives very hard. John was exiled to a small island called Patmos (see map on page 292) because of his witness for Christ. Christians needed to know that there is hope for the future. God showed John many pictures from the future to give them that hope.

The Bible begins with the book of Genesis—showing us the beginning of the world. Here, in Revelation, we see the ending of our world as we know it. We see Christ's complete and eternal victory over Satan.

Genesis
◄ God created the heavens and the earth.
◄ Satan tempted Adam and Eve. They sinned.
◄ Fellowship with God was broken.
◄ God promised a Saviour.

Revelation
◄ Satan is defeated.
◄ Christ, our Saviour, is triumphant.
◄ God makes a new heaven and a new earth.
◄ God lives in fellowship with His people.

In Genesis, Satan tried to separate the people God created from fellowship with God. Satan tempted them to sin. When Adam and Eve sinned, God promised that He would send a Savior from sin. God repeated that promise many times in the Old Testament. In the Gospels the promised Savior Jesus Christ came and took the punishment for our sin. Jesus made it possible for us to have fellowship with God by trusting Jesus as our Savior. In Acts and the New Testament letters, the good news of the gospel was sent throughout the world. In Revelation we see every promise fulfilled. Christ is triumphant. Satan is defeated. God lives with His people and has fellowship with them in a new heaven and a new earth.

When Events Happened

▲ = PROBABLE DATE OF WRITING   BC/AD

LOCATION: Revelation is a book of Prophecy. It tells what will happen in the future. Revelation is the twenty-seventh, and last, book in the New Testament.

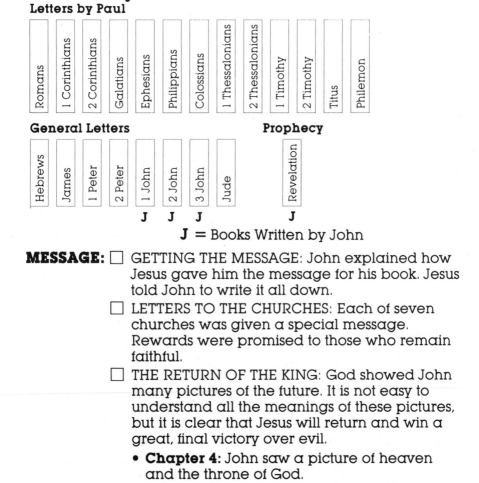

The Gospels

Matthew | Mark | Luke | John
J

History

Acts

Letters by Paul

Romans | 1 Corinthians | 2 Corinthians | Galatians | Ephesians | Philippians | Colossians | 1 Thessalonians | 2 Thessalonians | 1 Timothy | 2 Timothy | Titus | Philemon

General Letters

Hebrews | James | 1 Peter | 2 Peter | 1 John | 2 John | 3 John | Jude
          J   J   J

Prophecy

Revelation
J

J = Books Written by John

MESSAGE: ☐ GETTING THE MESSAGE: John explained how Jesus gave him the message for his book. Jesus told John to write it all down.

☐ LETTERS TO THE CHURCHES: Each of seven churches was given a special message. Rewards were promised to those who remain faithful.

☐ THE RETURN OF THE KING: God showed John many pictures of the future. It is not easy to understand all the meanings of these pictures, but it is clear that Jesus will return and win a great, final victory over evil.

• **Chapter 4:** John saw a picture of heaven and the throne of God.

- **Chapters 5-7:** Because of all Jesus has done, He is the One who is worthy to open the Book of Judgment. The Book of Judgment is closed by seven seals. As they are opened, pictures of coming death and disasters are shown. But God will protect His people.

- **Chapters 8-15:** When the seventh seal is opened, seven angels blow trumpets announcing Satan's terrible effort to conquer. During all the trouble, God will send messengers who will warn of the things to come. They are killed by God's enemies but brought back to life.

- **Chapters 16-18:** John saw the seven angels empty seven bowls which show God's power in attacking Satan. The devil himself comes to fight, and brings his own helpers. Many of the people still alive believe the devil's lies and worship him. The kingdoms of the earth are destroyed.

- **Chapters 19,20:** All of heaven praises the KING who is about to return. John saw a rider on a white horse, leading the armies of heaven. On His robe is written King of Kings and Lord of Lords. It is Jesus Christ, come to earth to take away the power of the devil. Jesus rules the earth for one thousand years. Once more the devil tries to take over, and Jesus destroys him.

- **Chapters 21,22:** The earth that we know is ended and a new one is made. Jesus judges all people and rewards those who have believed in Him. Jesus sits on the throne in His new city of Jerusalem and says, "I am making everything new!" (Revelation 21:5). Chapters 21 and 22 describe the new heaven and the new earth.

Where It All Happened

John wrote the book of Revelation from the island of Patmos. Find the little island of Patmos on the map. It is in a line with two other islands, Cos and Rhodes.

Chapters 2 and 3 mention the seven churches. Find them on the map. They are Ephesus, Smyrna, Pergamum (Pergamos), Thyatira, Sardis, Philadelphia and Laodicea. Read what the Lord says about each one.

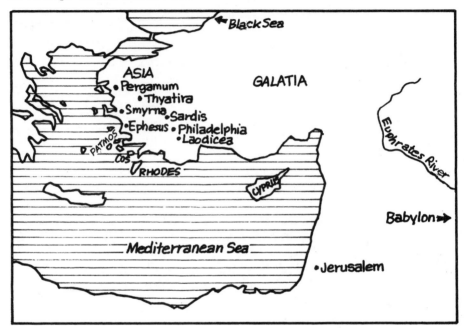

Christh

in the Book of Revelation

Christ appears everywhere in the book of Revelation. It is the prophecy of what He will do when He comes again. Christ is shown as the triumphant One. He is also referred to as the Lamb—the One who took the punishment for our sin. Everything that has been written in God's Word comes true. Christ called Himself "the Beginning and the End" (Revelation 21:6). In Genesis, He was there at the beginning of all things. In Revelation we learn that He will be there when the earth ends and afterwards! Jesus says that He will come quickly (Revelation 22:20). We do not know how soon but all Christians know how happy they will be when Jesus comes!

A Dictionary of Bible Words

Abba (Ab-uh)
An Aramaic word which means "Daddy." Aramaic was the language spoken by Jesus and other Jews living in Palestine.

adultery (uh-DUL-ter-ee)
Sexual union between a man and a woman when either of them is married to someone else. Adultery is a sin.

adversary (AD-vuh-sair-ee)
An enemy or someone who is against you.

advocate (AD-vuh-kit)
Someone who supports, comforts, gives help to or speaks up for another person. Jesus and the Holy Spirit are *advocates* for members of God's family.

affliction (uh-FLICK-shun)
Great trouble or pain.

alien (AYL-yun or AY-lee-en)
A person from another country; a foreigner.

altar (AWL-ter)
A place where sacrifices were made to worship God. An *altar* could be a pile of dirt or stones, a raised platform of wood, marble, metal or other materials.

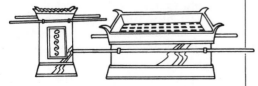

amen (ay-MEN or ah-MEN)
"Let it be so!" or "This is the truth!" *Amen* is often said after a prayer to show that people agree with what has been said and believe that it will happen.

Ancient of Days
A name for God that describes Him as the everlasting ruler of heaven and earth.

angels (AYN-juls)
Heavenly beings created by God before He created Adam and Eve. *Angels* act as God's messengers to men and women. They also worship God.

anoint (uh-NOINT)
To pour oil on a person or thing. A person was *anointed* to show that God had chosen him or her to do a special job. Samuel *anointed* David to show God had chosen him to be king.

antichrist (AN-tih-christ)
A great enemy of Christ Jesus who pretends to be the Messiah. The Bible tells us that before the second coming of Christ, an *antichrist* will rule over the world.

apostle (uh-PAH-sul)
A person chosen and sent out as a messenger. In the New Testament, *apostle* usually refers to one of the twelve men Jesus chose to be His special disciples. Paul and some other leaders in the early church were also called *apostles*.

appeal to Caesar (SEE-zer)
If a Roman citizen accused of a crime felt that the trial or verdict was unfair, he could request that the emperor hear the case. Paul, a Roman citizen, once did this.

ark of God ark of the covenant
A special wooden chest that was covered with gold. God told Moses exactly how to make the ark because it was to show the people of Israel that God was with them. The ark was about 4 feet long, 2½ feet tall and 2½ feet wide. On top, two golden figures of angels faced each other. The two tables of stone on which the Ten Commandments were written, a pot of manna, and Aaron's rod that budded were kept inside the ark. The ark was placed in the most holy place in the Tabernacle.

Aramaic (air-uh-MAY-ik)
The main language spoken by Jesus and other people who lived in Palestine when Jesus was alive.

armor-bearer
(ARE-mur-BARE-ur)
A person who carried the large shield and necessary weapons for a king or army officer.

archangel (ARK-ayn-jul)
A leader of other angels; the highest rank among angels.

Artemis (AR-tuh-mis)
A Greek goddess whose Roman name was Diana. Her most beautiful temple was built in Ephesus.

ascend (uh-SEND)
To go up. Jesus *ascended* to heaven to return to God the Father.

atonement (uh-TONE-ment)
To make up for a wrong act; to become friends again. In the Bible, *atonement* usually means to become friends with God after sin has separated us from Him. In the Old Testament, the Israelites brought sacrifices to *atone* for their sins. The New Testament teaches that Jesus Christ made *atonement* for our sins when He died on the cross. Because Jesus died to "make up" for our sins, we can have peace with God.

Baal (bale)
The name *Baal* means "master." *Baal* was the name of many false gods worshiped by the people of Canaan. They thought the *Baal* gods ruled their land, crops and animals. When the Israelites came to the Promised Land, each area of the land had its own *Baal* god. Names of places were often combined with the name *Baal,* such as Baal-Hermon, to show that Hermon belonged to *Baal.* Eventually, *Baal* became the name for the chief male god of the Canaanites. They believed that *Baal* brought the sun and the rain and made the crops grow. The Israelites were often tempted to worship *Baal*—something God had told them they were never to do.

balm
A sticky, sweet-smelling sap that was used as a medicine to heal sores or relieve pain. The plant or tree from which the sap was taken is unknown today.

balsam trees (BAL-sum)
Trees that grow in the Jericho Plain. The sweet-smelling sap of the trees and the oil from their fruit were used as medicine.

baptize (BAP-tize)
In the Old Testament, to *baptize* meant to wash with water. But in the New Testament, when John the Baptist called the people to be *baptized,* he was using water to show that people were truly sorry for the wrong things they had done and that they were asking God to forgive their sins. Today, a person is baptized to show that he or she is a member of God's family.

barren (BEAR-un)
A woman who could not have children was called *barren.* Fields that did not produce crops or fruit trees that did not grow fruit were also called *barren.*

Beelzebub (bee-EL-zee-bub)
A god the Philistines worshiped. In the New Testament, *Beelzebub* (or Beelzebul) is another name for Satan—the prince of the demons.

believe
To have faith or to trust that something is true. The Bible tells us that we can *believe* that Jesus Christ is God's Son and trust Him to keep His promise to forgive sins. We show that we *believe* that God loves us and wants what is best for us by obeying His commands.

betroth (be-TROTHE)
Engaged to be married.

bier (beer)
A stretcher or platform on which a dead body was carried to the place where it would be buried.

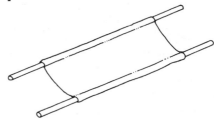

birthright (BURTH-rite)
The special rights the oldest son in Hebrew family enjoyed. When his father died, the oldest son received a double share of all that his father owned. He also received the right to make decisions for the entire family. Esau sold his *birthright* to Jacob for a bowl of soup.

bitter herbs (urbs)
A bitter green salad eaten at Passover to remind the Israelites of the sorrow, pain and bitter hardships they suffered as slaves in Egypt.

blaspheme (BLAS-feem)
To say bad things against God, to swear using God's name, or to do actions that show disrespect to God. The Bible says that *blasphemy* is a sin. The Jews punished *blasphemers* by stoning them to death. Jesus and Stephen were falsely accused of *blasphemy*.

blemish (BLEM-ish)
A spot or mark that makes something not perfect.

bless
The word *bless* is used three different ways in the Bible: 1. To ask God to do good things for another person; 2. To praise and worship and thank God; 3. To give good things or to show kindness. The Bible says that God *blesses* all people by giving them many good things and showing great kindness to them.

bondage (BON-dij)
Being in slavery. In the Old Testament, the Israelites were in *bondage* to the Egyptians for many years. In the New Testament, *bondage* means slavery to sin. Jesus died and rose again to set people free from sin. Christians are no longer slaves to sin, but are free to love and obey God and His Son, Jesus.

breastpiece or **breastplate**
1. A square of colored linen cloth worn by the high priest when he entered the Holy Place. The *breastpiece* was decorated with twelve precious stones. Each stone represented one of the twelve tribes of Israel. The *breastpiece* reminded the priest to pray for each of the tribes of Israel. 2. A piece of metal armor that protected a soldier's throat and chest.

burnt offering (OFF-ring)
A sacrifice, or gift, to God which was burned upon an altar. The offering was a perfect animal, such as a goat, sheep, lamb or ram. *Burnt offerings* were always given for cleansing, or atonement, for sin.

Caesar (SEE-zer)

The family name of Julius Caesar, a famous Roman leader. Later the name *Caesar* was added to the name of each Roman ruler, so it became a title that meant the same as "emperor" or "king."

capstone (KAP-stone)

The stone that holds two walls together; the final most important stone that finishes a wall. When the Bible calls Jesus a *capstone,* it reminds us that He is the head of the church and that He holds all Christians together.

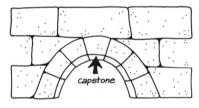

capstone

caravan (CARE-uh-van)

A group of people and their belongings, who traveled together for protection from robbers and wild animals. When families moved, they often traveled in a *caravan.* Traders also traveled in *caravans.*

census (SEN-sus)

The counting of the number of people living in an area or country.

centurion (sen-TOUR-ee-un)

An officer in the Roman army who was the leader of 100 men.

chaff

The worthless husks removed from grain. Farmers in Bible times got rid of *chaff* by throwing grain in the air on windy days. The light *chaff* blew away on the wind; the heavier grain fell to the ground. In the Bible, the word *chaff* often means something bad or worthless.

chariot (CHAIR—ee-ut)

An open, two- or four-wheeled cart pulled by horses.

chief priest

See *high priest.*

Christ

The Greek word which means "God's Chosen One." "Messiah" is the Hebrew word meaning the same thing. Jesus was the *Christ.*

This is my Son, whom I love.

Christian (KRIS-chun)

In the Bible, the word meant "Christ's person" or "little Christ." Today people who believe Jesus Christ is God's Son and follow His teachings are called *Christians*.

circumcise

To cut an unneeded flap of skin, called the foreskin, from the penis. For the Israelites, *circumcision* was a sign of the special agreement (or covenant) they had with God: If they worshiped and obeyed Him, He would be their God and they would be His people. Abraham was the first Hebrew to be *circumcised*. After Abraham, Hebrew baby boys were *circumcised* when they were eight days old. Leaders in the early church said that it was not necessary for men or boys to be *circumcised* to become part of God's family.

cistern (SIS-turn)

A hole dug in the earth or a rock to collect and store water. Empty *cisterns* were sometimes used to store grain or as prisons.

City of David

City of David has three meanings: 1. It is another name for the town of Bethlehem where David was born; 2. Part of the city of Jerusalem was known as the *City of David*; 3. The entire walled city of Jerusalem was sometimes called the *City of David*.

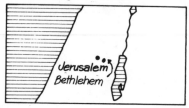

city of refuge (REF-uj)

One of six cities set aside by Moses where a person who had accidentally killed someone could stay until a fair trial could be held. While the person was in a *city of refuge*, he would be safe from family or friends of the dead person who might want to kill him.

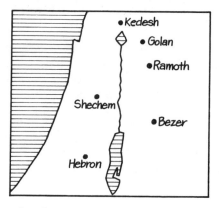

cloak (kloke)

A long, loose fitting robe people in Bible times wore over their other clothing.

commandment
(kuh-MAND-ment)

A rule or teaching people are to follow. Moses received the Ten Commandments from God. The Bible gives commandments for Christians to follow because they love Him and want to obey His Word.

conceive (kun-SEEV)
1. To become pregnant; 2. To think up or imagine something.

concubine (KON-ku-bine)
A slave woman in Bible times who lived with an Israelite family and had children by the father of the family. She was considered an extra or second class wife.

condemn (KUN-dem)
1. To find someone guilty of doing something wrong and to declare or pronounce a punishment. 2. To be against or disapprove of something because it is wrong.

confess (kun-FESS)
To *confess* means to tell or agree about what is true. *Confess* sometimes means telling God your sins. *Confess* can also mean to say in front of other people that you believe that Jesus is God's Son and that He died and rose again to forgive you of your sins.

conscience (KON-shuns)
A feeling about what is right and what is wrong; a sense of knowing what is good and what is bad.

consecrate (KON-see-krate)
To set apart something or someone to serve God in a special way.

convert (KON-vert)
A person who has changed from one belief or way of thinking to another. A person who decides to follow God's way instead of his or her own way, has become a *convert*.

cornerstone
A large stone in the foundation of a building at the corner of two walls. It holds the two walls together. The *cornerstone* is the first and most important stone laid when a building is started. Jesus is called the *cornerstone* of our faith in God because He is the most important part of our knowing who God is.

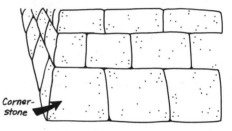

Corner-stone

counselor (KOUN-sel-or)
One who gives advice or help. Sometimes the Bible uses the word *Counselor* as another name for Jesus. In the New Testament, the Holy Spirit is also called the *Counselor* of Christians.

covenant (KUV-uh-nunt)
An agreement. Sometimes *covenants* were made between two people or groups of people. Both sides decided what the agreement would be. However, in the Bible, the word usually refers to agreements between

God and people. In a *covenant* between God and people, God decides what shall be done and the people agree to live by the *covenant.*

covet (KUV-et)
Wanting very much to have something that belongs to someone else.

I wish that was mine.

create (KREE-ate)
To cause something new to exist or to happen. God *created* everything that exists.

crucify (KROO-si-fy)
To nail or tie a person to a cross until he or she is dead. *Crucifixion* was a slow, painful punishment the Romans used for their enemies and the worst criminals.

curse (kurse)
In the Bible, to *curse* does not mean to swear or to use bad language. When a person *cursed* something, he or she wished evil or harm to come to it. When God *cursed* something, He declared judgment on something.

deacon (DEE-kun)
Helpers or servants in the church. In the New Testament, men and women deacons were chosen to take care of the needs of people in the church. Today churches give their deacons many different jobs to do.

debt (det)
Something a person owes someone else—usually money. In the Lord's Prayer, the word *debt* means sins or wrongdoing. The word *debtor* means those who sin against us.

decree (duh-CREE)
An order or law given by a king or ruler. A *decree* was often read in a public place so that many people would hear the new law.

dedicate (DED-i-kate)
To set apart for a special purpose. In the Bible, the word usually means that a person or thing is given to God to serve Him in a special way.

demon (DEE-mun)
An evil spirit working for Satan (the devil). A *demon*-possessed person was controlled by evil spirits. Jesus ordered evil spirits to come out of many people.

denarius (duh-NAIR-ee-us)
Roman money. A *denarius,* which was a small silver coin, was the payment for about one day's work.

detest (dee-TEST)
To hate.

devote (dee-VOTE)
To set apart for a special purpose or reason.

disciple (dih-SY-pul)
Someone who follows the teachings and example of another. In the New Testament *disciple* usually refers to a person who believed that Jesus is God's Son and loved and obeyed Him. Sometimes *disciples* means the twelve men Jesus chose to be His special friends and helpers. At other times, it refers to all people who love Jesus and obey His teachings.

edict (EE-dikt)
A written law or order given by a king or ruler.

elder (EL-dur)
In the Bible, the word *elder* has several meanings. 1. In the Old Testament, an older man in a family, tribe or town was called an *elder.* 2. Also in the Old Testament, each town had a group of older men known as *elders.* They made major decisions for the town. 3. The first four books of the New Testament usually refer to the Sanhedrin— the group of men who governed the Jewish people in Jesus' time— as elders. 4. In the early church, the church leaders were often called *elders.*

enmity (EN-muh-tee)
Hatred or bad feelings that make two people or groups enemies.

envy (EN-vee)
A strong feeling of jealousy caused by something someone else has or does well. *Envy* can cause a person to try to make him- or herself better than the other person. The Bible says *envy* is sin.

eternal (ee-TUR-nal)
Lasting forever; without end. God is *eternal* and members of God's family have *eternal* life.

301

eunuch (YOU-nuk)

1. The title *eunuch* was sometimes given to the man who was the most important helper or advisor to a king or queen. 2. Men who could not have children because their sex organs were damaged or defective were also called *eunuchs*.

everlasting

Never ending; forever.

exile (EG-zyl)

To make someone leave his or her country and live somewhere else. The Jews were in *exile* in Babylon for seventy years.

faith

Faith has two meanings in the Bible. 1. To be certain about the things we cannot see or to trust someone because of who he or she is. For example, a Christian has faith that Jesus is God's Son. 2. "The faith" means the whole message about Jesus Christ—that He is God's Son and that He came to take the punishment for our sin so that we may become members of God's family.

faithful

Always loyal and trustworthy. God is *faithful.* We can always trust Him to do whatever He has promised. We are also to be *faithful* in doing what is right.

famine (FAM-in)

A time when there is not enough food to keep people and animals alive. *Famines* can be caused by lack of rain, wars, insects that eat crops, and bad storms.

fear

Today, *fear* most often means being afraid of something or someone. However, the Bible often uses the word *fear* to describe the sense of respect or awe that people should have for God because of His greatness and His love.

feasts

1. Dinners, celebrations and banquets are often called *feasts* in the Bible. 2. Jewish religious holidays and celebrations are also called *feasts*. See page 43 for more information about religious *feasts*.

fellowship (FELL-o-ship)

A time when friends who are interested in the same things come together. In the Bible, *fellowship* often means the friendship Christians share because they love God and His Son, Jesus.

fig

A brownish, pear-shaped fruit that grows on trees. *Figs* are plentiful in Palestine. They can be eaten raw, cooked or dried.

firstborn

The first child born into a family. A *firstborn* son received special rights and power. He became head of the family after his father died and he received twice as much money and property as his brothers.

firstfruits

An offering to God of the first vegetables, fruits and grains the Israelites picked from their fields. The people offered their *firstfruits* to God to thank Him for supplying their food.

flax

A useful plant grown in Palestine. The seeds of the plant were used to make linseed oil and the fibers of the plant were woven into linen cloth.

flint

A very hard stone that can be sharpened to a fine cutting edge.

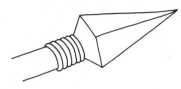

flog

To beat with a whip or stick.

forefather (FOR-father)

A person from whom one is descended—an ancestor. Your father, your grandfather, your great-grandfather and your great-great-grandfather are some of your *forefathers.*)

foreigner (FOR-uh-nur)

A person who is from another country.

forgive

To stop feeling angry and to stop blaming a person for something wrong he or she has done; to be friends again. God *forgives* everyone who believes that Jesus died to take the punishment for his or her sins. When God *forgives* a person, God forgets the person's sins forever. God instructs Christians to *forgive* each other in the same way He has *forgiven* them.

That's OK! I forgive you.

forsake
To leave, to go away from, to leave completely alone.

frankincense (FRANK-in-sense)
A very expensive, hard gum made from the sap of a terebith tree. *Frankincense* was used to make sweet-smelling perfume. The Israelites used *frankincense* in religious ceremonies: One of the special gifts the wise men brought to Jesus was *frankincense.*

Galilee (GAL-uh-lee)
The northern part of Palestine in Jesus' day. Jesus grew up, preached, and did most of His miracles in *Galilee. Galilee* is also the name of a large lake in this area.

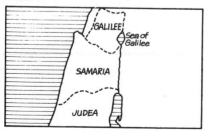

gall (gawl)
A bitter poisonous plant. The juice from the plant may have been used to make a painkiller. Jesus refused a drink of *gall* mixed with wine when He was dying on the cross.

generation (jen-uh-RAY-shun)
All the people born at about the same time. Grandparents, parents and children are three different *generations.*

Gentiles (JEN-tiles)
All people who are not Jewish.

glean (gleen)
To pick fruits or grain that the harvesters missed. The Bible told farmers to leave some crops in the field for hungry people to *glean.*

glory

Great beauty, splendor, honor or magnificence that can be seen or sensed. The Israelites saw the *glory* of the Lord in the cloud that filled the Tabernacle. The shepherds saw the *glory* of the Lord when the angels told them Jesus had been born. *Glory* can also mean to praise; to be proud or happy; to boast.

Golgotha (GAHL-gah-thah)

The place outside Jerusalem where Jesus was hung on a cross. In Aramaic, *Golgotha* means "the place of the skull."

gospel (GOS-pel)

Gospel means "good news." The good news of the Bible is that God sent His son Jesus to take the punishment for sin and then raised Him from the dead so that any person who believes may have new life. The story of the life, death and resurrection of Jesus Christ told in the first four books of the New Testament is also called the *gospel*. The books are also called the four *Gospels*.

grace

The love and kindness shown to someone who does not deserve it—especially the forgiveness, love, and kindness God shows to us. We don't deserve God's *grace* because we sin against Him. God showed *grace* to all people by sending His Son, Jesus, to be our Savior. God's *grace* allows us to become members of His family (see Ephesians 2:8). God's *grace* also keeps on helping us live as God wants us to (see Acts 20:32). A person cannot earn God's *grace* by trying to be good; it is God's free gift.

guilty (GIL-tee)

Having done wrong or broken a law. A person who is *guilty* deserves to be blamed or punished.

Hades (HAY-dees)

A Greek word that means "the place of the dead." Another word used in the Bible that means the same as *Hades* is "Sheol." *Hades* was thought to be a dark, shadowy place. Hell, or Gehenna was a much more fearful place— it is not the same as *Hades*. If a person has asked Jesus to forgive his or her sins, that person does not need to fear either of these places because he or she will live forever with Jesus.

Hallelujah (HAL-uh-LOO-yuh)

A Hebrew word that means "praise the Lord!"

harlot

A prostitute; a woman who gets paid for having sexual relations with another person. The Bible says *harlotry* is a sin, but like other sins, it can be forgiven. Sometimes the Bible uses the word *harlot* to describe people who turn away from God to worship idols.

harvest (HAR-vust)
To gather ripe fruits, vegetables, grain and other crops from fields, vineyards and orchards.

Hebrew (HEE-broo)
A name of the nation God chose to be His special people—the Israelites. It is also the name of any member of that nation, as well as the language they speak. Most of the Old Testament was written in the *Hebrew* language.

heir (air)
Someone who has the right to receive the property or position of another person when that person dies. In Bible times, the *heir* was usually a son. The Bible says that anyone who is a member of God's family is His *heir.* God will never die, but because we are His children, God keeps on giving us great love, care and kindness.

herbs (urbs)
Plants or parts of plants used to make teas, medicines and to flavor food.

Herod (HAIR-ud)
The family name of five kings appointed by the Roman Emperor to rule Palestine in New Testament times. Jesus was born during the rule of *Herod* the Great. The names of the other four kings are *Herod* Archelaus, *Herod* Antipas, *Herod* Agrippa I, and *Herod* Agrippa II.

high place
Altars and places of worship built on the tops of hills or mountains. Sometimes altars to God were built at *high places.* However, the *high places* were usually for the worship of idols. The Israelites were told to destroy the *high places* in their land where idols were worshiped.

high priest
The most important priest of all the priests who served God in the Tabernacle and later in the Temple. In the Old Testament he offered the most important sacrifices to God for the people. In New Testament times he was also a powerful political leader. He was the head of the Sanhedrin— the group of men who governed the Jewish people. He even had a small army. The *high priest* wore special clothing described in Exodus 28:1-39. Aaron was the first *high priest.* All other high priests were his descendants.

holy (HO-lee)
Chosen; pure; set apart; belonging to God. God is *holy*. He is perfect and without sin. Jesus is *holy*, too. He is without sin and dedicated to doing what God wants. Because Jesus died to take the punishment for sin and then rose again, people who believe in Him have the power to be *holy*, too. God helps them to become more and more pure and loving, like Jesus.

Holy Spirit
The personal but unseen power and presence of God in the world. The book of Acts tells us that the *Holy Spirit* came to followers of Jesus in a special way after Jesus had gone back to heaven. The *Holy Spirit* lives within all people who have had their sins forgiven. Jesus said that the *Holy Spirit* is our helper and comforter. The *Holy Spirit* teaches us truth about God. He helps us understand the Bible and helps us pray in the right way. He gives us the power and strength to do what Jesus wants.

Hosanna (HOE-zan-uh)
A Hebrew word that means "Save now!" The Hebrews shouted the word to praise someone important.

hypocrite (HIP-uh-krit)
A person who pretends to be something different from what he or she really is. In the Old Testament, *hypocrite* means a godless person. In the New Testament, it means a phony. Jesus called the Pharisees *hypocrites* because they did many things to make themselves seem very religious, but they would not listen to God.

idol (eye-dul)
A statue or other image of a god that is made by people and then worshiped as if it had the power of God. Idols are often made of wood, stone or metal. Sometimes, the Bible calls anything that takes the place of God in a person's life an *idol*. God tells us not to worship *idols*, but rather, to worship only Him.

Immanuel (im-MAN-you-el)
A name for Jesus which means "God with us."

incense (IN-sens)
A mixture of spices held together with thick, sticky juice that comes from trees and plants. *Incense* is burned to make a sweet smell. In the Tabernacle and Temple, *incense* was burned on a small golden altar to worship God.

inheritance (in-HAIR-ih-tunce)
Money, property or traditions received from another person. Often, a person receives an *inheritance* after another person's death. The Bible tells us that everything that is God's belongs to Jesus Christ. By His death on the cross, Jesus made it possible for us to share His *inheritance* with Him.

Israel (IZ-ray-el)
In the Bible, the word *Israel* has several meanings.

1. It is the special name God gave Jacob (meaning "Prince with God")

Israel
(Jacob)

2. It is another name for the Hebrew nation—God's chosen people.

Nation of Israel

3. It is the name of the nation ruled by the judges and the first three Hebrew kings—Saul, David and Solomon. See "United Kingdom" map.
4. It is the name given to the northern kingdom after Jeroboam led ten tribes to separate from Rehoboam and the two southern tribes. (The southern kingdom was called Judah.) See "Divided Kingdom" map.
5. After the northern kingdom of *Israel* was captured by the Assyrians, the word *Israel* was sometimes used to mean the southern kingdom.
6. It is also a name used for the people of God. The Bible often uses the term "children of *Israel*," meaning they were descendants of Jacob.

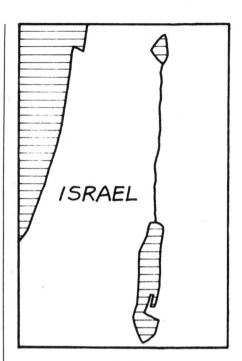

United Kingdom

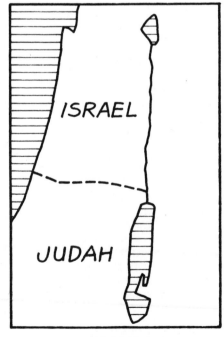

Divided Kingdom

308

Israelite (IZ-ray-e-lite)
A citizen of the country of Israel; a descendant of Jacob (Israel).

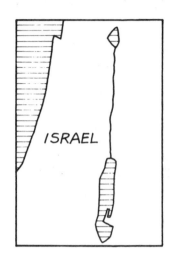

Israelites
Descendants of Israel
(another name for Jacob)
Also called "children of Israel"

jealous (JELL-us)
Jealous has several different meanings. 1. It can mean being careful to guard or keep what one has. This is the kind of *jealousy* the Bible is talking about when it says that God is a *jealous* God. He loves His people and wants them to turn away from sin and to love and worship Him. 2. Another kind of *jealousy* is to be angry and unhappy when someone else has something you want. The Bible calls this kind of *jealousy* a sin. 3. Another kind of *jealousy* is being afraid of losing someone's love or affection.

Jehovah (je-HOV-ah)
This is an English translation of one of the Hebrew names for God. A more accurate name is Yahweh. This name was considered to be very holy.

Jerusalem (ju-ROO-sah-lem)
The most important city of Bible times. It was the capital of the united kingdom of Israel and the kingdom of Judah. The Temple was built in *Jerusalem,* so many people traveled to the city to worship God. In 587 B.C. *Jerusalem* was captured and mostly destroyed by Babylonian armies. The city was rebuilt when the Jews returned after seventy years of exile in Babylon. Jesus taught in the city of *Jerusalem,* was crucified outside the city wall, was buried near the city, and then rose again. The first Christian church began in *Jerusalem* after the Holy Spirit came to the believers there.

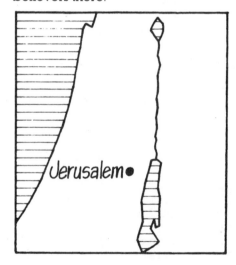

Jews
At first, *Jew* referred to anyone who was a member of the tribe of Judah. By New Testament times, however, it meant anyone who was a descendant of Abraham or who was a follower of the Jewish religion.

Judah (JOO-duh)
1. One of the sons of Jacob and Leah. 2. The descendants of *Judah,* who became the tribe of *Judah.* 3. The southern kingdom when the Israelites divided into two separate countries after the death of King Solomon. (The northern kingdom was called Israel.)

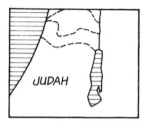

a son
of Jacob

tribe of
Judah

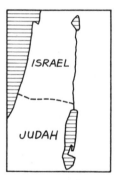

**Southern
Kingdom**

Judaism (JOO-day-izm)
The teachings of the Jewish religion. *Judaism* is based on worshiping the one true God, circumcision as a sign of being one of God's chosen people, worship on the Sabbath (Saturday), obeying God's laws, and following the traditions given from one generation to another.

judge (juhj)
In the time of Moses, a *judge* helped people settle their disagreements. When the

Israelites were settling the Promised Land after the death of Joshua, God chose leaders, called *judges* to rule the people. Often these *judges* led the people in battle against their enemies. Some of the *judges* were Deborah, Gideon and Samuel. After kings began to rule Israel, *judges* once again settled disagreements and took care of official business.

judgment (JUHJ-munt)
1. In the Old Testament, *judgment* can mean God's laws of instructions. 2. *Judgment* can also mean God's punishment of a person or nation for disobeying Him. 3. In the New Testament, *judgment* can mean to criticize or disapprove of someone. The Bible says Christians are not to *judge* each other. 4. *Judgment* can also mean the end of the world as we know it when God will *judge* sin, and reward those people who have lived for Him.

justice (JUS-tiss)
That which is right and fair. Most of the prophets in the Bible emphasized that God is *just,* and that He wants His people to act *justly.* Many of the warnings given by the prophets were because the leaders and people were guilty of *injustice,* cheating others, especially the poor.

justification
(jus-tih-fih-KAY-shun)
God's action of treating sinners who have faith in Jesus Christ as if they had never sinned. God

forgives their sin and becomes their friend. God also gives them the power to live right. *Justification* is possible because Jesus Christ died to take the punishment for sin.

justify (JUS-tih-fy)
To erase someone's sin; to announce that someone is right.

kingdom of heaven
The *kingdom of heaven* is also called the "kingdom of God." It means God's rule in the lives of His chosen people and His creation. In the Old Testament, the people in God's kingdom were the Israelites. In the New Testament and now, the people over whom God rules are Christians—people who love God and want to serve Him. A person becomes part of God's kingdom by trusting Jesus as his or her Savior and Lord. When Jesus comes again, then God's kingdom will become visible to all people.

kinsman
A relative.

Lamb of God
A name for Jesus that tells us that He died to take away our sins. When a Jewish person had sinned, he or she offered a lamb as a sacrifice to God. Jesus became like one of those lambs when He gave Himself as a sacrifice to die so that our sins can be forgiven.

law
The word has several meanings in the Bible. 1. It can mean all the rules God gave to help people to know and love Him and to live happily with each other. The Ten Commandments are part of God's *law*. 2. The first five books of the Bible are called the *Law*. 3. The entire Old Testament is sometimes called the *Law*. 4. Any rule which must be obeyed, whether it was decided by God or by people is a *law*. 5. God's rules in the Old Testament plus other rules added by Jewish religious leaders are sometimes called the *Law*.

leprosy (LEP-ruh-see)
A name used for several serious skin diseases. People with *leprosy* were called *lepers*. The Jewish law said that *lepers* had to stay away from people who did not have the disease. *Lepers* lived outside their cities and towns, either by themselves or with other *lepers*, until the disease showed signs of healing.

Levites (LEE-vites)
Descendants of Levi, one of the sons of Jacob and Leah. Some of the *Levites* were religious teachers. Others took care of the Tabernacle, and later, the Temple. Only *Levites* could become priests, but not all *Levites* were priests.

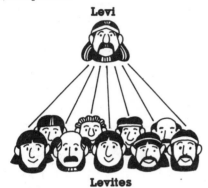

Levi

Levites

locusts (LOW-kust)
A *locust* is a large insect like a grasshopper. Sometimes *locusts* travel in huge swarms, eating all the plants they can find. In Bible times, *locusts* were sometimes eaten as food.

lute (lute)
A stringed musical instrument. It has a pear-shaped body and a neck. It is played by plucking the strings.

lyre (lier)
A small harp with three to twelve strings. A *lyre* was held on the lap when it was played.

Magi (MAY-ji)
Men who lived in the countries of Arabia and Persia and who studied the stars. People thought the *Magi* had the power to tell the meaning of dreams. Several of the *Magi* followed a star to Bethlehem and brought Jesus expensive gifts. The *Magi* honored Him as a newborn king.

manger (MAIN-jur)
A box in a stable where food was placed for cattle, donkeys or other animals. When Jesus was born, His first bed was a *manger*.

manna (MAN-uh)
The special food God gave the Israelites for the forty years they traveled in the desert. The Bible says that *manna* looked like white seeds or flakes and tasted sweet.

mantle (MAN-tul)
A loose fitting outer robe or coat.

master (MAS-tur)
1. A name for Jesus. It means "teacher." 2. An overseer, boss, or owner of a slave.

mediator (MEE-dee-ay-tor)
A person who settles differences or arguments between two or more people. Jonathan was a *mediator* between David and Saul. Moses was a *mediator* between God and Israel. By paying the punishment for sin, Jesus became the *mediator* who makes it possible for us to have peace with God.

mercy
Showing more love or kindness to a person than he or she expects or deserves.

Messiah (mu-SIE-uh)
The Savior whom God promised to send. Jesus is the *Messiah.* In Hebrew, *Messiah* means "the Anointed One." In Greek, the word for "the Anointed One" is "Christos." "Christ" is the name used in the New Testament to show Jesus is the Savior.

This is my Son, whom I love.

millstone
One of a pair of large stones used to grind grain into flour.

miracle (MEER-uh-kul)
Some event or wonderful happening done by the power of God.

Moabite (MOE-uh-bite)
A person from the country of Moab, located just east of the Dead Sea. Moab often fought against Israel and at times was under the control of Israel's kings.

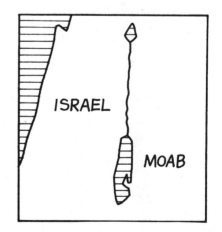

ISRAEL

MOAB

mortal (MOR-tuhl)
Able to die. All people, plants and animals are *mortal.* God is not *mortal;* He lives forever and will never die.

myrrh (murh)

The sap of the *myrrh* bush. *Myrrh* was used to make anointing oil smell good, as a perfume, as a pain killer, and to prepare a body for burial. The Magi brought Jesus a gift of *myrrh*.

nard

A pleasant-smelling oil made from the roots and stems of spikenard plant. This plant grew in India. Since the oil had to be brought from India to Palestine, it was very expensive. Mary poured *nard* over Jesus' feet.

Nazarene (NAZ-uh-reen)

A person who lived in the town of Nazareth. Because Jesus lived in Nazareth for almost 30 years, He was often called a *Nazarene*. Later, Christians were sometimes called *Nazarenes* because they were followers of Jesus.

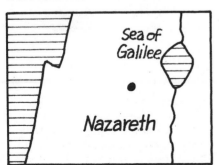

Sea of Galilee

Nazareth

Nazirite (NAZ-uh-rite)

A Hebrew person who promised to serve God in a special way for a certain length of time. The time could be anywhere from 30 days to a lifetime. To show dedication to God, a *Nazirite* would not cut his or her hair, eat or drink anything made from grapes, or touch a dead body. At the end of the time, the person lived like other people. Samuel and Samson were *Nazirites* all their lives. Some scholars believe John the Baptist was also.

nomad (NO-mad)

A person who lives in a tent and moves from place to place. *Nomads* usually move when seasons change or when they need to find grass for feeding their animals. Abraham was a *nomad* for much of his life.

oath

A serious promise that what a person says is true. In Bible times, people often made an *oath* by saying, "God is my witness." The *oath* often asked for God's punishment if what was said was not true. Jesus taught that people who love and obey Him do not need to make *oaths* because they should be known for saying only what is true.

offering (OFF-ring)

A gift of money, time or other possessions a person gives to God because he or she loves Him. In Old Testament times, people brought food and animals to the Tabernacle or Temple as *offerings* to God. The *offerings* were often burned on the altar. Animal offerings were always killed. Their blood symbolized sins being forgiven by death. Christians believe that we no longer need to offer sacrifices for the forgiveness of sins because Jesus' death is the once-for-all sacrifice through which our sins can be forgiven. (See Sacrifice)

offspring

For humans, *offspring* are sons and daughters. For animals, *offspring* are their young.

oil

In the Bible, *oil* almost always means olive *oil.* Oil was squeezed from the olives and used in food, as a fuel for lamps, as a medicine for wounds, and as a hair dressing and skin softener. Olive *oil* was used to anoint priests and kings. It was also used in religious ceremonies in the Tabernacle and later in the Temple.

ordain (or-DANE)

The word *ordain* has several meanings in the Bible. 1. It can mean to cause to happen. Psalm 65:9 says that the streams are filled with water to provide people with food because God has *ordained*—or caused—it. 2. To appoint or set apart a person to do special work. Paul was *ordained* to be a missionary to the Gentiles. 3. *Ordain* can also mean to decide or command.

overseer (OH-vur-seer)

A person who watches over and takes care of others. Joseph was an *overseer;* he watched over and directed other people who worked for Potiphar. In the New Testament, leaders in the early church were sometimes called *overseers*. Paul told these leaders to take care of the people in the church in the same way a good shepherd cares for his sheep.

ox, oxen

Strong male cattle. They were used for pulling plows, wagons, and other heavy loads.

pagan (PAY-gun)

A person who does not worship the true God, especially a person who worships idols.

parable (PAIR-uh-bul)

A story that teaches a special lesson or truth. Jesus often told *parables* to teach important lessons.

paralytic (PAIR-uh-lih-tic)

A person who has lost the ability to move one or more arms and/or legs.

Passover

One of the Jews' most important feasts. The Jews celebrate *Passover* every spring as a reminder that God freed them from slavery in Egypt.

The word *Passover* comes from the way the angel of death "passed over" the homes of Israelites on whose door posts the blood of a lamb was sprinkled. In Egyptian homes, where there was no blood on the door posts, all the firstborn sons died.

This terrible disaster convinced the Egyptian Pharaoh to let the Israelites leave Egypt.

At the *Passover* feast, the Jews eat bread made without yeast (unleavened bread), bitter herbs and lamb. The unleavened bread reminds them that the Israelites left Egypt in a hurry. There was no time to let bread rise.

The bitter herbs remind them of their suffering in Egypt.

The lamb reminds them of the lamb they killed for the first *Passover*.

The *Passover* feast was the last meal Jesus ate with His disciples before He was crucified.

Passover Lamb
The lamb killed at Passover as a sacrifice. The Bible says that Jesus is our *Passover Lamb.* He was sacrificed to deliver us from sin, just as the first *Passover Lamb* was sacrificed to deliver the firstborn sons of the Israelites from death and to provide them with escape from Egypt. (See Passover.)

patriarch (PAY-tree-ark)
The word usually refers to either Abraham, Isaac or Jacob—the founders of the Hebrew nation. Jacob's sons and David are also called *patriarchs.*

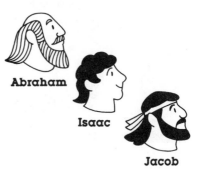

Abraham

Isaac

Jacob

317

Pentecost (PEN-te-cost)
A Jewish feast celebrated fifty days after Passover. (See page 43.) Today the Christian church remembers *Pentecost* because on the first *Pentecost* after Jesus' resurrection, the Lord sent the Holy Spirit to His followers as He had promised. (See Acts 2.)

persecute (PUR-suh-cute)
To continually treat someone cruelly or unfairly, even though the person has done nothing wrong. The early Christians were *persecuted* for teaching that Jesus is God's Son.

Pharaoh (FAY-row)
A title of the rulers of ancient Egypt, just as "president" or "king" or "prime minister" are titles of top officials in countries today.

Pharisee (FAIR-uh-see)
A Jew in the time of Jesus who tried very hard to obey every part of the Jewish law. Many sincerely tried to please God and to be holy. Some of the *Pharisees* worried more about keeping every little rule than about caring for people. Jesus often scolded the *Pharisees* because on the outside, they seemed very holy, but on the inside, they were full of lies and hate (see Matthew 23). Saul of Tarsus (later called Paul) was a *Pharisee.*

plague (playg)
1. A very serious disease that spreads quickly among people in an area. It often causes death. 2. Anything that causes great harm or suffering. For example, sometimes crops were destroyed by a *plague* of locusts. 3. The ten great disasters God sent to the Egyptians to convince their king to free the Israelites. Read about these *plagues* in Exodus 4—12.

plunder

1. To loot or rob, especially during a war. 2. The property taken by *plundering*.

pomegranate

(PAHM-uh-GRAN-ut)
A fruit about the size of an apple. The *pomegranate* fruit is encased in a tough, reddish skin. The fruit is ruby red, very juicy—and filled with edible seeds. *Pomegranates* grow on small, bushy trees.

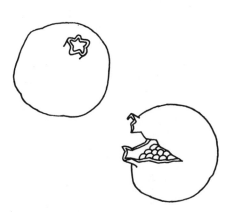

precepts (PREE-septs)
Commands, rules or laws.

predestined (pree-DEST-uhned)
Decided or chosen beforehand. In the Bible, the term refers to God's choice.

priest

Among the Jews, a *priest* was a man who offered prayers and sacrifices to God for the people. They led the public worship services at the Tabernacle, and later at the Temple. Often the *priests* also taught the Law of God to the people. The *priests* of Israel were all descendants of Aaron's family.

The New Testament says that Jesus Christ is now our High Priest, the One who offered Himself as the perfect sacrifice for our sins (see Hebrews 8,9). Also, all Christians are *priests* (see 1 Peter 2:9). We are to help others learn about and worship God.

proconsul (PRO-kon-sul)
A ruler in the Roman government. The Roman empire was divided into provinces or states. The highest Roman official in each province was called the *proconsul*.

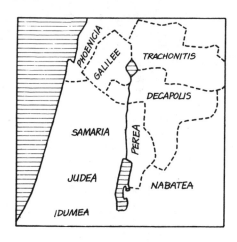

prophecy (PRAH-fuh-see)
The message from God that a prophet spoke or wrote to people. Some prophecies told about what God would do in the future.

prophets (PRAH-futs)
Men and women in the Old and New Testaments chosen by God to tell His messages to people.

"I have loved you," says the Lord.

prostitute (PRAH-sty-tute)
(See Harlot.)

proverb (PRAH-verb)
A short, wise saying. The Bible book of *Proverbs* is made up of many wise sayings.

provoke (pruh-VOKE)
To make angry; to cause trouble on purpose.

psalm (salm)
A Hebrew song or poem. A *psalm* usually praises God or tells the deep feelings of God's people. The Bible book of *Psalms* is made up of many Hebrew poems and songs.

purge (purj)
To make clean and pure.

Purim (POOR-im)
A Jewish holiday to celebrate the victory of Queen Esther and the Jews over wicked Haman. (See page 119.)

rams
Mature male sheep. Rams were used for sacrifices and food. Their wool was used to make warm cloth and their horns were often used to make musical instruments called rams' horn trumpets.

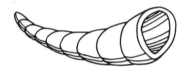

ransom (RAN-sum)
The price paid to buy the freedom of a captive or slave. The New Testament says that all people are held captives to sin and death. When Jesus died on the cross, He paid the price—the *ransom*—to rescue us from the powers of sin and death. (See **redeem**.)

raven (RAY-vun)
A large, black bird.

reap
To gather ripe grain and fruit. The
Bible also uses the word *reap* to
describe the reward or
punishment people receive for
their actions (see Galatians 6:9).

rebuke (ree-BUKE)
To correct someone sternly; to
scold someone.

reconcile (REK-un-sile)
To help people who have been
enemies become friends. In the
New Testament, the word usually
refers to bringing God and
people together again through
Jesus' life, death and resurrection.
Sin separates people from God,
but by dying, Jesus took the
punishment for sin. When a
person comes to know and love

Jesus, he or she learns to love God
instead of being His enemy. When
this happens the person is
reconciled to God.

redeem (ree-DEEM)
To buy back. In Bible times, a
person could pay a slave's owner
whatever the slave was worth
and then set the slave free. The
slave had been *redeemed* by the
person who had bought the slave
and then set him or her free.

The New Testament tells us that
by dying, Jesus paid the price to
"buy us back" and set us free from
our slavery to sin. (See ransom.)

reeds
Different plants growing in
swamps or along the edges of
water.

refuge (REF-uj)
A place where one is safe from danger; a shelter. (Also see "city of refuge.")

remnant (REM-nunt)
A small part that is left over. In the Old Testament, *remnant* usually refers to the few Israelite people who remained faithful worshipers of God after their exile in Babylon.

remnant

repent (ree-PENT)
Repent means to turn around and go in the opposite direction. In the Bible, to *repent* means that you stop doing wrong action and start doing what God says is right. *Repentance* always involves making a change away from sin and towards God.

restore (ree-STORE)
1. To bring back; to establish again. 2. To bring back to a former or original condition. 3. To return something lost, stolen or taken.

resurrection (rez-ur-RECK-shun)
1. To come back to life after being dead. Jesus died, and was buried. After three days He rose from the dead. That event is called the *Resurrection*. It shows Jesus' power over sin and death.
2. A future time when everyone who has ever lived will live again in new, spiritual bodies that will never die. Those who do not love God will be separated from Him forever.

Jesus   **Thomas**

retribution (re-truh-BYOU-shun)
A payment that is deserved, revenge. The punishment that comes to a person because he or she has broken God's law is called *retribution*.

revelation (rev-uh-LAY-shun)
To make known something that was hidden or unknown. In Old Testament times God *revealed* Himself through His mighty acts and through His words to the prophets and to other people such as Abraham, Moses, and David.

"I have loved you," says the Lord.

In the New Testament, God made Himself known by sending Jesus Christ. As Jesus lived on earth, He *revealed* God's love, His holiness and His power. Jesus helps us know what God is like.

This is my Son, whom I love.

One of the ways God *reveals* Himself to us is through His word, the Bible. The last book of the Bible is called The *Revelation* of Jesus Christ because it shows how Jesus will triumph over evil.

REVELATION Chapter 1

revenge (ree-VENGE)
Punishment, injury or harm done to pay back a wrong.

reverence (REV-er-unce)
A feeling of deep love and respect. *Reverence* should be our feeling about God and His holiness, power and love.

righteous (RYE-chuss)
Thinking and doing what is *right* and holy. The word is used in three ways in the Bible: 1. To tell what God is like: He does only what is *right* and holy. 2. A person who has accepted Jesus as Savior is looked at by God as being free from the guilt of sin. God sees the person as being *righteous.* 3. People who are members of God's family show their love for Him by living in *righteous* ways. They do what is *right* and holy.

Roman
1. A person who lived in the city of *Rome.* 2. A person who was a citizen of the Roman empire. A *Roman* citizen enjoyed special rights and protection. For example, he or she could not be punished without a fair trial, nor could a citizen be crucified.

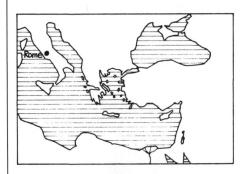

Rome

Sabbath (SAB-uth)
The weekly day of rest and worship God set apart for all people. In the Old Testament it is the seventh day of the week (Saturday). For the Jew, *Sabbath* starts at sundown on Friday and

lasts until sunset on Saturday. Many Jews and some Christians observe the *Sabbath* on Saturday.

Because Jesus rose from the dead on a Sunday, most Christians set aside Sunday as the day of rest and worship. (See Acts 20:7.)

sackcloth (SAK-kloth)
A rough, dark cloth usually woven from goats' hair. When someone died, the peron's friends and family wore clothes made of *sackcloth* to show that they were very sad. A person would also wear *sackcloth* to show that he or she was sorry for sinning.

sacred (SAY-kred)
Holy; belonging to God.

sacrifice (SAK-rih-fice)
A gift or offering given to God. A *sacrifice* usually involved the killing of an animal to pay for sin. The New Testament tells us that Jesus died as the once-for-all *sacrifice* for sinners and that no further *sacrifices* for sin are necessary.

Sadducees (SAD-you-seez)
Jewish religious leaders in New Testament times. They said that only the laws in the first five books of the Old Testament had to be obeyed. They did not believe in the Resurrection or in angels or spirits. When the New Testament speaks of the "chief priests" it is referring to the *Sadducees*.

saints
The word means "God's people." The New Testament says that all Christians are *saints*. Paul often addressed his letters "to the *saints*."

salvation (sal-VAY-shun)
Sometimes *salvation* means to be rescued from evil. Sometimes it means to be kept from danger or death. In the New Testament, *salvation* usually means to be rescued from the guilt and power

of sin. By His death and resurrection, Jesus brings *salvation* to people who believe in Him.

Samaritan (suh-MARE-uh-tun) A person who lived in or came from the area in Palestine known as Samaria. The *Samaritans* were only partly Jewish. They worshiped God differently than the other Jews. The Jews and *Samaritans* hated each other—perhaps because of the differences in the ways they worshiped. Jesus showed that He loved the *Samaritans* as much as any other people by traveling through Samaria, teaching the *Samaritans* about God. Jesus told the story of the *Good Samaritan.*

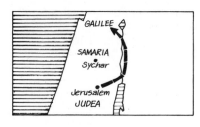

Most Jews traveled **AROUND** Samaria.

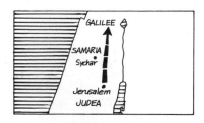

Jesus traveled **THROUGH** Samaria.

sanctify (SANK-tih-fie) To set apart for God's use. A Christian's *sanctification* is an ongoing process. When a person becomes a Christian, he or she is *sanctified.* The Holy Spirit continues helping him or her become more and more like Jesus, which is the process of *sanctification.*

sanctuary (SANK-choo-air-ee) A holy place; a place where God is worshiped. In the Bible, *sanctuary* usually refers to the Tabernacle or to the Temple.

Tabernacle

Solomon's Temple

New Testament Temple

Sanhedrin (san-HEE-drun)
The highest Jewish political and religious court. In New Testament times the *Sanhedrin* was made up of 71 men who were experts in Jewish laws. The *Sanhedrin* included the high priest, members of wealthy or prominent Jewish families and members of the Pharisee and Sadducee religious groups.

Satan (SAY-tun)
The most powerful enemy of God and all people. Other names for *Satan* include: the devil; the evil one; the prince of this world; the father of lies. *Satan* is the ruler of a kingdom made up of demons. He hates God and tries to destroy God's work. The Bible tells us that in the end, God will destroy *Satan* and the demons.

Savior (SAVE-yur)
A word which means "he who saves." The Old Testament almost always speaks of God as the *Savior* of His people. Sometimes God sent someone to help His people, and that person was called a *savior.* In the New Testament *Savior* refers to Jesus. He died and rose again to rescue or save us from our sin.

scepter (SEP-tur)
A short rod held by a king or queen to show that he or she was the person with the most authority and power.

scorpion (SKOR-pee-un)
A small animal, something like a spider. It has a long tail with a poisonous stinger on the end. Its sting can kill a small animal and is very painful to humans.

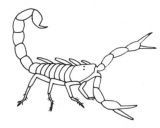

scribe
1. An expert in understanding the Jewish law. *Scribes* taught the people God's laws. They also copied the Old Testament writings onto scrolls. Ezra was a *scribe.* By New Testament times, the *scribes* often served as judges in Jewish courts because they knew so much about the law. 2. A writer or secretary who earned his living writing letters or important papers for other people.

Scripture (SKRIP-chur)
The Bible. Before the New Testament was written down, *Scripture* meant the Old Testament. After the New Testament was written down, Christians began calling both the Old and New Testaments *Scripture.* The word *Scripture* means "writing."

scroll (skrole)
A long strip of papyrus or parchment with writing on it. A stick was attached to each end of the strip so that it could be rolled up to make it easier to read, store and carry.

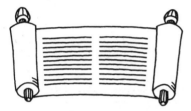

seal
A small tool or ring that had a design cut into one side. The owner of each seal had his or her own special design. When the owner wanted to put his or her own special mark or brand on something, the person would press the seal into hot wax or soft clay. As the wax or clay hardened, it kept the design in it. *Seals* were used in many ways. Some of them were: to show that two people had reached an agreement; to seal a letter; to show who owned something. Also called a signet.

seer (SEE-uhr)
A prophet; a person who, with God's help, could see what would happen in the future. (See prophet.)

sensual (SEN-shoo-uhl)
1. Appealing to the body's senses.
2. Caring too much for physical pleasures.

servant
A person who works for the comfort or protection of others. Jesus said that He is a servant. He instructed His followers to be servants to each other instead of trying to have authority over each other. In the Bible, the word *servant* sometimes means slave.

sexual immorality
To use *sex* in ways that God says are wrong; sexual union between two people who are not married to each other is a sin.

sheaf, sheaves (sheef, sheevz)
A bundle or bundles of cut grain stalks.

sheep pen, sheepfold
A protected place for sheep to stay.

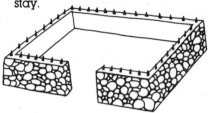

shekel (SHEK-uhl)
A small weight of silver or gold that was used as money.

shepherd (SHEP-herd)
A person who took care of sheep. *Shepherds* found grass and water for their sheep, protected them from bad weather and wild animals, brought them safely into a sheepfold at night, and cared for sick or hurt sheep.

sickle
A tool with a sharp curved blade that is attached to a short handle. A *sickle* is used to cut stalks of grain.

siege (seej)
The surrounding of a city or town by an army so that nothing can go in or out. The purpose of a *siege* is to make the city or town surrender.

signet
See seal.

sin
Any act or thought that is against the way God wants us to act or think. The Bible says that all people have *sinned. Sin* separates us from God. God sent Jesus to die to take the punishment for *sin.* Because Jesus died, our *sins* can be forgiven and the separation between God and us can be removed.

I have done wrong. Forgive me.

slander
To say untrue things about a person in order to hurt his or her reputation. The Bible says that *slander* is sin.

slave
A servant who is owned by his or her master and could be bought or sold like property. People became *slaves* if they were defeated in battle by an enemy or if they were unable to pay their

debts. A *slave* had to do whatever the master ordered.

Son of Man
A name for Jesus. Jesus called Himself the *Son of Man* many times. The name means that Jesus is a real man and that He is the One God promised to send in Daniel 7:13.

soothsayer (SOOTH-say-er)
A person who said he or she could tell what would happen in the future—a fortune-teller. Both the Old and New Testaments say that *soothsaying* is wrong.

sorcerer (SORE-sir-er)
A person who claimed to be able to make evil spirits work for him or her. The Bible says that *sorcery* is a sin.

soul
In the Bible, the word *soul* usually refers to the part of a person that cannot be seen but controls what a person thinks, feels and does. Sometimes *soul* means the whole living person. The words *soul* and "spirit" usually mean about the same thing.

sovereign (SOV-run)
Having authority and power over everything. God is *sovereign*.

sow
To plant seeds. In Bible times, a farmer *sowed* seeds by scattering them by hand over a plowed field.

spirit
The unseen part of a person that controls what he or she thinks, feels and does; soul. The Bible says that God is a spirit, showing that He does not have a physical body. (See **soul**.)

staff
1. A strong stick used for support when walking or climbing. 2. A strong wooden rod with a hook on the end used by a shepherd as he cared for sheep.

statute (STAT-chewt)
A law or command. In the Bible, *statutes* usually refers to God's laws.

stiff-necked
Stubborn, rebellious and unwilling to learn.

stone

To throw large stones and rocks at a person until he or she is dead. *Stoning* was the way people were punished for disobeying certain parts of the Jewish law. Stephen was *stoned* for teaching that Jesus is God's Son. (See Acts 7.)

submission

To choose to work with or to obey another person in a thoughtful, gentle way. The Bible says that Christians are to *submit* to each other in the same way Jesus *submitted* to God when Jesus came to earth.

synagogue (SIN-uh-gog)

A place where Jews meet together to read and study the Old Testament and to worship God.

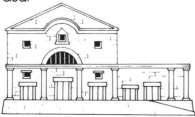

Tabernacle (TAB-er-nack-ul)

The portable tent where the Israelites worshiped God. They used it while they wandered in the desert after they left Egypt and for many years after they entered the Promised Land.

Moses and the people built the *Tabernacle* following God's instructions. The *Tabernacle* was used until it was replaced by a permanent place of worship called the Temple. The *Tabernacle* is described in detail in Exodus 26.

talent

A large amount of silver or gold worth a huge amount of money. One *talent* was considered to be the amount of money a working man would earn in about ten years.

Temple (TEM-pul)

The permanent place in Jerusalem where the Jews worshiped God. The first *Temple* was built by King Solomon and the people following the instructions God had given Solomon's father, King David. The *Temple* was a very beautiful place. It was destroyed and rebuilt twice. In A.D. 64 the *Temple* was destroyed again. It has not been rebuilt.

Solomon's Temple
(See 1 Kings 6—8.)

Second Temple
(See Ezra and Nehemiah.)

Herod's Temple
(See Matthew—Acts)

tempt

In the Bible, the word *tempt* has two meanings. 1. To test a person to improve his or her spiritual strength. 2. To try to get someone to do something wrong.

testimony (TEST-ih-MOAN-ee)
In the Bible, *testimony* has more than one meaning. 1. In the Old Testament, it often refers to the Law of God. 2. In the New Testament, *testimony* usually means giving proof that something is true.

Jesus is God's Son.

tetrarch (TET-rarck)
When a country in the Roman Empire was divided into sections, the head of each part was called a *tetrarch*. In the New Testament, Herod Antipas is sometimes called a *tetrarch* and sometimes a king. He was the ruler of Galilee in the time of Jesus.

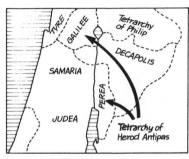

threshing floor

The place where grain was trampled by oxen or beaten with a stick to separate the heads of grain from the stalk. A *threshing floor* was usually a large, flat rock or a large area of clay that was packed hard. *Threshing floors* were usually built where wind would blow away the chaff and leave the heavier grain. (See winnow.)

tithe

To give God one-tenth of what you earn. For example, if you had ten dimes, you would *tithe* by giving one dime to God.

tomb (tume)
A place where dead people were buried. In Bible times, *tombs* were often natural caves or caves dug into stone cliffs.

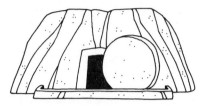

trance (trans)
In the Bible, a *trance* is the deep, dreamlike state in which a person received a message from God. Peter was in a *trance* when God showed him the vision of the animals in a sheet (Acts 10:10).

transfigured (tranz-fig-yurd)
To have been changed in appearance or form. The Bible tells us that Jesus' physical appearance was changed—*transfigured*—as three of His disciples watched. His face glowed and His clothes became shining white. Moses and Elijah appeared and Jesus talked with them about His coming death.

This is my Son, whom I love.

transgression (trans-GRESH-un)
A sin; disobeying the law of God.

treaty (TREE-tee)
A formal agreement between people, or groups, or countries.

trespass (TRES-pass)
To go against the rights of someone else. We *trespass* against people when we do something unfair to them or when we break laws made to protect people. We *trespass* against God when we break His laws. In the Bible, another word for *trespass* is "sin."

I didn't take it.

tribute (TRIB-yoot)
In the Bible, *tribute* usually means money or services a weaker nation was made to pay to a stronger nation.

trumpet
A straight tube that was bell shaped at one end. *Trumpets* were played at every Temple service. (Also see trumpet of rams' horns.)

trumpet of rams' horns
A curved ram's horn, blown as a signal. *Trumpets of rams' horns* were used in religious ceremonies and in battle.

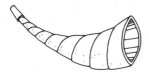

tunic (TOO-nik)
A loose shirt reaching to the knees. A *tunic* was usually worn as an undergarment.

turban (TER-bun)
A head covering made by twisting cloth and wrapping it around the head.

unclean
Unclean does not just mean dirty. It also means any action, thought, food, person, or place that God had said is displeasing to Him. One of the ways a Jewish person could become *unclean* was by eating food God had said not to eat. Other ways a person could become *unclean* were by touching a dead body or by getting a skin disease called leprosy. A person could become clean again by going through certain ceremonies.

unleavened bread
(un-LEV-und)
Bread made without yeast. *Unleavened bread* is usually flat, like a pancake or cracker.

vengeance (VEN-juhns)
Punishment for wrongdoing. In the Old Testament, a person was told exactly how much he or she could do to punish someone for a wrong he or she had done. But the New Testament tells people not to punish those who have wronged them. Instead, they are told to trust God to take care of the punishment because He is the only one who is completely fair and just.

333

vile
Disgusting or evil.

violate (VIE-oh-late)
1. To break the law. 2. To force someone to have sex; to rape. 3. To make something unholy.

viper (VIE-pur)
A poisonous snake.

virgin (VIR-gin)
A person who has never had sexual intercourse.

vision (VIH-zuhn)
A *vision* was a way God showed someone a truth that would otherwise not be known. God used *visions* to show a message of truth in pictures. Sometimes, people were asleep when God gave them *visions* (see Ezekiel 8:1-4 and Acts 10:9-29).

vow
A promise made to God.

wail
A long, loud cry to show sorrow.

widow
A woman whose husband has died.

wilderness (WILL-der-ness)
A large area of land where few people lived. Depending on the amount of rainfall, the land might be a barren desert or it might grow grass and other vegetation on which sheep and other herds of animals could graze.

wineskin
A bag made from an animal skin. Wine, milk, water and grape juice were stored in *wineskins*.

winnow (WIN-oh)
To separate the kernels of grain from the worthless husks removed from the grain. This was done by tossing the grain into the air when there was a strong breeze. The breeze would blow away the

light husks and the heavier kernels of grain would fall to the ground.

witness
1. In the Bible, a *witness* was a person who told what he or she had seen. 2. To tell others what you have seen. Jesus told His followers to be *witnesses*. We are to tell what we have seen Jesus Christ do in our own lives.

woe
Misery, sorrow or great suffering.

womb (woom)
The part of a woman's body where a baby grows until it is born.

wonder
A miracle. A thing or event that causes surprise and awe. God did many *wonders* to convince Pharaoh to let the Israelites leave Egypt.

world
1. The planet Earth. 2. People who follow Satan. 3. Anything that belongs to life on earth instead of eternal life with God.

worldly
Being part of life on earth instead of eternal life with God. The Bible warns against loving the things of the *world* more than the things of God.

worship (WUR-ship)
Anything a person does to show love and respect. Some people worship idols. Some people worship the one true God.

wrath (rath)
Very great anger.

Yahweh
An English equivalent of the Hebrew word for God; also translated "Jehovah."

yoke

1. A wooden bar that goes over the necks of two animals, usually oxen. The *yoke* holds the animals together when they are pulling something such as a cart or plow.
2. Two oxen *yoked* together.

3. The word *yoke* is sometimes used as a word picture for any burden or demand. Slavery, imprisonment, taxes or unfair laws were called *yokes*.

4. A partnership.

Zealot (Zel-ut)

A member of a Jewish group in the time of Jesus that wanted to fight against and overthrow the Roman rulers in Palestine. Jesus' disciple, Simon (not Peter), was a Zealot.

Zion (Zie-un)

Zion has several different meanings: 1. One of the hills upon which the city of Jerusalem was built was called Mount *Zion;*

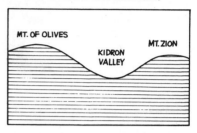

2. The entire city of Jerusalem was sometimes called *Zion;*

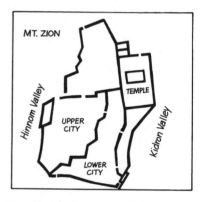

3. *Zion* is another name for the nation of Israel.

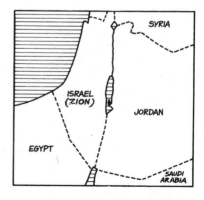

4. *Zion* is another name for heaven.

The Lands of the Bible

The arrow points to a place that is a very special part of God's plan. This place has been called by several names: Canaan, Palestine, Israel.

Thousands of years ago, God told Abraham* to leave his home in Ur and go to a land that God would show him. Abraham did as God said. He led his family and flocks to Canaan. There God said to Abraham, "SOMEDAY all of this land will belong to you and your descendants (Abraham's children's children's children)."

Abraham, and then his son Isaac, and then his grandson Jacob, lived in Canaan as shepherds. And THEN—after many years—something happened that made Jacob's family leave Canaan. There was a great famine in Canaan—a time when there was not enough food.

Jacob's family moved to Egypt. His descendants lived there 400 years—first as shepherds, and then as slaves. During this time God made them into a nation—the people of Israel. God brought this nation back into Canaan, the land God promised to Abraham.

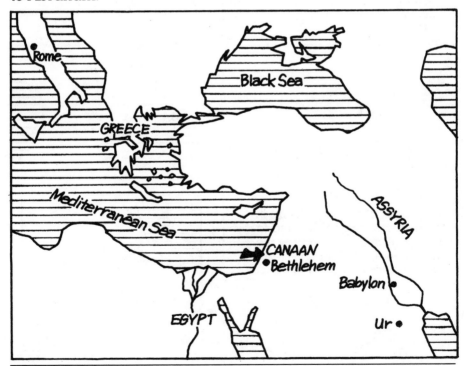

---

* When we first read about this man, his name was Abram. Later his name was changed to Abraham.

God blessed His people—the people of Israel—with good things, just as He promised. But as the years went on, many of the people forgot God. Some of them even worshiped idols (false gods). And so, God allowed His people to be taken as captives to foreign lands—some to Assyria and some to Babylon.

After a period of time, God in His faithfulness allowed His people to return to the land He had promised them. (The land of Canaan became known as Palestine and was a very important part of God's plan.) It was here in THIS land—and through THIS people (the people of Israel) that God planned to send the promised Savior.

And so it was, that hundreds of years later—at the time and in the place God planned—God sent His Son Jesus, the Messiah (Savior), just as He promised. Jesus was born in Bethlehem, a city in Palestine.

After Jesus died and rose again, He told His followers to tell everyone about Him. For the good news about Jesus, the Savior, was not just for THIS land and THIS people. It was to go out . . .

- FROM this land to ALL lands, and
- FROM this people to ALL people.

And that includes you and me!

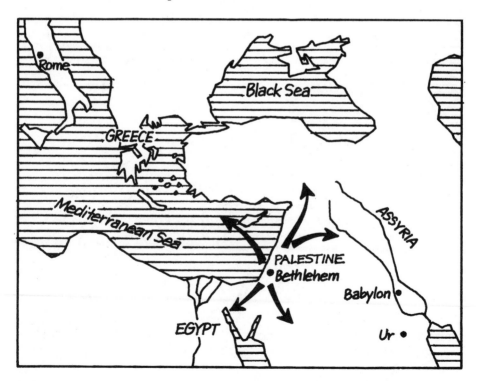

The Geography of Canaan (Palestine)

You can understand Bible events better if you know something about the land where those events happened. The map below shows how the land divides into four natural sections.

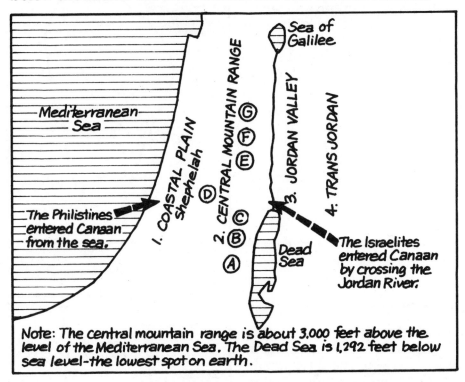

Mediterranean Sea

Sea of Galilee

1. COASTAL PLAIN — Shephelah

2. CENTRAL MOUNTAIN RANGE

3. JORDAN VALLEY

4. TRANS JORDAN

The Philistines entered Canaan from the sea.

The Israelites entered Canaan by crossing the Jordan River.

Dead Sea

Ⓐ Ⓑ Ⓒ Ⓓ Ⓔ Ⓕ Ⓖ

Note: The central mountain range is about 3,000 feet above the level of the Mediterranean Sea. The Dead Sea is 1,292 feet below sea level—the lowest spot on earth.

When the Israelites crossed the Jordan River into the Promised Land, they settled primarily along the central mountain range. These cites were on the central mountain range: Ⓐ Hebron, Ⓑ Bethlehem, Ⓒ Jerusalem, Ⓓ Gibeon, Ⓔ Bethel, Ⓕ Shiloh, Ⓖ Shechem. After the land was conquered, some of the Israelites made their home across the Jordan River, in the Transjordan. ("Trans" means "across.")

About the time that Joshua and the Israelites crossed the Jordan River, the Philistines arrived by sea and settled on the coast. The shephelah (she-FEE-la) was a section of low hills that helped to protect the Israelites from the Philistines. In the book of Judges we read about a lot of the cities in the shephelah. Both the Philistines and the Israelites wanted to control these cities. The Philistines kept trying to cross the shephelah so they could attack the Israelite cities on the central mountain range. The battle between David and Goliath took place in the shephelah.

Sea of Galilee

The water in the Sea of Galilee is blue and fresh (not salty). Fishermen still fish in this lake today. Some of Jesus' disciples were fishermen who lived at Capernaum, a town on the shore of the Sea of Galilee.

Read these Bible verses to find some other names for the Sea of Galilee.

- Numbers 34:11
- John 6:1
- Luke 5:1

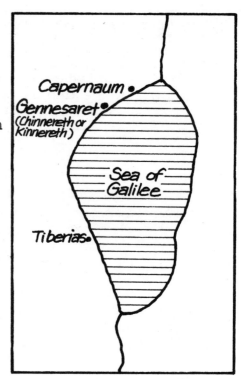

Jordan River

The Jordan River starts north of the Sea of Galilee and ends in the Dead Sea. The distance between the beginning of the river and the end, when measured in a straight line, is only about 80 miles (128 km). But the river twists and turns so much that it is 200 miles (320 km) long!

The river begins as a clear mountain stream. But farther south it becomes muddy.

This is the river Joshua and the Israelites crossed (Joshua, chapter 3). It was in the Jordan River that Naaman was healed of leprosy (2 Kings 5:10-14). This is the river where Jesus was baptized by John the Baptist (Mark 1:9).

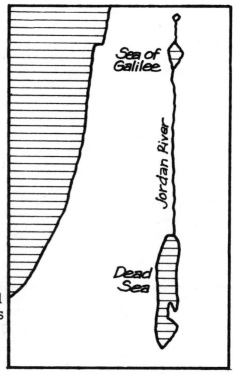

340

Places in the Old Testament

Bible Lands Information

Jerusalem

The city that David captured from the Jebusites (see 2 Samuel 5:6,7) was a very small city. But it was in a very good location. It was near a spring that provided water for the people. And it was on a hill that could be defended from enemy attacks.

The photo on page 353 shows part of Jerusalem as it looks today. The diagram below shows where the Canaanite city of Jebus was. David captured this city from the Jebusites and called it the City of David.

Gihon Spring, which furnished water for the city, was outside the city wall. When Hezekiah was king he built a tunnel to bring the water inside the city of his day (see diagram below and diagram on page 354). Can you find the numbered places on the photo on page 353?

① Gihon Spring
② Pool of Siloam
③ Hezekiah's tunnel (see also photo on page 355)
④ Location of Solomon's Temple (an Arab place of worship is there today— see building with large round dome)
⑤ Today's city wall

The photo and diagram on page 354 show how Jerusalem grew as the years went on.

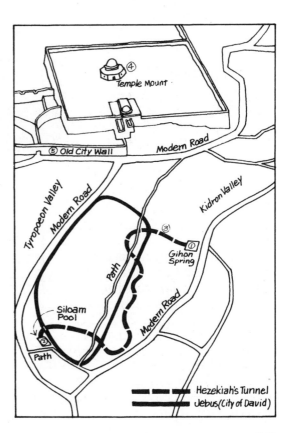

Babylon

In Bible times Babylon was a great city with huge walls. (See drawing below.) This is the city to which Daniel, Ezekiel and other captives from Judah were taken.

Jeremiah 51:58 says, "This is what the Lord Almighty says: 'Babylon's thick wall will be leveled and her high gates set on fire.'" Isaiah 13:20 says of Babylon, "She will never be inhabited or lived in through all generations."

Today Babylon is in ruins—just as God said when He spoke through the prophets. For centuries Babylon has lain desolate. Only the beasts of the desert live there. The once-magnificent city of Babylon is today a heap of fallen bricks. What a remarkable fulfillment of prophecy!

Places in the Gospels

Bible Lands Information

The map below shows the location of many places mentioned in the Gospels. The photos on pages 360-362, 366 show how some of these places look today.

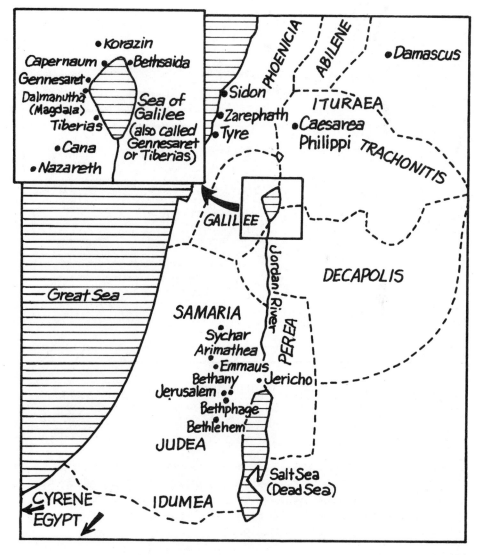

New Testament Jerusalem

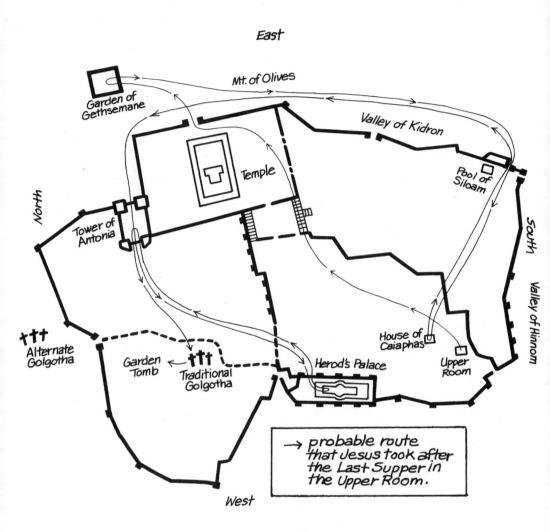

Can you find where these events happened?
1. The crowds welcomed Jesus. Matthew 21:9-11
2. Jesus taught. Mark 11:17-19
3. Peter and John prepared the Passover feast. Luke 22:8-13
4. Jesus prayed. Matthew 26:36
5. Jesus was arrested. Matthew 26:36,47-50
6. Jesus was brought before the High Priest. Matthew 26:57,58
7. Jesus was crucified. John 19:17,18
8. Jesus was buried. John 19:40-42
9. Jesus rose again. Mark 16:5-8

Temple

The Bible tells about three Temples built on the same spot, but at different times.

1. **The First Temple (Solomon's Temple)** was built under the leadership of King Solomon. When the Babylonians captured Jerusalem in 587 B.C., this Temple was destroyed.

2. **The Second Temple** was built by Jews who came back to Jerusalem after being captives in Babylon. (See Ezra.)

3. **Herod's Temple** (see model of this Temple on page 362) was built over and around the existing Second Temple. It was destroyed in A.D. 70 by the Romans.

This is how Solomon's Temple looked.

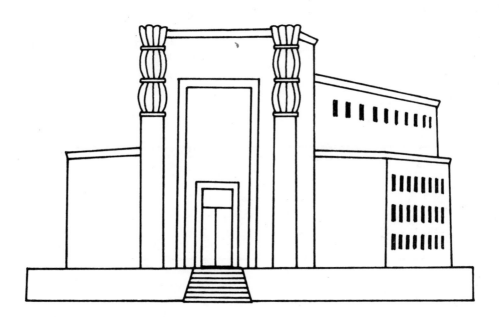

Old Testament Time Line

Founding of Jewish Nation

Israel in Egypt

Exodus and Wilderness Wanderings

Creation

*Abraham
*Isaac
   *Jacob   * Joseph   * Moses

B.C. (Before Christ)   **2100**   **1900**   **1700**   **1500**

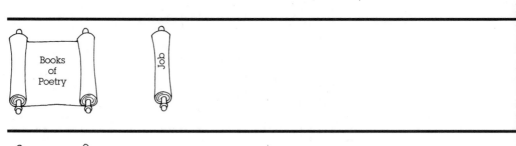

Books of Law and History   Genesis   Exodus   Leviticus   Numbers

Books of Poetry   Job

Books of Prophecy

Note: Times of events within each book are approximate.

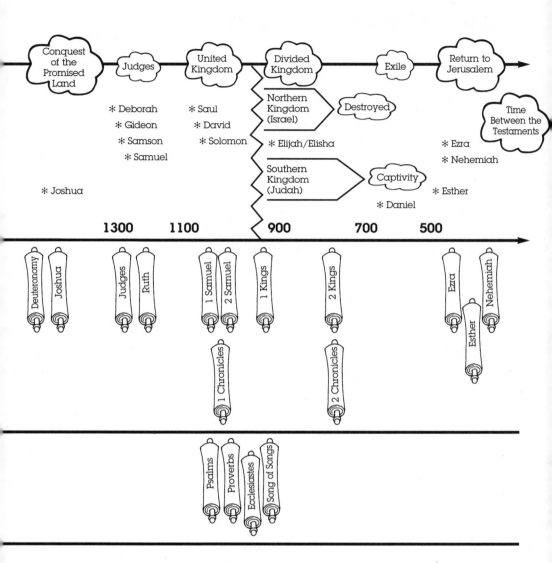

Conquest of the Promised Land
Judges
United Kingdom
Divided Kingdom
Northern Kingdom (Israel) → **Destroyed**
Southern Kingdom (Judah) → **Captivity**
Exile
Return to Jerusalem
Time Between the Testaments

* Deborah
* Gideon
* Samson
* Samuel

* Saul
* David
* Solomon

* Elijah/Elisha

* Joshua

* Daniel

* Ezra
* Nehemiah
* Esther

1300 **1100** **900** **700** **500**

Deuteronomy | Joshua | Judges | Ruth | 1 Samuel | 2 Samuel | 1 Kings | 2 Kings | Ezra | Esther | Nehemiah

1 Chronicles | 2 Chronicles

Psalms | Proverbs | Ecclesiastes | Song of Songs

The 17 Books of Prophecy were written during the Divided Kingdom, the Exile and the Return to Jerusalem. To see the dates of individual books, look at the chart on pages 136, 137.

New Testament Time Line

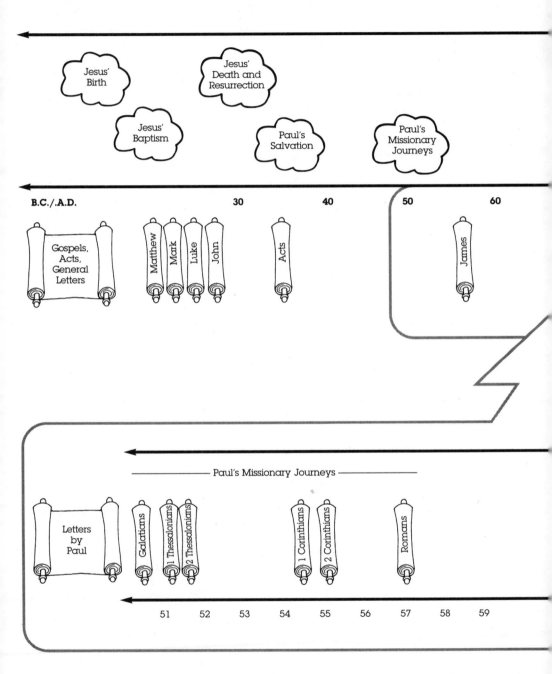

Jesus' Birth

Jesus' Death and Resurrection

Jesus' Baptism

Paul's Salvation

Paul's Missionary Journeys

B.C./A.D.   30   40   50   60

Gospels, Acts, General Letters

Matthew Mark Luke John

Acts

James

Paul's Missionary Journeys

Letters by Paul

Galatians 1 Thessalonians 2 Thessalonians

1 Corinthians 2 Corinthians

Romans

51   52   53   54   55   56   57   58   59

Note: We do not know exactly when the New Testament letters were written. The writers did not date their letters as we do today. People who have studied the Bible very carefully think the letters were written at about the times shown here.

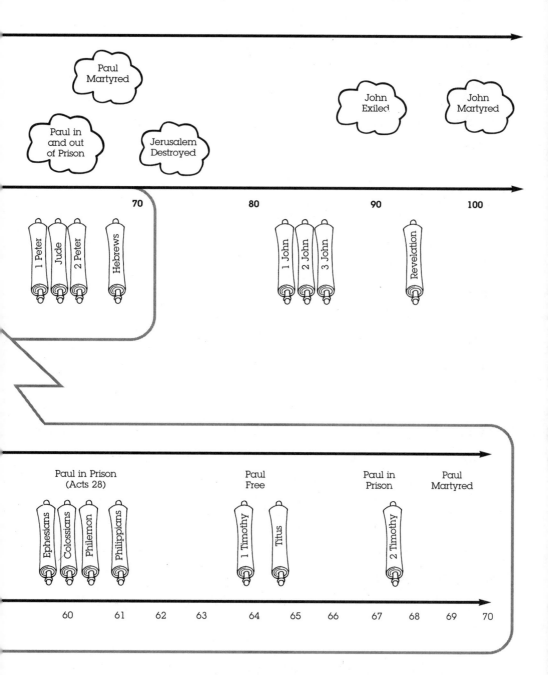

Index to Bible Lands Photographs

Many people think this is Mount Sinai. Read Exodus 19,20 to find what happened when the Israelites reached Mount Sinai.

There is a large space at the base of the mountain. This may have been where the Israelites camped.

351

© FRANCES BLANKENBAKER

🔺This is an acacia tree. Acacia (shittim) wood was used in building the Tabernacle and its furniture (see Exodus 25-27).

🔻Can you imagine how the Israelites felt when they came to an oasis like this? Exodus 15:27 tells about one of these times.

© FRANCES BLANKENBAKER

This is how part of Jerusalem looks today.

ZEV RADOVAN

This is how Jerusalem looks today from the air. The diagram shows how the city of Jerusalem grew in Old Testament times.

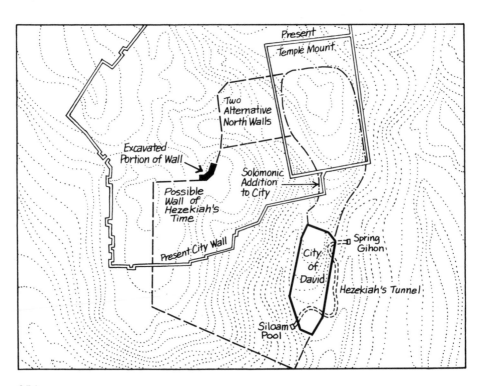

354

If you visit Jerusalem today, you can walk through the water in Hezekiah's tunnel. Read about this tunnel in 2 Kings 20:20.

En Gedi (see map on page 76) is one of the places where David hid from Saul. Can you find a cave in the photo?

355

⬆**Babylon:** This wall has been rebuilt to show how part of the wall of Babylon looked in Bible times.

⬇**Babylon:** This is how Babylon looks today—a city of ruins. Read Jeremiah 51:58; Isaiah 13:20.

Edom: These high cliffs form the only entrance to Petra, a great rock city in the land of Edom. © JOYCE THIMSEN

357

© JOYCE THIMSEN

◆**Edom:** In Jeremiah 49:16 God refers to the people of Edom as those "who live in the clefts of the rocks."

◆**Egypt:** This is the country that made slaves of God's people (see Exodus 1-14). Read what God says in Ezekiel 32:15.

358

© FRANCES BLANKENBAKER

▲Nineveh: (capital of Assyria): Sheep now graze on what was once the mighty city of Nineveh. Read Zephaniah 2:13.

▼Moab: This is the land Ruth and Naomi left (see the book of Ruth). Moab was also an enemy of Israel. Read Amos 2:2.

359

◄Jericho is an oasis—a green area in a dry land. A spring of water comes up from the ground. Read Mark 10:46-52.

◄This is the garden of Gethsemane where Jesus prayed just before He was arrested. Read Mark 14:32-50.

⬆️Some people think this is the place the Bible calls "Golgotha" or "Calvary"—the place where Jesus died on the cross.

⬇️This empty tomb (grave) is cut out of a hillside. It is in a garden near the place pictured above.

361

This is a model of the Temple that was in Jerusalem in New Testament times. The Temple was a place to worship God.

Archaeologists digging at Jerusalem are finding many clues about what Jerusalem was like in Bible times.

➤ God led His people to the good land He promised them. They plowed the land using plows and oxen like these.

➤ When the grain was ready, they threshed and winnowed it. See "winnow" and "threshing floor" in the dictionary that begins on page 293.

363

⬆Many Israelites were shepherds. David was a shepherd (see 1 Samuel 16:11-13; 17:34-37). He wrote Psalm 23.

⬇A sheepfold (sheep pen) is a protected place for sheep to stay. Read John 10:1-18.

This village has homes like those in Bible days. Notice the stairs leading up to the flat roof. Read 2 Kings 4:10.

In some places today, people and donkeys still carry loads as in Bible times.

Fishermen on the Sea of Galilee still use nets to catch fish—just as they did in Bible times. Read Matthew 4:18-20.

The Jordan River is the longest and most important river in Palestine. This is where it leaves the Sea of Galilee.